Zenana

Zenana

EVERYDAY PEACE IN A
KARACHI APARTMENT
BUILDING

———— Laura A. Ring

Indiana University Press • Bloomington and Indianapolis

The photographs in this book are by Sheheryar
Hasnain.

This book is a publication of

Indiana University Press
601 North Morton Street
Bloomington, IN 47404-3797 USA

http://iupress.indiana.edu

Telephone orders 800-842-6796
Fax orders 812-855-7931
Orders by e-mail iuporder@indiana.edu

The paper used in this publication meets the minimum
requirements of American National Standard for
Information Sciences—Permanence of Paper for
Printed Library Materials, ANSI Z39.48-1984.

Manufactured in the United States of America

Library of Congress Cataloging-in-Publication Data

Ring, Laura A., date
    Zenana : everyday peace in a Karachi apartment
building / Laura A. Ring.
        p. cm.
    "The photographs in this book are by Sheheryar
Hasnain."
    Includes bibliographical references and index.
    ISBN-13: 978-0-253-34824-1 (cloth : alk. paper)
    ISBN-13: 978-0-253-21884-1 (pbk. : alk. paper)
1. Intergroup relations—Pakistan—Karachi—Case
studies. 2. Conflict management—Pakistan—Karachi—
Case studies. 3. Ethnic conflict—Pakistan—Karachi.
4. Women and peace—Pakistan—Karachi. 5. Sex
role—Political aspects—Pakistan—
Karachi. 6. Karachi (Pakistan)—Social
conditions. 7. Karachi (Pakistan)—Ethnic
relations. I. Title.
    HN690.5.K33R56 2006
    305.48'8009549183—dc22
                                        2006016280

1 2 3 4 5 11 10 09 08 07 06

Contents

Acknowledgments

In the writing and researching of this book, I was aided by the generous support of many people to whom I wish to acknowledge my debt—intellectual, emotional, and material.

I am grateful to Arjun Appadurai and Leora Auslander, who provided guidance and direction from the earliest stages of the project to its completion. For their careful readings and warm friendship, I wish to thank Kimberly Mills, Krisztina Fehervary, and Elise LaRose. For their thoughtful criticism and advice, I am grateful to Barbara Yngvesson and Mary Hancock. Many thanks to John Kelly, Kamran Ali, Sylvia Vatuk, and Rebecca Tolen for their comments and suggestions. I am especially grateful to Sheheryar Hasnain for providing all the photographs for the book.

My fieldwork was made possible by a generous Fulbright IIE fellowship. During the write-up period, I was supported by a generous grant from the Committee on Southern Asian Studies at the University of Chicago.

To my friends and colleagues in Chicago, especially Jim Hannan, Deborah Cromley, Manan and Kitty Ahmed, Ed Yazijian, Lisa Knight, Caitrin Lynch, and Matthew Hull, I am grateful for the conversation and companionship. To my husband, Sheheryar, and sons, Faizan and Rameez, and to our families in New England and Karachi, I offer a world of thanks.

Finally, for their goodwill and candor, I thank my neighbors, informants, and friends in Karachi, whose willingness to welcome me into their lives was a kindness beyond measure. I hope this project honors them, although they remain anonymous.

Note to the Reader

For the sake of readability, I have employed a simple transliteration system for Urdu and Sindhi words that does not use diacritics. This system does not distinguish between long and short vowels (*a*, not *aa; i*, not *ee*) or between dental and retroflex consonants (*t*, not *tt; d*, not *dd*). A glossary of select terms with standard diacritical markings can be found at the end of the book. For Urdu and Arabic terms in common English usage (e.g., salaam, purdah), I have adopted the conventional English spelling.

Zenana

1

Introduction
The *Zenana* Revisited

We stood in the dimly lit hallway, my husband Sheheryar, son Faizan, and I. Our downstairs neighbor, Ruhi, had said to come at 9 PM, and we were late. "Oh, you people have come!" she exclaimed, throwing open the screen door and ushering us inside. As we turned toward the drawing room, Ruhi admonished, "Brother, this is the *zenana* (the women's space); the *mardana* (men's space) is over there." Reluctantly, Sheheryar and I separated. Faizan joined the other pre-schoolers shouting and playing in the corridor, and I stepped through the curtains to join Ruhi, her female relatives, neighbors, and friends.

For days, Ruhi had been reminding me to come to her dinner party: "If you want to learn about Karachi people, then you must come." The residents of the Shipyard were well aware of my interest in Karachi's ethnic "troubles." Ruhi's husband had been involved in Sindhi nationalism during his university days and was certain to have some interesting stories.

As the evening progressed, conversation in the *zenana* moved from marriage, to mother-in-law problems, to children, to sex, to hair removal. Eschewing their various native languages (Sindhi, Punjabi, Memoni), the women conversed comfortably in Urdu, the national language. They pumped me for information: Where were Sheheryar's parents from? How did I get along with my *sas* (mother-in-law)? Why didn't we have a second child? Had I converted to Islam? Did I prefer waxing or shaving?

From the *mardana*, I could hear snippets of conversation—something about migration, feudalism, roots, language. Casually, I attempted to elicit comments from the women on ethnic identity, on what it meant to be Sindhi, Muhajir, and so on, but to no avail. Time and again, I found myself glancing wistfully at the gap in the curtains, toward the *mardana*—imagining the political repartee, the debates, the arguments—as if somehow the truth about ethnic difference, conflict, the "troubles," could be found there in the men's room, but not here in the *zenana*.

Ethnic Conflict in the *Zenana*

In most scholarly accounts, this moment represents a stopping point. Those who write about ethnic violence often introduce women into the narrative, only to leave them stranded at the well, discussing "domestic" and "family" matters (e.g., Kakar 1996). Women are conflict's "victims"; they are "innocent bystanders"; they are, in the last analysis, incidental to the drama (if not the tragedy) of ethnic violence. Feminist critics of this position continue to present counternarratives of women stepping out into public, political life, protesting in the streets, rioting, aiding and abetting "insurgents" (or, if you prefer, "terrorists") (Aretxaga 1997; Jayawardena 1986; Stree Shakti Sanghatana 1989). But what of the women who, in fact, do stay home? What of the women at the well? Although it was not immediately apparent to me at the time, we in the *zenana* were equally involved in Karachi's "troubles" in significant and transformative ways.

As my example makes clear, there are many ways in which we have implicitly accepted the tenets of Western liberal ideology, which casts "home" as a private, feminine realm, cut off from the world of the political, uninvolved with matters of state. This "private sphere" is idealized by some as a realm of freedom of expression, love, and fulfillment; others see it as "women's incarceration" and "restrictive domesticity." But one serious consequence of our tacit acceptance of these tenets is that we have failed to adequately explore the spaces and the social relations of dwelling—of household, apartment building, neighborhood, backyard, balcony—as sites of political processes, not just of gendered and generational conflict but of class, ethnic, racial, and national struggles.

The considerable literature on domesticity in colonial India has established the centrality of "home" in Indian and Indian Muslim nationalist and reform discourses (Chatterjee 1993; Devji 1991; Metcalf 1990; Minault 1998). By appropriating and reconfiguring the "public" and "private" dichotomies of liberalism, anticolonial movements crafted visions of the home (*ghar*) or the *zenana* as sites of cultural authenticity, untouched by the emasculating and corrupting influence of colonial power. The home and the *zenana* would nurture not colonial subjects but national citizens. Such scholarship has indeed unsettled and complicated any easy understanding of these terms—public, private, masculine, feminine, home, nation—and has forced us to locate their emergence within specific cultural and historical practices. But despite this important intervention, the *content* of domesticity (if we choose to call it this)—the lived spaces, relations, and boundaries of dwelling—remains largely unexamined.

Still, one may ask, what do marriage, mother-in-law problems, children, sex, and hair removal have to do with ethnic conflict? Why look to the *zenana*, the apartment building, the dinner party for insight into Karachi's "troubles"? Because the everyday, intimate negotiation of "ethnicity" and "nationalism"—within gendered cultural and historical discourses and practices of home and outside, neighborhood and community, anger and honor, piety and civility—is deeply implicated in the broader conditions of possibility of ethnic violence in the city, as well as the possibility of peaceful coexistence.

Despite a wealth of information on ethnic violence, we actually know very little about the micromechanics of coexistence—about the neighborhoods and colonies that achieved and maintained intergroup peace in the midst of civic strife. There is a pressing need for scholarly analysis of the day-to-day poetics of intergroup cooperation. But even more pointedly, we cannot view this everyday life, this peaceful coexistence, as the static context or backdrop against which "things" (like riots, violence, or "breakdown") happen. Rather, peace itself is the product of a relentless creative labor. Coexistence, as much as conflict, needs to be explained. It is this notion that underpins my interest in the routine rituals and practices of social life in the middle-class Karachi apartment building I have termed "the Shipyard," and it is what has prompted me to return repeatedly to that moment of rupture—the seductive but obfuscating gap in the *zenana* curtains.

As I came to realize, women's refusals to engage with my direct questions about ethnicity in the *zenana* were not evidence of a de facto separation between women's domestic lives and the "broader" political world. On the contrary, such refusals were themselves political practices and would prefigure what was to become an ongoing research theme, namely, that ethnicity in the Shipyard was confounding, complex, shifting, and unpredictable. Ruhi, the "Sindhi" hostess, was "actually a Pathan," she informed me, who grew up in interior Sindh and married into a Sindhi family. Mustafa was a Muhajir, but more important, neighbors stressed, he was a "Syed," descendant of the Prophet. Aliya spoke Punjabi, but she was "actually Kashmiri," she insisted; the Ismaels were Sindhi, but "Memon"; Beenish's family was Muhajir, but "Shia."

"But the family in the corner flat—they're Sindhi, right?" I asked the party guests.

"Those people?!" the women laughed. "But they're Sheiks!" (Sheiks are considered a low-status *zat*—patrilineage, tribe, or caste.)

The repeated insertion of the particular—the insistent invocation of the complexity and the ambiguity of social identity—was critical to the very possibility of "sharing the shade" or *ham sayagi*, the Urdu term for "neighborhood." This example from the dinner party can serve to foreshadow for us the intricate and integral involvement of women's neighboring practices in the everyday maintenance and/or disruption of local, cooperative relations or, put more simply, peace.

But this example can only take us so far, for this labor of peace is less a rationally calculated series of diplomatic and strategic choices (whom to give food to, when to visit, what gossip to share, what to tell one's husband) than it is a fully embodied campaign to interpret, manage, and regulate emotional life, both personal and collective, on a daily basis. If emotions are embodied interpretations of the self-relevance of information (imagined or received) (Hochschild 1983) or cultural statements about personal involvement (Rosaldo 1984), then they are critical modes and moments where individuals and collectives decide the local salience of events, encounters, or ideas. It follows, then, that emotional discourse figures dramatically in the daily intersubjective processes of peace and violence.

There is, however, no simple or straightforward coherence between affect, peace, and violence, where peace is cool-headed reason and violence is unbridled emotionalism. While it may seem self-evident that women would labor to squelch anger, resolve tension, and foster intimacy in order to create peaceful relations, this is not precisely the case. "Anger," "tension," and "intimacy" answer to intricately woven ethnopsychologies and become involved in peace and violence in distinct and surprising ways. It is my contention that we cannot understand the play of interethnic peace and violence in Karachi without unpacking the gendered cultural logics and pragmatics of local emotion discourse and practice. On another note, paying attention to the play of emotional life in peacemaking can help us craft a vision of agency that rejects enlightenment fantasies of autonomous reason. For, while emotion may not altogether be the unwilled, instinctual, organic, universal, feminine, irrational soma that Western philosophical discourse makes it out to be (Lutz 1990), it does point us to nonrational links, motives, and developmental stories that render practice indeterminate, unpredictable, beyond calculation. Agency—even the political agency of violent action or peaceful détente—is not altogether a slave to conscious intent.

Peace Breaks Out

While the anthropological study of violence grows ever more sophisticated and nuanced,[1] the same cannot be said for peace, which remains something of a residual or even organic concept in the discipline. This is why the phrase "peace breaks out" strikes us as absurd: peace cannot "break out," for it is a kind of default setting or underlying context of action. There is something potentially politically positive here— that violence is viewed as aberrant and requiring explanation while peace is viewed as right and natural. But there are dangers as well, for if we relegate peace to the realm of the biological, we relinquish all the anthropological and sociological tools we could be using to understand it in all its cultural and historical incarnations.

The anthropological literature on violence in South Asia almost without exception strives to locate collective violence in social, cultural, and historical contexts. The actors to whom we are introduced are never autonomous individuals but social or colonial constructions: "ethnic warriors," "martial races," "criminal tribes," "terrorists," "religious nationalists." But the rescuer, the altruist, or the peacemaker is invariably represented as a lone, individuated figure, ruled implicitly by things like strength of character and free will. E. Valentine Daniel's stunning "anthropography" of violence in Sri Lanka ends with a tantalizing but terse story of such a rescue (1996). A Tamil man finds himself on a train that is being forcibly boarded by Sinhala nationalist "thugs." The thugs are moving from cabin to cabin, grabbing Tamil passengers (identifiable by their dark complexions) and killing them. The obviously Tamil man shares the compartment with only one other passenger, a Sinhala woman, fair of skin and dressed in obviously Sinhala village attire. Without a word, the Sinhala woman—a stranger—rises, sits next to the Tamil man, and takes his hand in hers. When the thugs enter their cabin, they are fooled by the ruse and move on to the next compartment.

The story is moving and rich with analytical promise. What motivates the Sinhala woman to take the hand of a Tamil stranger, dramatically transgressing gender and sexual propriety norms and risking her life in the process? Daniel refuses to interpret. He has nothing to say about the event, suggesting that nothing in fact can be said. Thrown back on the mystery of a good deed, we are left only with the autonomous, unenculturated individual standing apart from the mob. Peace, altruism, and rescue, when understood (however unconsciously) as universal human acts, humble us, for they profoundly satisfy our longing for the self-willed free agent. But they also silence us, for "character" and "free will" are not amenable to sociocultural analysis. The anthropologist is rendered mute.

Peace and rescue, like terror and violence, are social products, subject to an equally complex array of cultural discourses, narrative conventions, forms of authority, and lines of fissure. We need only consult Goffman's microsociology to appreciate the immense amount of labor that goes into securing the everyday, the ordinary, the normal, and the default (1959, 1967). Thus, in the chapters that follow, it is the everyday micropolitical labors of peace in Karachi that command my attention, and violence becomes peace's context.

Violent Contexts

By virtually all accounts, talk about Karachi in the 1990s—be it local gossip or CNN sound bites—began and ended with "ethnic conflict." Karachi entered the international scene as a city "under siege." "Carnage," "terrorism," "strife-ridden," "embattled"—such were the code words uniting its sprawling territories and its divided population of not less than 14 million. Since the partition of the Indian subcontinent in 1947, Karachi has been the destination of immigrants and migrant workers from throughout the region. The most ethnically diverse city in Pakistan,[2] Karachi has also suffered the most intergroup conflict, rendering the shifting coalitions and antagonisms between variously constructed communities (Muhajir, Sindhi, Baluch, Pathan, Punjabi) difficult to track.

In the 1990s, however, Karachi politics were dominated by the sometimes violent, sometimes dialogic efforts of the MQM—Muhajir Qaumi (national) Movement—to undermine or reform the then ruling (largely rural Sindhi and Punjabi) Pakistan People's Party (PPP). Demanding government representation, jobs, and an end to "Punjabi domination" (at times even demanding the creation of a separate Muhajir province), militant Muhajirs—the descendants of partition-era Indian immigrants—have been waging a battle against the state, meeting its terror tactics with sniper fire and sustained "confrontations." Thousands of Muhajirs have been killed since the mid-1980s in what are euphemistically labeled "the troubles in the city."

"Muhajir," the Urdu word for immigrant, refers specifically to those Urdu-speaking immigrants from North India, especially Uttar Pradesh, who settled in the cities of Sindh at partition (predominantly Karachi and to a lesser extent Hyderabad). While most of the Indian émigrés who settled in Pakistan's other provinces (Punjab, Baluchistan, and the Northwest Frontier Province, or NWFP) were ethnically similar to, and readily assimilated with, their host populations, Muhajirs remained culturally and linguistically distinct (Ahmed 1988: 34). At the same time, it would be misleading to construct "Muhajir" identity as simply one ethnic position among several in the increasingly diversifying landscape of Karachi; it represents, rather, an entirely different way of thinking about the nation and community.

Hailing from the intellectual centers of Indian Muslim reform and the Pakistan movement, Muhajirs provided the ideological content of Pakistani *sharif* (noble) nationalism. Therein, the nation is conceived as an "indissoluble Islamic unity" threatened by "inferior distinctions of tribal, local, or parochial interest" (Daultana in Maniruzzaman 1971: 155). This Muhajir vision marks the imagined continuation of a specific Muslim cultural community that developed through the twin forces of religious reform and embourgoisement in nineteenth-century north India. The Urdu-speaking, exogenous-identified *shurafa* (plural of *sharif*) community looked to neither ethnic nor regional roots in the land, but outside, to Mecca and Medina and a pan-Islamic identity (Devji 1991: 143). In *sharif* discourse, ethnic identity, indeed, any ties to the land or a vernacular language, become antinational and anti-Islamic, signaling a failure to fully convert (Kurin 1981: 122).[3]

In the dominant discourse of a Muhajir past, Karachi marks the actualization of ideological and personal struggle. After migration, Muhajirs viewed themselves as the architects and rightful inheritors of the nation. *Sharif* nationalism became, in effect, public policy. In an effort to unify West Pakistan, which was seen as dangerously divided by linguistic and cultural differences, provincial identity was dissolved and vernacular education outlawed, while an Islamic, Urdu national culture was promoted.[4] Ironically, while this Muhajir-centric ideology of Pakistan— and the anti-ethnic sentiments of *sharif* nationalism—still dominates, its authors find themselves disenfranchised. Excluded from the Punjabi-dominated civil-military apparatus, and all but absent from the government leadership, Muhajirs come together as a politically underrepresented urban "underclass," unemployed and underemployed, in perpetual violent conflict with the state (see Alavi 1987).

Certainly, in one sense, on the other side of *sharif* nationalism, ethnicity (difference) is all the same. Against the only wholly de-territorialized group in Karachi, all other groups, to a degree, serve as a foil for Muhajir universalism. But to so collapse them is to ignore the specific semantics of struggle through which ethnic conflict in Karachi gets narrativized. Indeed, while Muhajir claims to Karachi rest on a notion of political and religious inheritance, Sindhi nationalist claims rely on the cachet of indigenous "roots." Whatever the specific demographics of struggle—whatever the actual dynamic of relations between Muhajirs and

Sindhis (for their political efforts, at least, are not always opposed—notably, in their shared critique of Punjabi domination; Alavi 1987)—the symbolism is clear: the "troubles in the city" revolve around these competing nationalisms, Sindhi (ethnic) and Muhajir (*sharif*) (Ahmed 1988).[5]

In many ways, the creation of Pakistan decisively separated Karachi from the rest of the Sindh province. Before 1947, most of the Sindhi inhabitants of the city were Hindu, and when Sindh passed, unpartitioned, to Pakistan, most Hindus fled to India. The resulting urban vacuum was also rapidly filled and exceeded by Muhajirs. This radical demographic transformation, accompanied by the "Urduizing" policies of the fledgling Pakistani state (not to mention a Muhajir "failure to assimilate") have been bemoaned by Sindhi activists as effecting the "de-Sindhization" of Sindh (Singh 1986: 160).

Currently, Sindhis constitute one of the smallest ethnic minorities in Karachi, remaining both pragmatically and symbolically incarcerated in the interior. While the deposed Bhutto government had ties with rural Sindh, this did not result in real economic opportunities for the rural Sindhis flocking to the city. If anything, it exacerbated the tumultuous relationship between Karachi and Sindh—Muhajir and Sindhi—a relationship which is caught up with narratives of trespass: the cultural dominance of *sharif* nationalism renders Sindhis out of place in the city, anachronistic intruders, flashy feudal relics, or backward peasants. Similarly, Sindhi nationalism—and the Sindhi *daku* (bandit) raids on urban travelers in the interior—renders material this phantasmagoric barrier between metropolis and hinterland, a barrier that invests itself in ethnic bodies, proscribes mobility, and informs dwelling.

My first inkling that apartment dwelling could serve as a kind of metaphorical site for thinking about ethnic conflict in Karachi came when my husband and I were apartment hunting during my preliminary research trip in 1994. We had been looking at apartments for most of the day—after weeks of arguing with my husband's parents over whether or not we should "live separately" from them. Narrowly missing rush-hour traffic, we met the real estate agent at the Al-Habib Arcade, a towering apartment complex opposite the Tin Talwar (three swords) roundabout, in the center of Clifton, an elite neighborhood on Karachi's southern coast. We took the elevator up to the fourth floor, walked along the breezy corridor that hovered between the parking lot and the open sky, and found our way to the flat soon to be available for rent. The real estate agent knocked on the door, which was answered by a man wearing a white *shalwar kurta*, red and gold Sindhi *topi* (cap), and *ajrak*—articles of clothing that dramatically announce Sindhi identity. The agent and the tenant conversed briefly in Urdu and turned to address us. "He says only she can go in," the agent remarked, pointing to me. "Some of the women are still in bed." I followed the tenant into the apartment, and the door closed, clicking softly behind us.

Due perhaps to their imminent move—or, equally possible, the minimalist trends of small-time absentee landlords and their retinues—the flat was completely bereft of furniture. Quilts lay on the floor, rolled up against the wall of each room. The walls had obviously suffered serious water damage, perhaps from the previous season's monsoons or internal plumbing problems. My host gave me a tour of the flat, pointing out the largeness of the space and directing me to each window, for a view of its outer parameters. "Here's a room, here's another room," he was saying. "Look, here's a garden." In the largest room, which opened onto a balcony, sat four women and a toddler, on bedding and floor pillows, smiling politely as they drank their morning tea. I greeted them and made my way to the balcony, which was filled with fresh produce. The tour was over; I thanked the man and left.

Meanwhile, outside, the agent was indignant. "These people! Why couldn't the women just wait in the bedroom?" Shaking his head, he apologized for the disrepair of the apartment, promising that it would be fully refurbished before we moved in. My husband asked me for details: What were the bedrooms like? The drawing room? The dining room? Was there a TV lounge? I struggled to summon up the images of such rooms in my mind, but none were forthcoming. I hadn't been shown any bathrooms. The most I could say was that it seemed quite spacious.

At that moment, I realized that there was something more I needed to know in order to make sense of this interaction. Outside, the young Urdu-educated Muhajir real estate agent was attempting to collude with my equally young English-educated Muhajir husband to produce notions of the Sindhi as rural, backwards, a relic, out of place in the city. The soggy walls, the general disrepair confirmed the agent's opinion of Sindhis as "bad tenants." "They come here, and they move in, and they never leave," the agent told my husband. Sindhi dwelling was read as a kind of excess, a surfeit of rooting, an invasive, destructive dwelling, which penetrates and alters space—a convenient metaphor, homologous with notions of Sindhi rootedness as against Muhajir urban rootlessness. In urbanist discourse, which the agent, as a kind of "modernist practitioner of space," reproduces in practice, this mode of dwelling is unintelligible. It signals only failure: failure, above all, to follow the rational, functional layout of the space. Unlike the many agent-led tours we had been on that week, this one was pointedly nonutilitarian. Perhaps the women could not simply "wait in the bedroom," for "bedroom" and all that it implies was more diffusely present in the totality of the space.

Because the social relations of this space—the neighborhood of Al-Habib Arcade—were inaccessible to me, the interaction was limited to one of thresholds, and my analysis remained merely metaphorical. But my tenure as a resident in the Shipyard convinced me that the multistory apartment building could serve not simply as metaphor but as a kind of microcosm of ethnic relations in the city as a whole. It is to the Shipyard that I now turn.[6]

Field Site

If you take Khayaban-e Sahal heading west, you'll come to the Arabian Sea. First you'll pass Clifton's youth-dominated fast-food and commercial strip, known simply as "Boat Basin," gaudy with a trove of half-lit signs advertising everything from Broast Karachi to Baluchi embroidery. Interspersed between these dusty commercial lanes—packed with schools and flats and medical clinics—are transient colonies of refugees, beggars, day laborers, and their livestock. There is a stinking stream following one of these lanes, emptying into the polluted but picturesque bay. At the junction leading to Keamari Harbor, you'll see a now-tattered billboard advertising the forthcoming "Marine Park," a reminder of the ill-fated government scheme to use Karachi's population of blind dolphins for tourist dollars.

After negotiating a roundabout, you'll leave the main road for a series of unpaved, gridlike lanes, dotted haphazardly with date palm and hibiscus. These lanes sport the bungalows of the comfortably upper middle class. As date palm and hibiscus give way to mangrove and desert scrub, you arrive at Rasm Chowk, a commercial street facing the sea on one side and—though separated by an expanse of overgrown empty lots and squatter settlements—its more illustrious neighbors on the other. The Shipyard is one of many undistinguished, multistory apartment buildings on Rasm Chowk, sandwiched, both spatially and economically, between a ring of luxury high-rises housing the city's elite and the ubiquitous, vacant shells of buildings frozen in varying stages of construction, unlikely ever to be completed, thanks to some combination of wild speculation, embezzlement, land disputes, and unsafe building practices.

Everything on Rasm Chowk is affected by the sea. Metal hinges and runners on doors and windows are forever rusting and breaking down. Cars and motorcycles on the roadside depreciate at untold rates. Windows and storefronts must be washed daily to remove the opaque layer of brine and sand that the humid westerly winds slap mercilessly on their exposed surfaces. Those denizens of the coveted "west-open" flats get the full force of the breeze off the sea—cooling, indeed, but also dirty and destructive.

If you stand with your back to the wind, you can take in the public face of the Shipyard. It is three steps up to the portico that spans the length of the building, a shady stretch punctuated by concrete support beams that line up with storefront divisions. Almost all of these storefronts are shuttered and padlocked; only one is up and running—a real estate agency. Through the glass door, you can see two rows of neatly groomed young men, talking on telephones and sitting at desks crowded by fans and potted plants. Outside, their motorcycles lie in a tangle at the foot of the steps.

Each of the four floors above the portico sport open-to-sky balconies on each of the building's four sides. In the daylight hours, the balconies are strewn with wet laundry; at any given time, these spaces are alive with the sounds of chickens cackling, children playing, and women in conversation or at work.

There is a newly constructed building, Fairhaven, to the north of the Shipyard; the first floor of the Fairhaven hosts a Chinese restaurant and a dry cleaners. By the time we left, only a handful of families had moved into the upper ten floors of middle-income flats. A narrow gully winds between the two buildings and stretches on, bifurcating the Sindhi camel and cattle herders and Afghan refugee settlements that come and go on the overgrown "empty" lot behind the Shipyard, which is said to be municipal land earmarked for a park. After alighting from bus or rickshaw or after parking their cars or motorcycles in front of the western steps, residents of the Shipyard must walk along this gully to reach the entrance, avoiding brackish mud puddles, construction debris, and feral cats as they go.

Even a cursory glance across Karachi's landscape confirms the ubiquity of buildings like the Shipyard. Unlovely, patchy-gray reinforced concrete, its fixtures corroded by the briny sea air, the five-story walk-up shelters close to fifty households. Multistory living marks a recent change in urban housing trends, away from the more traditional single-story, single-family residence pattern of elite bungalows, lower- to middle-income colonies, historic *mohalla*s (city or town quarters), and *kachi abadi*s (squatter settlements). Introduced as government housing projects in the 1960s along Karachi's Superhighway, high-rise living was slow to catch on with the general population. It was not until the mid-1970s that multistory living became the housing of choice for the lower middle class (see Lari 1998).

The combined influence of colonial development (with its typical segregation of cantonment and native town), urban housing policies, and property values in Karachi has consigned the bulk of the lower middle class to the remote, suburban periphery of the city. Too poor to afford bungalows in the more central, elite neighborhoods but well-off enough to escape the crowds and the clutter of the ghettoized inner city, this class finds itself relegated to Karachi's outskirts. It is no coincidence that this "periphery" is also the main locus of ethnic violence, considering that the region's ethnic political movements draw their members largely from this socioeconomic stratum.

As families residing on this violence-ridden periphery become upwardly mobile, they tend to move toward the city's center, where jobs, services, safety, and the benefits of citizenship await them. Multistory living, for the most part, is a condition of this kind of upward mobility. Or to put it another way, the increased availability of lower-income, multistory dwellings has enabled members of the lower middle class to move in from the urban periphery. Many make small upward moves to less remote (but still peripheral) neighborhoods (like Gulshan-e Iqbal and Federal "B" Area). And a smaller number head for the more elite areas of District South (Clifton, Defense, KDA, PECHS), settling for cramped, poorly serviced economy flats in exchange for the opportunity to share in the region's imagined insulation from routine violence.

Residential communities in high-rises differ from those in more traditional urban quarters in one very important aspect: high-rises tend to be multiethnic. While slums, *mohalla*s, and colonies are generally homogeneous—reproducing caste groups, ethnic populations, or sectarian communities—the relations of dwelling in tenements like the Shipyard are largely abstracted from relations of kin, clan, ethnic group, and sect. Indeed, the ethnic and sectarian diversity of the Shipyard was pronounced, finding Sindhis, Muhajirs, Punjabis, Pathans, and Baluchis (not to mention Shias, Memons, and Bhoras) randomly scattered along the betel nut–stained hallways. Arguably, the multiculturalism of high-rise living marks a significant site of historical transformation in the social conditions of "neighboring" as well as pointing to the transformed, supraproximate conditions of practicing kin, clan, ethnic, and sectarian relations for these urban dwellers.

At this point, I wish to draw attention to one of the obvious problems that accompany research in an urban apartment building. How do we mark this space as giving rise to specific or new social forms without reducing it to a facile story of modernity versus tradition? Ethnographies of urban life are vulnerable to grossly simplified readings which assume that the complexity, turmoil, or labor depicted in social relations therein must necessarily be imagined as counterposed to an original, traditional simplicity, ease, and unreflective or "mechanical" identity or solidarity (Durkheim 1933). Certainly, any reader familiar with South Asia would grasp the absurdity of such a proposition. Village life in India is famously complex, and the anthropological archive on Pakistan is filled with descriptions of labyrinthine systems of affinal gifting (Eglar 1960; Werbner 1990) and other ways in which social relations are symbolically and pragmatically constructed. This is true from the most allegedly natural bonds of close kinship to the most abstract bonds of national citizenship. Let me make it clear, then, that my observations about the apartment building in no way imply that the labor of creating social relations is somehow new or uniquely "modern." But having said that, it is clear that this space—the multistory apartment building—does give rise to distinct forms and problems of sociality.

Sociologists of urban India have repeatedly noted the residentially segregated character of the greater part of South Asian cities—the grouping of neighborhoods based on caste, ethnic, linguistic, regional, and religious affiliations (Raju 1982: 1). In Karachi, slums or colonies may host a number of ethnic or religious groups, but internal lanes are usually relatively homogeneous. While South Asian governments bemoan the persistence of ethnic or kin-based residential enclaves as anathema to modern civil society, attempts to "distribute population on the basis of income homogeneity" have largely failed (Raju 1982: 20). Ties of kinship, clan, caste, ethnic group, language, sect, or natal region are not only not destroyed by a homogenizing modernity or urban way of life.[7] More often than not, such ties inform how people migrate, the forms of residence they take up in the city, and—where residential propinquity cannot be achieved—the forms of sociality they pursue beyond place of residence (Chandra 1977; Hasan 1976; Raju 1982).

It is clear that the extreme heterogeneity of the Shipyard population was something new for most of my informants. It is also clear that residents tried to bring forward preexisting social forms into this new context. Family members tried, often desperately, to buy or rent flats adjacent to one another. When Sheheryar and I rented a flat during my preliminary research in 1994, the landlord asked us to pose as his relatives because he did not want to offend the family next door, who for years had been asking that he rent the flat to their brother's family. "But how could I give the flat to them?" he explained. "Two brothers, side by side, they'd never leave!"[8] In the Shipyard, one family spatially preserved (and reconfigured) the joint family system by buying two nonadjacent flats in the building. This was far from uncommon.

The attempt to draw familiar social forms into the new space of the apartment building presented any number of problems and opportunities for Shipyard residents, as I will demonstrate later in the text. Now I want to return to outlining some of the general demographic characteristics of these residents, for, in addition to this broader, historical shift toward multistory dwelling, living in the Shipyard marks a significant site of *personal* transition for many of the inhabitants. Many had indeed migrated from poorer, violence-ridden areas of the city (most notably, Malir and Nazimabad) or peripheral suburban neighborhoods (like Gulshan-e Iqbal and Federal "B" Area). Some had arrived directly from villages or towns of Sindh, Punjab, Baluchistan, and NWFP. For a select few, living in the Shipyard represented a downwardly mobile move; families fallen on hard times had been forced to leave their better-serviced, more respectable flats for the shabby, commercial-lane tenement. There was even a young, elite couple sacrificing splendor for the chance at independent living outside the joint family household.

Despite their diverse origins, the majority of Shipyard residents did share a kind of social identity—that of the Muslim, Urdu-educated, newly middle class (pointedly *not* the English-speaking, Western-educated elite).[9] The men worked, for the most part, in low-paying but respectable government jobs (as teachers, revenue officers, engineers, police officers, doctors, and so on); only a handful of women worked—as Urdu and Islamiat (religious instruction) teachers—outside of the home. The families relied largely on public transportation, though some owned motorcycles and cars. Their children almost exclusively attended government Urdu-medium grammar schools, some (nearly all of the boys, very few of the girls) going on to study in a government college or university. Despite their different linguistic backgrounds, all of the men and most of the women were able to converse fluently in Urdu.

While this litany of demographic details does help set up the social historical context of buildings like the Shipyard, it fails to convey the ambivalence with which people make such geographic and symbolic moves. To grasp the tenuous ways in which the Shipyard gets constructed as a particular kind of "modern" space, we need to turn our attention to Shipyard dwellers and their stories.

Coming to the Shipyard

One morning, as on many other mornings, I sat with Zubaida in her corner apartment and talked about life in the Shipyard and the city in general. Zubaida grew up in the Sindhi interior, in a small village outside of Khairpur named for her father and his grandfather before him, small-time landlords holding sway over little more than one hundred acres of arable land. Zubaida had left her natal village seven years previously, upon her marriage to her patrilateral, parallel cousin, or her father's brother's son. Zubaida is the only woman in her family to have settled in the city; more commonly, landowners' sons migrate to Karachi, Hyderabad, or the smaller towns of Sindh for education and employment, while their wives remain in the *gaon* (village). Like the other women in her village, Zubaida initially moved into her father-in-law's house (which was simply two houses away in the extended-family compound) while her husband continued to work and live in the city. But Zubaida's husband, Babar, quickly tired of this arrangement and insisted upon bringing Zubaida to Karachi to set up their own household. "Why did I marry if I'm to live alone?" Babar had apparently quipped.

For Zubaida, then, coming to the city coincides with a number of dramatic life changes: the leaving of the natal home, the establishment of the marital household, the transition from unmarried woman to wife, and the assumption of all the duties and privileges and pleasures that may entail. In Zubaida's case, the move also represents an escape from the father-in-law's house and the everyday authority of her mother-in-law, which is no small matter.

But as a Sindhi immigrant, coming to Karachi means leaving behind the ubiquity of a vernacular Sindhi public. It means living among people who are *ghair* (strange, foreign) in many ways. As Zubaida's village was practically coterminous with *biradari* (patrilineage, or clan), neighbors were also already *rishtedar* (relatives), however intimately or vaguely reckoned. But the Shipyard brought the *na-mehram* (outsiders, non-kin, men from whom women must segregate) right to one's door. Neighbors were strangers—strangers one could reach out to, not through the language of home and family and *biradari* but through the national, civic language of Urdu and Islam.

Being of some, though comparatively modest, privilege, Zubaida had been educated up to interscience (university) and was fluent in Urdu. Urdu is rarely spoken in Sindhi village households in the interior, and women without formal education, in which Urdu language is compulsory, rarely become fluent (although, according to Zubaida, more and more Sindhi women in the villages are learning Urdu, thanks to satellite TV and the Hindi film channels).

Zubaida had much to say about the differences between village life and city life. Indeed, this was a favored topic among many of my women neighbors, both the newer and older village emigrants and the lifelong urbanites. But on this particular morning, Zubaida was reminiscing. A gifted storyteller, she related to me the details of her earliest memory of Karachi, and I was spellbound:

> "I was four years old. My mother, my father, and some of my aunts and uncles had won the lottery to go for Hajj that year.[10] They were to go by sea, and my youngest brother and I had come to Karachi with our *taya* (father's elder brother) to bid them farewell. I remember, we were standing in the Keamari harbor, holding hands, and there on deck we could see my mother. My brother started to cry, and I wanted to cry, too. But my mother was laughing and waving. She looked so happy and so carefree. I stood up straighter, and I hushed my brother and waved, calling out, 'Don't worry, Ammi, I won't cry. I'll be brave. You go and be happy.' We waved 'ta-ta' and watched the ship until it moved out of the harbor into the sea."

As soon as I heard this story and eagerly committed it to paper, I knew that it could somehow provide a focus for the myriad and contradictory portrayals my informants gave of Karachi and Village, real and apocryphal. Zubaida's story so elegantly allegorizes the ambivalence that Karachiites, old and new, express about their city—about what they have found and what they have left behind, what this city offers and what it restricts. Zubaida's is a story of loss and promise, opportunity and danger. Her mother, on the deck, is both lost to her and at the same time hinting at pleasures and possibilities Zubaida can only imagine. The remembered intimacy of the mother, home, childhood is juxtaposed with—or sacrificed for—the promise of new pleasures, growth, empowerment. It should not be forgotten that the traveler's journey is one of Hajj, a religious pilgrimage that offers the possibility of fulfillment, in terms of both spirit and status. Karachi, in Zubaida's story, is both a point of departure for one's dreams and a port of arrival of adult responsibility and self-reliance, thus she will be brave and not cry. Zubaida, the child, is both bereft and emboldened.

Throughout my residence in Karachi, the tales people told of the city were often dystopian and despairing. Iqbal,[11] the Punjabi Christian sweeper who came each morning to clean for me (and many others in the building), repeatedly warned me of the folly of studying Karachi if I'm to understand Pakistan. *"Karachi men tarah tarah ke log rehte hain,"* she would say. (In Karachi, all sorts of people are living.) "If you want to know about real Punjabis, you have to go to Punjab," she insisted.

"The Punjabis here, they're not real Punjabis." In fact, Karachi was said to be full of dangers, precisely because of its multiethnic, migrant, displaced populations—"*tarah tarah ke log.*" People in Karachi were not who (or where) they were supposed to be.

Similarly, Zubaida told me time and again that the Sindhis in Karachi were not *real* Sindhis. "When Sindhis come to the city, then their minds become bad (*dimagh kharab ho jate hain*)." When I asked her whether she and her husband, who had migrated to the city, were also not real Sindhis, she qualified her statement: "No, you see, we've come directly from the village," she explained, as if her ongoing practical and affective ties to the village preserved her authenticity, mitigating against a total migration.

It is not only rural immigrants who bemoan the conditions of living in Karachi; rather than glorifying a lost "rusticity," Muhajirs and urban Sindhis instead sing laments for "the ruined city."[12] For Kulsoom, a Muhajir Shia neighbor whose daughter Beenish was a frequent visitor at our flat, Clifton was a much safer, much more dignified (*sharif*) place before all the Sindhi landlords moved in. According to Junaid, an elite Muhajir friend of my husband's, our building was overrun with "Nazimabadi-types," by which he meant the grasping, social climbing, newly middle class. (Nazimabad, a western neighborhood of Karachi, was the destination of many partition-era Muhajirs and the site of a great deal of MQM factional violence in the 1990s. Despite the obvious presence of old money therein, Nazimabad nevertheless signals a kind of peripheral backwater for which Clifton and Defense are the figurative metropoles.) An Aga Khani Sindhi friend often lamented the (perceived) transformation of Garden East—a predominantly Ismaili area—from a tightly cooperative (homogeneous) neighborhood to a besieged enclave,[13] and Sheheryar's mother, also Sindhi Ismaili, took us through Nazimabad and Malir, pointing out the traces of long-gone farms and Ismaili mosques, crowded out by development and demographic changes. "They've taken it all. It's all theirs now," she said softly—"they" being perhaps developers or immigrants or "troublemakers"; it never became clear.

This concern with the city as social breakdown, people set loose from the structures of kin and clan, free to mix, mingle, and run amok in the disorderly city, is a familiar refrain for anthropologists. Much has been made of the moral tensions played out in contests over "city" and "country" in industrializing Europe (Williams 1973)—and of course, these historical tensions became universal evolutionary markers in anthropological scholarship, qua the infamous "folk-urban continuum" (Miner 1952; Redfield 1947). But decades of scholarship on colonial and postcolonial societies have established the culturally specific ways in which notions of modernity and tradition—and city and country—are caught up in locally meaningful (but globally engaged) moral struggles. Lest we presume to recognize this anxiety too easily, it should be remembered that the city has other pasts in South Asian and Islamic cultures. A convenient metonym for Western modernity, it is simultaneously a moral victory—the triumph of Islamic law over the heretical Sufi wilderness (Devji 1991). And on a more prosaic level, the dystopian trope of the city as "corrupt modernity" shares space with (and is itself informed by) the equally powerful, heady vision of the city as a setting for desire. Thus a Sindhi neighbor confided that most of the Sindhi village girls who stayed with her at Marvi Hostel in Sindh University faced a terrible dilemma: having seen "the city" (Jamshoro and Hyderabad), they never wanted to return to the *gaon*.

In the Shipyard, Sindhi residents received a continuous flow of visitors from the *gaon*, who would stay for two or three days of shopping and *samandar dekhna* (looking at the sea). The urban hosts get to be sophisticated and savvy. Returning to the *gaon* similarly performs these moral possibilities. Zubaida told me that when she goes to her village, "Everyone rushes to greet me. They like me because each time I come, they see that I haven't changed. I don't say, 'Oh, I don't like this,' or 'I won't sit on the floor,' or 'In Karachi we have this and that.' They see that I'm just the same." Ruhi, on the other hand, described how her women relatives in the *gaon* looked to her as a kind of translator of urban chic and the repository of new kinds of knowledge:

> "Last time I arrived, I was tired and dirty from the long trip, wearing a simple cotton suit,[14] like this one. And the women said, 'Oh, don't you want to wear something nice? Don't you want to put on a silk *jora*?'
> 'No,' I said, 'I like my cotton suit.'
> 'Oh, in Karachi they're wearing cotton suits?' someone said. 'Well, we also have cotton suits.'
> 'Yes, yes,' all the women agreed."

At times, the bald contradictions of urban imaginaries were jarring. About six months into my fieldwork, Zubaida's live-in *devar* (husband's younger brother) married a girl from Larkana (a small town in interior Sindh) and brought her to live with them in the Shipyard. During my many visits to Zubaida's flat, the bride, Tahira, would sit quietly, with a tight-lipped smile, while Zubaida and I conversed. "My *devrani* (*devar*'s wife), she doesn't like Karachi," Zubaida would say with approval. When I asked Tahira her reasons, she shrugged and said "*Bas, aise*"—just like that. Despite her demurrals, Tahira nevertheless seemed to be enjoying her "honeymoon," taking numerous seaside strolls with her husband and frequenting the many cloth and bangle markets in Saddar (the city center). After some time, it occurred to me that, just as it doesn't look nice (*acha nahin lagta*) for a bride to eat with gusto, smile with her mouth wide open, and look around boldly, so it doesn't look nice to *like* the city. Ironically, when I later asked Zubaida why Tahira wasn't living with her in-laws in Zubaida's village, Zubaida confided, mildly disparaging, "My *devrani* couldn't stand even one day in our *gaon*; she's not a country girl."

Perhaps even more glaring were the confusing opinions Shipyard residents seemed to have about their own neighbors and the building in general. Kulsoom warned me, soon after I moved in, that there were "not very many nice people living here." Zubaida suspected that many neighboring flats housed militant Sindhi-hating Muhajirs. She advised me often on which flats I should avoid and which I should freely visit. Male residents confided in my husband that our building housed "all types," even prostitutes. The Baluch customs official living above us was said to be a con artist and bribe-taker; a woman on the fourth floor was said to be the wife of an imprisoned Sindhi bandit; the Muhajir family downstairs had MQM connections; this and that man had two wives; the building president was a lecher. All in all, women in the Shipyard expressed a great deal of fear, disdain, and suspicion toward the people who were sharing their shade (*ham sayah*: neighbors).

But in the same breath, my fellow residents assured me of the safety, the affability, and the hominess of the building. Certainly, I shouldn't hesitate to let my son run freely in the halls. "In this building, everyone loves each other. No one will scold your child. They'll look out for him, just as if he were their own," Zubaida averred. "We're like family here (*sab apne hain*),"[15] Ruhi told me. "Everyone helps each other."

There is, or should be, nothing surprising about the internally contradictory nature of these narratives of the city. Surely, just as Zubaida's story suggests, Karachi, or more specifically the Shipyard, with its multiethnic population, presents both risks and opportunities to its inhabitants. Behind the fearful and disdainful talk, I suspect, lies the conception of this space, this condition of dwelling, as somewhat unscripted. There is a sense that structures, relations, and spaces must be forged where none can be said to exist. "Neighborhood," or being "neighbors," requires a kind of vigilant labor, under conditions of imperfect information and undetermined expectations. The dangerous, slippery, disordered circumstance of proximate living must be transformed, through practice, into *ham sayagi*. This is how neighbors can be at once feared outsiders and fictive kin.

Mobility

Chroniclers of the modern city have frequently noted the unprecedented opportunities for individual freedom that urban life offers—freedom of movement and freedom from local authority, kinship hierarchies, and the sanctioning power of small town gossip. But as Mrs. Sultan's story suggests, this scenario is far from universal.

Sultan Sahib and his family lived in the northeast corner flat on the ground floor.[16] The ground floor apartments were much coveted by the upper floor dwellers because instead of two separate back balconies, each flat boasted a large, walled, open-to-sky terrace. We on the upper floors looked down with longing at the green and flowering plants and vines in Sultan Sahib's garden and at his carefree children riding tricycles and playing ball in the shade.

Sultan Sahib and his wife were Pashto-speaking Pathans who had fled their native Nathiagali in the NWFP when a local feud threatened their safety. Not long after arriving in Karachi in the early 1990s, they purchased a flat in the Shipyard and started a family. By the time we moved into the building, the Sultans had two preschool boys, and Sultan Sahib was working as a barrister in the city courts.

Sultan Sahib was a very visible and vocal presence in the building. Most evenings and weekends, one could find him sitting on the portico conversing in Pashto with the young *chowkidar* (watchman, gatekeeper), a fellow native of Nathiagali. Sultan Sahib and the *chowkidar* were on very friendly terms, and whenever the Sultans were traveling, the *chowkidar* would take up residence in their flat. This close friendship, born, it was assumed, of a shared ethnic and linguistic heritage, was the cause of some grumbles among the other residents. With the *chowkidar* so clearly in his corner, wouldn't Sultan Sahib get special, perhaps unfair building privileges, like extra water at delivery time?

Sultan Sahib was also good friends with the building president, Ilahi Sahib, a Sindhi speaker, and with our hallmate, Qazi Sahib, a Punjabi. It was not uncommon to find Sultan Sahib chatting with them in Urdu in the hallways, alley, or portico and accompanying them to the Sunni al-Hadith mosque one block away. With his loud, good-natured presence and his obvious (but not necessarily offensive) self-importance, Sultan Sahib clearly enjoyed being in the middle of things and was accustomed to being the leader.

Things were quite different for Sultan's wife. The only times I saw her leave her flat were evenings and weekends, in full *burqa*, accompanied by her husband or other *burqa*-clad women. My neighbors and I surmised that she and/or her family were very strict about the observance of purdah (the veiling and segregation of women), and this undoubtedly limited her mobility both inside the building and beyond.

But the other difficulty Mrs. Sultan faced was that she did not speak Urdu. A number of times, while standing on a back balcony and chatting in Urdu with neighbors above or to the south of me, I would see Mrs. Sultan step into her garden. Unable to join in the conversation—and perhaps also unwilling, I cannot say—she would look up, salaam, and go back inside.

The rare times that the Sultan children—who also spoke only Pashto—came to play with Faizan in our flat, Mrs. Sultan would shout a request to the *chowkidar* to go and fetch them for dinner. These and other sorts of requests—and they were many, since her local life and transactions were overwhelmingly conducted through, or mediated by, the *chowkidar*—issued from their northside window, which opened onto the alley, at the western end of which the *chowkidar* habitually sat. As the main door of the building also opened onto the alley, this window was easily visible to passersby—and vice versa. While the window, like all the ground floor windows, was caged in by a security grate, someone had cut a head-shaped hole in the *jali* (screen or netting). Mrs. Sultan could thus stick her head out past the screen and look through the security bars at the neighborly comings and goings and, when needed, summon the *chowkidar*.

That head-shaped hole in the window screen was a poignant reminder of what so many women had to give up to come here, for, while moving to the city—or, even more specifically, to the kind of multiethnic, seemingly anonymous community of strangers that the Shipyard offered—may have represented opportunities for greater mobility for the men, for women it marked the opposite. Zubaida spoke of female friends and relatives who were reluctant to leave the village because of the greater *pabandi* (restriction) they would face in the city. The *burqa* (full body covering) and the *hijab* (headscarf) are urban affairs, Aliya insisted. Even in small towns or older city quarters, women can move about relatively freely. "There is no need for purdah in such places," Zubaida told me, "because women can find a path from house to house without being seen."

Since the area outside the building is unambiguously public, most women are loathe to traverse it without the accompaniment of male or senior female relatives. Thus the building itself becomes a crucial site of women's everyday social life and attachment. Those women, especially internal immigrants like Mrs. Sultan, who are insecure about their cultural competency and Urdu language skills, can find themselves virtually isolated in an environment that seems both hostile and denigrating.

But there is more to this story than the trope of "city versus country" can reveal. Pakistani women *expect* to live their lives largely in the company of other women, not ensconced in the privacy of the conjugal couple. With the growth of relatively nuclearized households and a concomitant transformation in local attitudes toward women's extrafamilial exchange relations, women's sociality in the Shipyard and other buildings of its kind is at once complicated and uncertain. The increased concerns with purdah in the city, combined with this class of women's limited geographic mobility, means that they are thrown back on their neighbors for sociality and support more than ever. A final look at the dinner party can throw into relief some of the cultural, ethnopsychological conditions within which this sociality gets constructed:

At 10:30, I heard my husband's voice outside the *zenana* curtains. "I'm leaving. I'll put Faizan to bed," he called. "You coming up soon?"

"Yes, okay. Soon." I turned and rejoined the conversation; half an hour later, I rose and made my apologies. "I really must go. Sheheryar's waiting for me."

The women began to bid me *khuda hafiz* (good-bye, God protect), when Ruhi fixed me with a wry smile and asked in a loud, teasing voice: "Laura! Are you leaving because *you* have remembered Sheheryar Bhai (brother) or because he'll be angry if you don't?" Nonplussed, I shrugged and grinned, and the women burst out laughing.

I pause at this round of laughter because it points, of course, to the normative. Leaving this neighboring public because you want to be with your husband is actually laughable; you're not supposed to want that. But even more sharply, Ruhi's comment helps bolster the notion that the site of "having a life" may not necessarily lie on the other side of those curtains, in the privacy of the conjugal couple, any more than it need lie in the masculine public of the *mardana*. This social space may be exactly where you want to be, the space where things happen, where words and practices have impact, where spontaneity, creativity, and attachment are all possible.

But the second part of Ruhi's utterance, the specter of my husband's anger, is also critical. It reminds that this space of sociality is produced within gendered power relations, within local cultural discourses and disciplines of male dominance. Women repeatedly invoke a naturalized and ethnicized discourse of male anger in order to explain their actions (and, as I discuss in chapter 4, to explain the differences between ethnic and sectarian groups). The threat of male anger marks the boundaries of the possible.

Indeed, this project is poised between two related conversations about gender and feminist theorizing in postcolonial contexts. On the one hand, a central aim of the book is to challenge those ubiquitous studies of the Islamic world that construct the practices of purdah as banishing women from the potential empowerment of public life. My research suggests, rather, that "neighborhood"—the spaces and social relations of the apartment building—served as an arena for the construction of women's political subjectivity, that the neighboring *zenana* was itself a kind of public, within which women could reconfigure as well as reproduce gendered power relations, ethnic enmities, and class hierarchies.

On the other hand, it is clear that women's political agency in this space of segregated sociality was fully contingent on, and reproductive of, gender difference and hierarchy. It is impossible simply to champion this agency or these political practices without marking the way in which they represent a reinscription of the very system of gendered power relations that underpins women's subordination. Maintaining a balance between these two agendas—between political recognition and critical distance—has been a key consideration in the presentation of my research.

The Anthropologist

Although I had much more freedom and mobility, and my Urdu language skills were certainly greater than Mrs. Sultan's, I had my own insecurities about cultural competence when I was first faced with the complex and uncertain social life of the building. When my family and I first moved into the Shipyard, I felt overwhelmed by all that I had to manage and understand on a daily basis. We had found the flat through my mother-in-law's close friend, who had purchased it for her daughter's dowry. Once the building construction was completed, however, her daughter and son-in-law could not abide the "low class of people" who settled there, and they chose instead to rent it out.

Sheheryar and I spent our first few weeks in the flat struggling to get water tanks and hot water heaters repaired, the telephone turned on, and the fuse boxes to work. With our limited experience with independent living in Karachi, simple matters like putting out the garbage, paying gas bills, and hiring a sweeper seemed like Herculean tasks. In those early days, I did little more than exchange friendly smiles with my new neighbors; rapport seemed ages in the future.

Our son, Faizan, on the other hand—then three and a half years old—was much more intrepid. Oblivious to language barriers, he immediately joined the Shipyard children in their games on the stairs and in the hallways, often following them into their own flats and bringing them to ours. Before long, the children's faces became familiar. Frequently, little girls would come to my door on what appeared to be reconnaissance missions, armed with simply phrased questions about things like my religious affiliation and Sheheryar's occupation.

But finally one day, while two of Faizan's friends, Meher and Zain, were playing in our apartment, their mother, Zubaida, knocked on my door in search of them. I invited her in, and we had a long, pleasant conversation about the building, our children, and how I came to be here. The next day, I received scores of visits from the women in the building. "We didn't know that you spoke Urdu," Hina's mother told me.

Hina was a mischievous five-year-old who lived across from us and was the chief reconnoiterer on the hall.[17] "That's why we stayed away."

Urdu proficiency was a kind of bare bones requirement for participation in Shipyard social life. But progressing from casual visits and passing conversations to more intense engagement and acceptance rested heavily, I suspect, on my own adherence to the norms of behavior deemed befitting of a wife, a daughter-in-law, a sister-in-law, or a friend in Pakistani society. Indeed, when I explained my research agenda to my neighbors, they viewed it as a kind of moral endeavor—as the effort on the part of the foreign wife of a Pakistani Muslim to understand Pakistani customs.

For my part, the desire for acceptance in this cultural milieu had a history rather longer than that defined by fieldwork. My husband grew up in Karachi, and the bulk of his family lives there still. Since our 1990 wedding in Pakistan, when I met my very warm and gracious in-laws for the first time, I have tried to fit in and find a place for myself in the family—and the land—of my husband's birth.

In some ways, my early experiences in Karachi were like the stuff of a regency romance, where the female protagonist—raised, perhaps, by an indulgent widower father, in the seclusion and freedom of a country estate—joins polite society and must suddenly conform to a host of bewilderingly strict and precise behavioral standards, if she is to maintain her reputation and win favor, friends, and, of course, a husband. In my case, some concessions to local expectations were easier than others; I was quite happy to wear *shalwar kameez*, for example. Restrictions on my mobility in public were somewhat harder to bear. When Sheheryar and I argued one day, I burst out of the house intending to take a long, solitary walk in the neighborhood, only to be driven back by a passing cyclist who, upon finding me lingering at the curb, admonished me to go inside.

The struggle both to adapt to the new and to hold on to the familiar collided most dramatically in the fracas created by my name. Shortly after I arrived in Karachi that first time, Sheheryar informed me, rather sheepishly, that it had been suggested that I be called "Sara." The problem, it seemed, was that *Laura* sounds a lot like *lora*, which is Urdu slang for "penis." I was devastated by this stroke of strange coincidence and bad luck. But to become "Sara"—to have this place so completely remake me—was unpalatable in the extreme. As a compromise, we settled on "Lori," my childhood nickname, which I had abandoned when I entered college (deeming "Laura" a more mature and dignified moniker for my newly liberated adult self). Ironically, in Urdu, *lori* means "lullaby." The contrast was staggering: Laura, quite literally, was "the phallic woman," but to me, the name signaled empowered, self-determining, self-willed adult identity. Lori was a lullaby, an infantilizing, experiential summons to my childhood, a place of subjection and submission to the wants of others. (Incidentally, this issue never arose with my neighbors, who called me Laura with no apparent qualms.)

The struggle over my name allegorized my difficulties in abiding by expectations which followed from beliefs, sentiments, and gut reactions that I did not share and systems of relations in which I had no naturalized place. Now, of course, I can see how embedded this conflict is in Western understandings of human development, where individual autonomy, self-will, and adulthood are seen to go together. For my in-laws and other Pakistanis, adult status was linked to other things that were at the time unknown to me, thus my efforts at self-assertion perhaps seemed childish to them.

The more I understood the meanings and systems behind these cultural expectations, the more "natural" they felt to me. This understanding rested, above all, on my induction into particular "structures of feeling" (Williams 1973). Years later, when I came to the Shipyard to conduct my fieldwork, I recognized, in my growing friendships with my informants, this same kind of emotional apprenticeship. My fellow neighbors taught me (or tried to teach me) not so much rules of conduct as *fitting sentiments* (not the least of which was "It is better to be with us than with your husband").

This brings me to the matter of methodology. It would be hypocritical, at the conclusion of research, to detail all the well-thought-out strategies I intentionally employed in order to find the data I was so pointedly seeking. The fact is that when I arrived at the Shipyard, I had little idea of what precisely I needed to know. I was alarmed by ethnic violence, but intrigued by ethnic discourse and curious as to how, or whether, ethnicity figured in the routine rituals, social relations, and sensibilities of urban life. Little did I know that, in place of a kind of simmering violence, I would find an edgy, intricate peace. Nor did I anticipate that this peace would be achieved with reference to, and through the medium of, personal and collective emotional life and its careful regulation—or that the burden of this regulatory labor would rest overwhelmingly with women.

The data upon which I have based my argument emerged almost exclusively through participant observation. I lived in the Shipyard for over a year. In the early months of research, I did a great deal of exploring in the city, visiting various embattled neighborhoods, thinking it would help me position my field site in a broader context. But despite my greater mobility (I had a car and possessed both the skill and permission to drive it), I was thrown back on this space of home almost as much as were my informants. Strikes[18] and general tension in the city would conspire to keep me home, as would the complications involved in balancing child care responsibilities with Sheheryar's work schedule and my disinclination to do certain things alone or go certain places unaccompanied. The bulk of my days were thus spent visiting in one flat after another, building friendships, observing the details of everyday life and social interaction, asking questions and also answering them. In such a context, props like tape recorders or notebooks were impractical and prohibitive. The few times that I did bring along a tape recorder to a neighbor's flat with the express purpose of "conducting an interview," it failed miserably. Women would clam up, claiming that they had nothing "of importance" to say and that I should ask such questions of their fathers, or husbands, or brothers, who "knew much more" about such things. I am not saying that, had I persevered in my (abortive) effort to conduct interviews, I would have failed to elicit anything of value. But such formal methods of information gathering quite simply took me too far away from that which I was seeking: the routine, the everyday, and the unremarked. Even carrying along pen and paper threatened the taken-for-granted access I gained to these social worlds by virtue of my status as a neighbor and through my participation in neighborhood life.[19] Thus I spent hours every evening, and many an afternoon as well, recording the events, conversations, and stories of the day in an endless stream of field journals. The conversations and stories I present in the pages to follow are thus not verbatim transcriptions, but they are faithful renderings, punctuated by exact (often unforgettable) phrases that stuck in my head for one reason or another. (In such cases,

I have included the Urdu term or phrase alongside the English translation.)

Let me end by stating that I did not simply "act" the part of interested, active neighbor as some kind of ploy to get information; I (often
quite unselfconsciously) lived the part. I ran out of things (like flour and
tea) just as often as my neighbors did and showed up at their doors for
the proverbial cup of sugar with the same regularity. Like them, I told
my share of stories, petitioned help with tasks impossible to do alone,
and certainly spent an equal amount of time wandering the halls and
knocking on doors in search of my son. And also like many of my neighbors, I was hungry for social interaction. Sheheryar was busy with his
own work, doing photo projects and teaching at the Indus Valley School
of Art and Architecture. With my own family far away and my in-laws
living across town, I sought out the company of my neighbors in search
of friendship as much as data. Indeed, the interpretation and management
of my own emotional life in the building is a part of this story as well.

Overview of Chapters

The chapters that follow mark my attempt to consider the problem of ethnic violence in Karachi from the vantage point of peaceful
coexistence. What does an "everyday peace" look like, and how is it
crafted on the ground in social practice? In chapter 2, I introduce the
social space of the building, taking readers through a "day in the life" of
its residents. My purpose here is to highlight the kind of routine "getting
along" that characterizes life in the Shipyard—both the ideas behind it
and the practices that make it up, the explicit values and "scripts" that
inform "neighboring," and the pragmatic efforts that both construct and
reflect it. I focus in particular on the myriad daily exchanges (e.g., borrowing, lending, helping, visiting, gifting) that take place between women
in the building and on the specific tensions and contradictions that underpin these exchanges.

Anthropologists have long recognized a link between practices of
exchange and peacemaking. How might casting a careful eye at this ne-
glected link provide us with renewed insight into the micropolitical processes by which an everyday peace gets forged? In chapter 3, I analyze
the logic and practice of local exchange in the building, with a specific

focus on the social and cultural tensions that underpin this exchange, the movement and management of tension in the exchanges themselves, and the gendered character of this exchange.

A central motif in the book is the inexorable contradiction between universalizing assimilative narratives of national identity (centered around Urdu and Islam) and narratives of ethnic difference (centered around vernacular language and heritage). I demonstrate that this tension is pivotal both to the how and why of local exchange and to its effects. The transformed conditions of neighborly exchange in multistory apartment buildings like the Shipyard demand new skills and sensibilities of my informants. Short of laying all my cards on the table, let me suggest that women's local exchange practices constitute a form of peacemaking that rests on an *ethic of suspense*, where sociocultural tension is laboriously sustained rather than resolved. This poses a direct challenge to academic and folk understandings of the flow of tension in violence, where peace is seen to rest on resolution, remission, or relief.

Finally, I show that the casting of women as peacemakers in this space emerges not from some essentialized "maternal body" or "feminine psyche." It follows, instead, from a complex set of circumstances in which peace may be but a by-product of, or condition for, other longed-for cultural ends. In chapters 4 and 5, I analyze what is at stake for women in local exchange—what it risks, what it costs, and what makes it worthwhile.

In chapter 4, I take up women's cultural understandings of male anger as pivotal to a sensibility or praxis of peace in the building. In their stories and routine practices, women celebrate male anger as iconic of masculine efficacy and group status, but at the same time they lament it as base impulse, irrational, dangerous, and unpredictable. Significantly, it is precisely men's perceived vulnerability to irrational anger that grants women's local exchange a kind of moral imperative: women must act as local mediators in this space so that men do not have to. At the same time, male anger sets limits on women's exchange and infuses it with palpable risk.

While the threat of male anger serves as an organizing principle in women's neighboring relations, it is offset by a countervailing force: the somewhat covert longing for intimacy in the form of female friendships. In chapter 5, I demonstrate that the apartment building makes available distinct forms of female sociality and new forms of self-other knowledge, which paradoxically both serve and contravene local and national imperatives of shame and modesty. Thus I propose that women's embodied and affective labors of peace—bearing tension and managing male anger—are aimed, in part, at protecting this "civic intimacy" and the new pleasures it affords.

Finally, the role of emotion in peacemaking is a theme that runs throughout the book. In the conclusion, I elaborate on my ideas about the relationship between emotion and the political subject, both in social and anthropological thought and in the everyday peace that prevailed in the Shipyard. It is to the Shipyard and this everyday peace that I now turn.

A View of Empress and Sadar Markets, Downtown Karachi

Mid-rise Apartment Buildings near I. I. Chundrigar Road, the Central Business District

Above: A City Bus Passes an Abandoned, Colonial-era Building in Kharadar, one of Karachi's Oldest Neighborhoods

Facing page: Women Cross in front of a Rickshaw in the Densely Populated Neighborhood of Lyari

Detached Family Homes House the City's Elite

Boys Playing Cricket in Baluch Colony, an Informal Settlement (*kachi abadi*) on the Outskirts of Defense

Women in *Burqa* at Funland, an Amusement Park in Clifton

A Mosque in Clifton after Heavy Rains

Supplicants at Abdullah Shah Gazi's Shrine

Facing page: The Shrine of Abdullah Shah Gazi in Clifton

2

A Day in the Life

Any Karachiite living near tree life—almond or walnut groves, guava trees, coconut or date palm—will almost certainly be awakened each morning by the singing of birds. Whenever we stayed at my in-laws' flat in Old Clifton, the ravens and koels nesting in the chiku tree outside our bedroom window would awaken us just before sunrise with chatter, shrieks, and song. But in the Shipyard, which is surrounded only by sand and desert scrub, residents awaken to the sound of the *azan*, or call to prayer. The Sunni mosque three blocks south of the Shipyard employed an exceptional *muezzin*, whose dulcet and ardent call to prayer was marred only by the intermittent crackle of the loudspeaker.

With the *azan*, women rise for ritual ablutions and prayer while the men make their way to the nearby mosque to pray in company. Many men say their *fajr* (sunrise) prayers at home, and of course not every Muslim man or woman prays the prescribed five times a day; some do not pray at all. But nearly every woman I knew in the building purported to relish these serene moments of devotion and tried to sell me on the purely pragmatic benefits of prayer (a feeling of peace, limber muscles from the obligatory prostrations, etc.) as well as the spiritual ones. But life with a small child had made me a jealous guardian of sleep, and I usually managed to doze through the morning *azan* and its hauntingly sung pronouncement that "it is better to pray than to slumber."

Even for those women who do not rise to pray, the day must begin early, for there is breakfast to be made. It was the rare family that would breakfast on cornflakes and Weetabix; most of my neighbors were frying flat bread and omelets or preparing stew for the morning meal, all washed down with several cups of strong, sugary tea.

After breakfast, the men would make a hasty departure, most of them taking buses to their place of work in the city center or beyond, which meant a half-mile walk to the nearest bus stop in ovenlike heat (except for the winter months). A smaller number would hop on their motor-cycles—the second sleep-shattering sound that met my comparatively lazy mornings—and still fewer sped away in tiny economy cars.

With the men gone, women would turn their attention to getting children ready for school. Children bathed every morning, and as far as I was able to gather, adults did the same (this in addition to the ritual washing, or *wuzu*, that precedes each of the five daily prayer sessions).[1] Bathing in the Shipyard generally entailed heating a large pot of water and mixing it with cold water in a bucket (*balti*); the bather would then stand or crouch down, pouring cups full of water over his or her head and body. While many Shipyard bathrooms had showerheads affixed to the walls, most were not connected to water tanks, and thus would func-tion only at water delivery time. Moreover, the showers offered no tem-perature control; if one's water heater (which few people owned) was on, the water was scalding; if off, frigid. *Balti*-bathing was not surprisingly a preferred option (and incidentally, one that made far more efficient use of water in situations of habitual scarcity).

Clean and dressed, children were sent off to school. If they were old enough, they walked with a group of kids. If they were young, they were walked to school by their mothers. This was an ambivalent experience for women. Aliya complained that it was a tiring task, interfering with the multitude of household chores that occupied her mornings. Zubaida complained that she felt self-conscious walking along the wide streets and fearful of strange men, wild dogs, and potential kidnappers.

Meeting male neighbors along the way was even more awkward. Zu-baida told me how one day, returning from taking her children to school, she met Ilahi Sahib on the path. She kept her head down and quickly walked past him without a word. Later, in a huff, he complained to his daughter-in-law, Ruhi, that Zubaida had failed to greet him when they passed on the street. "But where I come from, women never call out to men," Zubaida told me. "We only greet in reply, and sometimes not even then. What will people think if I'm calling out to men on the street?"

When one woman was sick or busy with houseguests, another mother would walk her children to school. For a while, Aliya and Zubaida talked about hiring a van to collect their children, but in the end their husbands could not be persuaded. Parveen, who taught Urdu and Islamiat at an English-medium school not within walking distance, would ride to school with her children (who attended the school for free) in taxis and rickshaws. I usually left the building a little before nine to drop Faizan at his Montessori school several miles away, and if Parveen was running late, she and her daughters would catch a ride with me. After the summer, when Ruhi got a job teaching Urdu and Islamiat at a school some distance away, her husband began driving her and their daughter to school. Although he worked in the real estate office on the ground floor of the Shipyard and thus had no need of the car, there was no question of Ruhi driving herself to work; like nearly every other woman I knew in the building, she had never learned to drive.[2]

On returning from dropping the children, women would begin their array of morning chores. Garbage had to be gathered together for the building's sweeper, Bashir, and handed to him at the door. After sweeping the halls and stairwells and collecting each resident's garbage, Bashir would lug the trash to a dumpsite a quarter of a mile away. Frequently, before Bashir's arrival, residents would already have been visited by Afghani children from the adjacent squatter camp, asking for *kachra* (trash), which they would take back to their tents to rifle through for any usable or edible items. On days when the *batliwala* came, women would call him to come and take away their bottles, newspapers, old sandals, and other recyclables in exchange for small tidbits or practically worthless coins. Sometimes the barter was more creative, featuring "*chusa*s for *chapal*s" (chicks for sandals) and other unlikely trades.

On various days in the month, women could expect a morning visit from the *chowkidar*, delivering gas bills, electric bills, and a request for the building fees. Each flat paid 300 rupees or so a month to cover the building sweeper's salary, water delivery, the *chowkidar*'s salary, and the cost of lighting the hallways. Gas and electric bills were invariably paid by the men in the family, who would go and stand in interminable lines at local pay windows in shopping plazas. I, however, always paid because women were never expected to wait in line at such places, and men always graciously stepped aside to let me or other women (who were few) go first.

Every morning shortly after sunrise, the newspaper deliveryman would silently slide the newspaper under one's door. But once a month, he would ring the doorbell, requesting payment. He had the annoying habit of doing this right after *fajr* prayers—as early as 6 AM. For many households, this was not inconvenient; husbands or brothers-in-law, finished with their prayers, would answer the door and handle the matter. My household, however, would be deep in sleep. My husband or I would open one eye in disbelief, look at the clock, and fall back asleep. Eager to collect payment, the newspaper seller would try the next day, and the next, until finally, bleary-eyed, my husband would make it to the door before the seller had given up in disgust. This pattern so confused my body that for months I would wake up at 6 AM and insist that the doorbell had rung. Furious, Sheheryar would jump out of bed and run to the door, only to find no one there. I suspected that the newspaper seller—a surly man who hadn't appreciated Sheheryar's request that he refrain from ringing the doorbell before 9 AM—was playing tricks on us. It wasn't until our trip to Kalaam some months later that I realized the power of my imagination, for that first morning in a guest house in the frosty hills, I awoke at 6 AM as always to the imagined sound of a doorbell.

Nearly every household in the building employed a woman sweeper, always referred to as *masi* (mother's sister), to do some of the dirtier and more taxing of the household chores. Bashir's wife, Sharifa, and his sister-in-law, Iqbal, each cleaned four or five flats in the building. While the *masi* swept and mopped the floors and cleaned the bathrooms from top to bottom, women residents would dust furniture, finish washing the breakfast dishes, and sort laundry. Some households sent their dirty clothes to the *dhobi* (washerman), who also collected and delivered in the morning, or, like Parveen, did the washing themselves. Most, however, paid the *masi* to help with the washing at home.

Clothing was always washed in the morning to give it plenty of time to dry on the line before sunset. The morning water delivery happened at around 9 AM, and those households that lacked storage tanks almost always did their laundry at this time. It is, in flats, a system bereft of labor-saving aids; there is no washboard, no wringer, no Latin American–style *pila* (although a handful of lucky souls had washing machines that, while incapable of agitating, would spin the clothes dry—wringing out wet clothes being by far the most physically draining part of doing laundry). Clothes are worn once and washed daily, due to the dusty, humid, and sweaty living conditions and a significant concern for cleanliness (for one thing, clothes must be unstained for ritual purity in prayer).

In most of the households that I visited, this was a cheerful time of day. While some women had little interest in chatting with the *masi* and took little pleasure in their daily chores (as was the case, according to Iqbal, with Kulsoom and the Baluch woman who lived above us), most women seemed to enjoy their work and had friendly, teasing relationships with the *masi*. When she helped clean my flat, Iqbal and I talked nonstop about our children, other families in the building, and life in Karachi in general. When cleaning in Zubaida's flat, Iqbal was forever laughing and fending off Zubaida's teasing chatter: "Look, my *masi* is so 'smart' (meaning trim and attractive—and she was, in fact, stunningly beautiful); that's why she has so many children. Her husband can't keep his hands off her!"

In some households, the sweeper was left to do the work without help, which Iqbal resented. In Zubaida's flat (as in mine and Parveen's), the work was done together. Aliya said that she always closely supervised her *masi* Sharifa (the phrase she used means to "keep standing on her head"), because it ensured that the work was done correctly. But even this supervision was filled with laughter and friendly teasing.

The relationship women had with their sweepers was also one of patronage; most women—who were themselves struggling financially—would save bits of food, medicine, or used clothing for their *masi* and, whenever possible, undertake to hire her for "extra" jobs (like acid-cleaning the bathrooms or, in Iqbal's case, leg waxing). Of course, however pleasant the atmosphere or warm the relationship with her employer, a sweeper still holds a low-status occupation with dreadful insecurity and backbreaking labor, undertaken in the best and the worst of health, from respiratory infection to late pregnancy. And for women residents, she is still a servant, who will quite likely try to cheat one by overcharging or doing shabby work.

From the time men left in the morning until their return for lunch, it was not at all uncommon to see all the outer doors of the flats on one's floor slung open, with just the screen door separating the private space of individual residences from the semipublic space of the hallway. In fact, I quickly came to view a closed door as a signal that men were home and that I (or other visitors) should take care before entering. It was at these times, when doors lay open, that the connection and exchange between women neighbors was at its height.

Alongside the scuff of the broom on the cool tiled floors and the hum of the generator as it pumped tanker-purchased water up to the roof, one would invariably hear loud staccato knocks on the doorjamb and the squeak of screen doors opening as neighbors visited neighbors. Requests for kitchen items were manifold: a cup of flour, a teaspoon of cumin seeds, boiled water. Information was at a premium: Has Iqbal come yet? Did you receive your gas bill? Did you hear what happened to so-and-so? Help with chores was petitioned: My brother's wife is coming for lunch. Will you help me make flatbread? My mattresses need airing. Can you help me turn them?

At any given time in the morning, someone was visiting someone somewhere. It was rare that I spent a morning in someone's flat without being joined by at least one other neighbor. When dashing over to Parveen's flat to borrow coriander, I found Zubaida there, showing Parveen how to make *suji ka halwa* (semolina pudding). When I was drinking tea at Zubaida's, Seema stopped by to commission some embroidery work from Zubaida's relatives in the village. When I was giving Ruhi English lessons in her drawing room, Mahvish stopped by just to chat. When I was visiting Mrs. Habib in her corner flat, Qazi Sahib's wife dropped in and joined us for tea. When returning a plate to Kulsoom's flat, I found Sakina, Seema's *bhabi* (brother's wife), chatting with Kulsoom in the doorway.

The informality of visits like these was marked by the manner in which visitors (or borrowers or petitioners) would dress. Without exception, women in the Shipyard wore *shalwar kameez* on a daily basis.[3] The national dress of Pakistan, the *shalwar kameez*—often referred to by women simply as a suit, or *jora*—features a long-sleeved, knee-to-calf-length tunic over baggy, pleated, and tapered pajama-type pants. The *dupatta*, or scarf, is a long strip of cloth worn either draped over the shoulders or on the head. When stepping into the hallway en route to another flat, women will most likely be wearing their simple everyday suits; throwing a *dupatta* over their shoulder and slipping on *chapal*s, cheap flip-flops, women make their visits. In contrast, when walking their children to school, women don proper, dressier sandals and cover themselves more carefully—usually over their heads—with their *dupatta*s. Thus the variability between bare feet, flip-flops, and shoes—and the absence or degree of presence of *dupatta*—enacts a continuum of privacy and publicity, informality and formality, ease and discomfort, that the flat, the hallway, and the street represent.

As the morning drew to a close, women turned their attention to the midday meal. Vegetables purchased from the *thailawala* (vendor) outside one's window that morning were pared and chopped; sometimes chicken or meat was marinated and fried; curry dishes or lentils were prepared, *chapati*s (thin, unleavened bread) were kneaded and rolled, or rice was rinsed and soaked. It was at these times that I got some of my best cooking tutorials: how to make *shami* kebabs that don't crumble, how to make the ultrathin *phulka chapati*, and what in the world to do with the gag-inducing *karela* (bitter gourd).

Around 1 PM, the children were collected or they made their way home from school, and the final lunch preparations were begun: *chapati*s dry-fried on the *tawa* (concave cast iron frying pan) or rice set to boil. Fresh-faced and changed out of their school clothes, children were often deputized to distribute tasty samples of their mother's cooking—from pumpkin kebabs to *dal gosht* (lentils cooked with meat)—to select flats in the building. Husbands arrived home, doors would close, and lunch was served.

Lunch was generally a private affair during the work week. The few times Sheheryar and I ate lunch at neighbors' flats, it was on Saturdays, with neither school, nor office, nor the lengthy Friday afternoon prayers on the schedule. While Sheheryar, Faizan, and I would eat a comparatively pathetic meal of fast food or makeshift sandwiches on weekdays, my neighbors would enjoy a leisurely, heavy lunch. Those residents who owned a dining table would set the food and plates there, with or without silverware, and parents and children would take their seats around it. A greater number of residents would spread *dastarkhan*s (tablecloths) out on the floor and lay their food and plates on top of it. The family would then sit, cross-legged or loosely kneeling, around the *dastarkhan* and eat, using bite-sized pieces of *chapati* to break off bits of meat and soak up rich and spicy gravy.

Food and the manner in which it was eaten were understood by Shipyard residents—and city dwellers as a whole—to be linked with class status. That some people owned dining tables and others did not was no small matter. Middle-class status hinged, to some degree, on the possession of such items as drawing room sofas, armchairs, and coffee tables, dining room tables and chairs, and beds complete with headboards and mattresses. There was also the ideal—unattainable for most Shipyard residents—that children have their own bedroom, separate from their parents (although even in those households, like Aliya's and Parveen's, where the children did have their own bedrooms, they nevertheless slept each night in their parents' room).

But more specifically, women often spoke as if food encoded some social hierarchy in which they came out far from on top or in the know. In one of my first meetings with Zubaida, as we stood in my dining room talking about the long day she had spent cooking in preparation for her in-laws' impending visit, she exclaimed, with perplexed amusement: "Women in this city are going to restaurants, and look at me!" On another occasion, Zubaida told me that her brother, upon graduating from Sindh University, was invited to a Chinese restaurant by his professor: "When they asked that the chef make them his most special dish, he brought out onions! Onions!" Zubaida laughed in amazement. "Eh, we also have onions, and we don't think they're something special." To Zubaida and other Shipyard residents, restaurants and hotels constituted an unknown, incomprehensible world of secret modes of judgment—an intimidating world in which women fear they may be judged lacking.

It was not simply a matter of financial limitations that kept Zubaida and other similarly positioned families from such places (although it was unquestionably a prohibiting factor). When my Urdu tutor was invited to dinner by a British client, he balked: "What will they serve? How will I know how to eat it?" he worried. Speaking of expensive hotels and restaurants, Ruhi said, "We don't like to go to such places. See, we are afraid. What if we have to go to the bathroom and we can't find our way and we have to ask the clerks for help? When our men can't speak to them in English, they'll look down at us, as if to ask, 'Oh, why are you here?'" In another context, Ruhi was deeply offended when her employers at an English-medium grammar school requested that she learn English so she could better communicate with students' parents. "It makes me feel very strange," she said, "that in my own country, I'm made to feel that speaking my own language is not good."

Women rarely spoke directly about perceived class or status differences in the building. If the topic of so-and-so's car or this or that person's new sofa came up, a woman might shrug and say, "We are not rich people" (*ham amir log nahin*). Disapproval of income disparities might emerge through criticisms about so-and-so's "ultramodern" behavior, but for the most part, such differences (beyond the extremes of rich [*amir*] and poor [*gharib*]) were denied, explained away as misperceptions (e.g., "They spend all their money on furniture; we're saving ours to buy a flat," or "He may earn a lot, but he has two households to support," and so on). Perhaps it is more accurate to say that women were reluctant to *concede* higher status, income, or class to others; at the same time, an ethos of egalitarianism—preached in Islam, and evident in ordinary discourse—inhibited, or rendered suspect, direct assertions of status superiority.[4]

After lunch, when the men had returned to work, the tempo of the building slowed. It was common practice, after the dishes were washed and *dastarkhan*s or tables wiped down, for women to take a nap. Considering their late-to-bed and early-to-rise schedule, this extra rest was much needed. Children would often nap, too. Or they would sit or stretch out on the floor doing homework or quietly playing, occasionally making subdued forays into the hall in search of playmates. Sometimes naps were rejected in favor of slightly more formal visits. A neighbor might send a daughter to a friend's flat to reconnoiter: Is Auntie sleeping? Would she like a visitor? The anticipated pleasure of such visits (and the dictates of hospitality) would rouse any woman from her bed. Tea would be made, and hostess and guest would settle comfortably in the drawing room for leisurely conversation.

These were the kinds of visits I received from those neighbors with whom I had fewer dealings, and it was my sense that this was generally the case. Kulsoom, Mrs. Habib, and Hina's mother were most likely to call on me in this manner, as were Seema (Hina's mother's *devrani*) and Batool (Kulsoom's daughter), who often came to see me when they were visiting their families in the Shipyard. Unlike morning visits, during which cleaning, tailoring, cooking, or other household duties were rarely halted, these visits required the host to set aside other business and give full attention to the guest—to the extent that appointments were often missed and other engagements, duties, or plans unquestioningly were postponed.

By late afternoon, most children were busily engaged with "tuitions"—after-school lessons in a variety of subjects, from English, to Urdu, to Sindhi, to math, and so on. Whether this widely felt need to hire home tutors was due, as some suggested, to the outrageously rigorous curriculum of British-influenced grammar schools or, as others suggested, to the efforts on the part of underpaid teachers to earn extra money tutoring on the side, I cannot say. In the Shipyard, much of the tutoring was done by barter: e.g., Zubaida would tutor twelve-year-old Beenish in Sindhi, and Beenish in turn would tutor Zubaida's children in English.

By early evening, men would begin returning home from work. The family would often take tea together—complete with biscuits, store-bought bread, snacks, or sweet dishes—and the pace of life in the building would once again increase. Men would head to the nearby mosque for *maghrib* (sunset) prayers, while children raced into the hallway with shouts of laughter accompanied by the endless crack of screen doors slamming. Indeed, it seemed to me that this time of day was dominated by the comings and goings—the kind of roving antics—of Shipyard children.

Because men were in residence once again, women's casual traffic between flats was inhibited. Children, at these moments, became a useful pretext, or opportunity, for sociality. Women were forever wandering up and down the halls, stopping at various doorways and inquiring after their children. This is how I first met Zubaida and Ruhi. Zubaida had come in search of Meher and Zain and found them happily doing puzzles on my living room floor. Ruhi had come asking after her daughter Sana, but neither Sana nor Faizan were with me. After a long stroll up and down the hallways chatting and asking after our children, we found them in Aliya's flat, sneaking chocolates from a candy jar in her drawing room.

Children thus enabled women's continued sociality even after men came home from work, largely because keeping track of children was an expected part of women's duties, and husbands could hardly expect their wives to return home without chatting with the mothers of their children's playmates; that would be unthinkably rude.

On the other hand, children could also be handy if one wished to avoid social interaction. If a woman was busy with housework or guests, children could be sent out to hunt down siblings, return something borrowed or borrow something else, or conduct reconnaissance. I have already described how, in my first few weeks in the Shipyard, children would appear frequently at my door in search of information: Where was I from? What was my son's name? and most important: Were we Muslim or "Christmas"? But children also came to our door on reconnaissance missions when I was out of town in Islamabad; while it might not "look nice" (*acha nahin lagta*) for a woman to seek out my husband and ask after me, it was perfectly acceptable for her daughters (e.g., Hina, Nazu, Anam, or Meher) to do so. "When is Auntie coming back?" they would ask. "How is her health?" "Who is that auntie who keeps coming in the evenings?" (Nothing improper: It was my sister-in-law Fauzia.)

Aside from its utility in enabling the continued socializing of their mothers, children's play had its own relatively autonomous character. Children made their own visits, played in one another's flats (at times they were sent to play in the hall when they became too disruptive, although the tolerance level for this was very high), and raced up and down the hallways on bicycles or roller skates, with balls and boxes and a multitude of props found and imagined. Children had no fear that their play would disturb the adults and bring about criticism or scoldings. "Why would we scold?" Ruhi asked me. "They are all our children."

Indeed, children were treated extremely well by adults strange and familiar. Older children were teased and plied with sweets, while younger ones were fed, petted, and picked up. Parents had little fear for their children—as young as two—wandering in the hallways, for all adults looked out for and seemed to share a stake in the fate of any child. When Faizan fell down the stairs on his bike with loud cries and clamor, innumerable doors were flung open and concerned neighbors rushed to help and comfort.

Sometimes the twin urges to indulge and protect children came into conflict, as was the case when Qazi Sahib's daughters began keeping stray cats in the public areas of our floor. These feral, mangy cats would habitually sleep on our northside balcony (the lower two feet of this balcony was open, but security-barred, from the stairwell, providing the stairwell with illumination and giving the cats a place to hide). Iqbal complained that they shat all over the place and increased her workload, and Bashir said the same of their presence in the halls. Parents complained that the cats were dirty and disease-ridden and should be removed, but Qazi Sahib did not have the heart to get rid of them. "You know, the children, they love them. What can one do?"

However, when Faizan developed a serious allergic reaction shortly after playing with the cats, Qazi Sahib was devastated. He immediately sent the *chowkidar* to gather up the cats and take them away, and he came to our door, his face grave, to inquire about Faizan's health. "He's *my* son," Qazi Sahib kept saying with remorse. "He's *my* child."

While children were unquestionably treated with indulgence by adult neighbors, this was not what children could expect to receive from an adult when they transgressed in particular ways. What constitutes legitimate, illegitimate, permissible, or scold-worthy behavior is far from self-evident, as I discuss in chapter 4. Neighbors scolding other people's children was so rare that I only saw it happen once. Qazi Sahib's daughters had been criticizing Zubaida's son, Zain, calling him a "dirty little boy" and telling him to clean up and get new clothes. Zubaida was more upset at the implication of status inequality that their criticisms suggested than at the fact of their bullying (which would otherwise have been ignored). Zubaida reprimanded the girls for it, without obvious rancor, but they nonetheless looked suitably abashed.

As children were such an integral part of local social life, women who were childless were the object of great pity. Aliya often talked with me of her great joy in her children, Anam and Shan, for they were born, in quick succession, after eight years of unexplained, heart-wrenching infertility. Ruhi, who had a six-year-old daughter, Sana, lamented that she was thus far unable to conceive a second time. "I pray and pray, but it's not happening. *Allah malik hai* (God is sovereign). What can I do?" My women neighbors (as well as my cousins and other in-laws) were always asking me when the next child was coming, reminding me that it is not good for children to be alone and that I needed a girl. When I did find myself pregnant with my second child several months before my fieldwork ended, my neighbors became ever more solicitous, sending me plate after plate of food, lending me looser clothing, and advising me not to wear heels or work in the heat.

As all these stories suggest, children in the building were genuinely cherished, moving in and out of adult life all day and usually sleeping in their parents' bedroom at night. But because children were always present, they were also less focal; adult schedules were not molded around children's bedtimes or set naptimes. Moreover, I discerned no strongly expressed desire on the part of women for peace and quiet, for time away from children, or for privacy.

Like Elizabeth Fernea's Iraqi informants in *Guests of the Sheik* (1965), women in the Shipyard loathed isolation. When struck with a respiratory flu or stomach virus—times when I would want to shut the world away and crawl into the privacy of my bed—women longed for company. In fact, the expectation that friends and acquaintances would visit one's sickbed was so extreme that a failure to visit could be read as a severing of relations. When Zubaida was sick with malarial fevers, I met neighbors I had never seen before gathered around her bedside; women who were not in the habit of everyday exchange with Zubaida nevertheless flocked to her sickbed.

Meanwhile, my disinclination for company in times of illness or other trouble was somewhat puzzling to my neighbors. Zubaida chided me for failing to visit her one day when I was suffering from food poisoning. "*Pagal!*" (crazy), she told me. "You could have just used my bathroom." This kind of physical intimacy between friends, however, was foreign to me, just as more emotional or confessional forms were far from second nature for my neighbors. To Shipyard women, the sickbed vigil was one (if not the only) type of visit that was unambiguously permitted and expected, even religiously dictated, and it was welcomed as an occasion for intimacy—an intimacy framed in physically expressive, caretaking, or nurturing terms.

While children go about their socializing and men entertain themselves, women prepare the evening meal in much the same manner as they do midday. Unless relatives or a husband's friends are visiting, dinner is a family affair. This was equally true for my household, which habitually piled into the car at 8:30 PM and drove northeast two miles to eat

dinner with my in-laws. That my husband's family remained such a central referent in my life (despite our nuclear, neolocal residence) served
as a reminder to me that, while women pass their everyday lives in buildings like the Shipyard, much of what they consider permanent, relevant,
and determinant of their actions, desires, and decisions rests in their
ongoing relations with their extended family, natal and affinal. Women
talked together often about the alternately baneful and salutary influence
of sisters- and mothers-in-law, and they reminisced about warm relationships with siblings and parents. Aliya was regularly visited by her
elder brother, bearing gifts from Dubai, where he lived and worked;
Zubaida spoke on the phone daily with her favorite *bhabi*; and Ruhi told
me of the conflicted desires she felt to return to her father in the village
and yet to stay here with her husband: "A woman has so much love
(*pyar*) and concern (*pareshan*)—for father, husband, child—that the heart
fills (*dil bhar jata hai*)."

Not everyone in the Shipyard was living in a nuclear, neolocal household. Some flats housed three generations, and many others housed the
joint families of two or more brothers. In one case, two separate flats in
the building were occupied by the same extended family: parents and a
grown son with his wife and children on one floor, and three brothers
(one married with children) on another (and they were also related by
marriage to another household in the building).

But even for those households where the extended family is not in
residence, the influence of in-laws in particular is ever apparent. Like
me, Shipyard women were routinely welcoming in-laws or—accompanied by their husbands—heading to affines' houses or villages for religious holidays and ceremonies, weddings, circumcisions, or funerals. And
by reputation, mothers-in-law have a more nefarious influence, controlling, even from afar, things like their daughter-in-law's visiting habits and
other aspects of her—and the conjugal couple's—life.

In contrast, I could hardly have survived, much less conducted fieldwork, without the influence (and at times interference) of my mother-
in-law. Because I knew so little about the pragmatics of life in Karachi,
her advice was welcome, and because my anticipated stay in Karachi was
finite, the control that her advice and involvement implied was (generally) tolerable. In fact, it was thanks to my mother-in-law's involvement

and her contacts that we ended up taking a flat in the Shipyard, and it was with her that we had our first encounter with the building president, Ilahi Sahib.

We had just finished unloading the last of our belongings from my sister-in-law's trunk when Sheheryar's mother, doubling back, brought Ilahi Sahib to our door. "Here, you must meet the building president," she said. "He's a very responsible man. I've met him now, and he'll give you help if you need it."

Sheheryar shook Ilahi Sahib's hand, and I smiled and nodded, taking a few steps backward as he lumbered into the room. "Before I met your mother," he said to Sheheryar, "I thought all Aga Khanis were *kafirs* (infidels). *Kafirs!*"[5] My mother-in-law smiled benignly, and they left us to our unpacking, which we undertook after a good, rip-roaring laugh.

The anecdote that opens chapter 1, where Ruhi's dinner party guests hesitate to directly label or classify their neighbors in terms of stark ethnic divisions, prefigures a broader discomfort with announcing ethnic difference in the building. Like class or status distinctions, the expression of ethnic and sectarian differences is, in many ways, suppressed in everyday contexts. Some weeks after moving in, I related Ilahi Sahib's amusing (I assumed) comments to my new friends Aliya and Zubaida, and they reacted with vitriol rather than laughter. Such comments were "beyond belief," "nonsensical," and "rubbish," they told me. In a city where people were killing and dying in the name of such differences, his comments were truly seen as no laughing matter.

But just a few weeks later, Zubaida told me, in her customarily ebullient tone, that when we first moved in, she said to herself, "Oh, I think he's Sindhi. I *hope* they're Sindhi!" When I asked her what difference it made, she shrugged and said, with a sheepish grin, "*Hamari biradari hai* (It's our clan)." The line between a kind of pleasurable play with difference or different degrees of belonging, and the more threatening *ranking* or excluding that such differences implied rendered talk about ethnicity awkward and even out of place between neighbors.

This was similar to residents' efforts to imagine the building as a kind of unified community, with norms of neighborly assistance, affection, and togetherness, but at the same time incontrovertibly divided into units of private property, interests, and priorities. When Hina's family moved out of the Shipyard and another moved in, our new neighbor asked if he could place one end of a split unit air conditioner on our balcony, so that it would not ventilate into the hallway. We agreed, but my mother-in-law disapproved and phoned the building president to put a stop to the proceedings. Later I complained to Ruhi about my mother-in-law's interference, but Ruhi, to my surprise, took her side. "She did the right thing. People here, they grab things (*qabza karte hain*); first, you let them keep the AC on your balcony, and soon they'll be saying, 'This is our flat' (*yeh hamara flat hai*)." The contradictory pulls to invoke or deny ethnic bonds and to open up and close off one's space came together— and were fascinatingly upended—when an electrical fire shook the building.

Sometime after dinner, and most often between 11 PM and 1 AM, Shipyard residents prepared for sleep. Those children who had fallen asleep on floor cushions or sofas were carried to the bedroom, and their parents retired for the night after completing their individualized grooming routines (involving such bathroom shelf staples as Dr. Forhan's dental powder, face and body creams, hair tonics, and moustache combs). Outer apartment doors generally remained closed, and the building was bathed in silence and darkness until dawn. But one night in late summer, this silence was broken by frantic shouts from the *chowkidar*, and the darkness was illuminated by a riot of sparks flying from the building's entryway. The electrical boxes were on fire. Male residents who rushed to the scene immediately noted the alarming proximity of the fire to a gas line, and fearing an explosion, they ran up the stairs and down hallways to knock on each door and warn the residents to evacuate.

We evacuated in two lines: the men went out the north entrance, which meant passing the scene of the (pretty much self-limiting) fire in the entryway; the women and children went down the south stairs and out the south exit, which was ordinarily locked and barred, so that the *chowkidar* need keep watch over only one entrance. Despite their assertions about the possibility of an explosion, the men remained in the gully, no more than ten or fifteen feet from the fire; the women and children gathered at the portico facing the sea, many of them barefoot and bereft of *dupatta*—a sure sign of the frame-breaking nature of the situation (Goffman 1974).

Despite the inconvenience—the bare feet, the sleeping children in arms—the atmosphere on the portico was festive. Women chatted breathlessly about the evacuation and speculated about the dangers. Hina's brother Imran would periodically race over from his watch in the gully and provide updates on the fire and the efforts to extinguish it. But from the midst of these excited murmurs, an angry voice was raised: "It's your fault," an old woman blurted, gesturing at me. "You have such a big AC."

I glanced around at the suddenly discomfited crowd, and Zubaida leapt to my defense: "What rubbish! Everyone runs an AC," she retorted, adding, under her breath, "Crazy old woman."

Our rented flat did, indeed, have a large air conditioner installed on the northside bedroom wall, though, like many other families in the building, we rarely ran it, for the electric bills were prohibitively steep. But there were other ways—besides the obvious cachet of my American passport—in which our comparatively elite economic and social status must have been marked. We owned a car, we spoke English, and we occupied a northern corner flat (the only three-bedroom flats in the building). That this economic disparity would create some resentment was not surprising. But it is significant that any such feelings—or their expression—were inhibited in everyday interaction. Something about the context of crisis—the spatial reorderings, the unaccustomed proximity and visibility of all one's (women) neighbors at once, outside of the context of everyday exchange—enabled the direct expression and criticism of perceived status inequality—or, from another perspective, it allowed the *suspension* of everyday civility that is such a central part of neighborly coexistence.

Meanwhile, as my husband told me later, the men were hard at work trying to get the bureaucrats at the electric company, KESC, to shut off power to the Shipyard so the fire could be put out. This necessitated numerous drives to the KESC building and heated arguments with the technicians over what it would cost (in bribes). Far from festive, the mood in the gully was one of frustration, with the men watching helplessly as electrical boxes burned beyond repair.

The roving boys, however, seemed exhilarated, sharing in the festive mood of the portico, while at the same time sampling the adventure and danger of the gully. As Sheheryar stood watching sparks fly from the entryway, a Sindhi boy between ten and twelve years old sidled up to him and asked gleefully,

"So you're Sindhi?"

Nonplussed, Sheheryar answered, "Yes. Well, my mother is Sindhi, and my father's Muhajir."

"So you're half Sindhi," the boy prompted.

"Yes," Sheheryar nodded, his attention caught between the more immediate drama of the fire and the—what seemed to him—rather incongruous conversation.

"But you speak Sindhi."

"No."

"Oh well, then, you're one-third Sindhi!" the boy announced with a laugh and ran off toward the portico.

Clearly, the same set of disordered circumstances that allowed a neighbor to publicly criticize my socioeconomic advantage was at play in the above interaction. The Sindhi boy was empowered by the intensity and simultaneous presence of neighbors—separate from the privacy and restricted access of flats—to directly approach Sheheryar (his senior both generationally and in terms of social status). Significantly, at this moment of extreme (universalizing) identification, when building people are unified physically in unprecedented ways, bonds of ethnic affinity—normally suppressed—become articulable (if only by a child and, even then, still read by the adult interlocutor as incongruous). There was even space for playing with this affinity, probing the degree to which this (vaguely illicit, particularizing) identification (Sindhi? One-half? One-third?) could be imagined.

There is more to this story, I suspect, and in order to access it, we need to briefly lay out some of the popular and academic discourses surrounding ideas of the "ethnic" and the "civic." In most cases, ethnicity comes to our attention as a problem: of violence, oppression, discrimination, or ethnocentrism. Ethnic identity is largely disparaged by governments and intellectuals alike as a regressive, primordial bond that threatens the more rational elective ties of national citizenship. Civic nationalism, as a much vaunted form of political modernity, claims to represent the transcendence of the parochial and the cultural.

Of course, there are obvious problems with this. As numerous scholars of nationalism have noted, citizenship carries with it the price of cultural assimilation.[6] While civic identity is promoted as a transcendence of ethnic difference, it promotes its own specific ethnic heritage—in Pakistan, that linked to the Urdu-speaking gentry of reform-era India. This suppressed cultural dimension of citizenship ensures, among other things, that ethnic difference is indeed ranked, marking not only the asymmetrical ordering of cultural groups under the political auspices of the nation (Comaroff and Comaroff 1992) but also the differential access that differently marked subjects can claim to the cultural capital of citizenship.

Moreover, while civic discourse engages an evolutionary motif, where we progress *out of* ethnic primordia *into* universal citizenship, it must be remembered that ethnicity is a form of political modernity as well. In Pakistan, ethnic narratives and movements have their origins in colonial policies of provincial administration; vernacular education and language standardization; knowledge projects like folklore studies, anthropological tracts, and historiography; and anticolonial movements (e.g., the movement to separate Sindh from the Bombay Presidency, in which all these policies were called upon to justify the status of Sindh province as a separate nation).

Finally, both Zubaida's aforementioned plea ("I hope they're Sindhi") and the Sindhi boy's appeal to Sheheryar's Sindhi identity cast some doubt, for me, on our reduction of ethnicity to problem, rank, and disruption. Counter-Enlightenment figures like Herder stressed not the divisive but the creative dimensions of ethnic, primordial-claiming identities (Berlin 2000). As a rich language of attachment, the appeal to ethnicity perhaps confesses urges to connect better, more persuasively than does the more elective, rational, and anonymous civility of citizenship.

In the chapters to come, this contest is evident in the dramas and details of everyday life—the contest between ethnic identification (both as a claim to status and as a source of nonrational attachment that is disparaged by intellectuals and states alike) and a much lauded civic nationalism (to which people have differential access and commitment). For all the reasons stated above, we would be ill-advised simply to take the side of transcendence. I do not wish to anticipate my argument, so for now let me just suggest that we leave these contradictory pulls in their felicitous state of tension and return to the story.

After the power was turned off and the fire extinguished, Shipyard residents returned to their beds, only to awaken to an unpleasant reality. Those residents who occupied flats in the northern half of the building were without power and could expect to be so for at least two weeks, until the electrical boxes could be replaced. Flats on the southern half of the building were unaffected. With lavish and unhesitating generosity, residents in the southern half of the building opened their doors to their affected neighbors, running extension cords from one flat to another so the beleaguered residents could operate at least one light and a window fan to stave off the mosquitoes.

For those two weeks, the Shipyard had an uncommonly open feel to it, with doors left open day and night, both to accommodate extension cords and to facilitate a cross breeze. The temporal character of neighbor interaction was upset, as the comings and goings of men no longer was marked by the opening and shutting of flat doors. Socializing stretched way into the night, as the darkened hallways became the stage for men's conversations and women's shuffling forays from flat to flat. Indeed, it seemed that the division of building space into sealed-off units of private property had suddenly become a moral problem. Those residents who did not open their doors to neighbors (and they were few) became the object of (for the most part, unspoken) bitterness, and the rest of the residents did their best to deny or subvert these divisions by leaving doors open and by lingering outside.

This short period following the fire seemed like a brief fulfillment of the neighborly norms of unity and assistance that people often asserted, but it was not ordinary life and could not be sustained. As with the ephemerality of Turner's *communitas*, structure (with its hierarchies and lines of fissure) was reasserted in the end. To my mind, however, the structure of everyday life in the Shipyard, the everyday peace that characterized local relations, is no less astounding. While I will revisit the fire in my concluding chapter, my main goal in presenting it here has been to foreground the "normal" that it lays bare.

In this chapter, I have tried to provide a picture of, and ethnographic context for, everyday life in the Shipyard. In particular, I have demonstrated the intensity of women's local exchange practices, and I have introduced some of the sociocultural tensions that both divide and connect Shipyard residents. In the chapter that follows, I look more closely at this exchange and at the flow of tension therein for what it can tell us about peace as social practice.

3

Tension

ten-sion 1. the act of stretching or straining. 2. the state of being stretched or strained. 3. mental or emotional strain; intense, suppressed suspense, anxiety, or excitement. 4. a strained relationship between individuals, groups, nations, etc.

tense 1. stretched tight, as a cord, fiber, etc.; drawn taut; rigid. 2. in a state of mental or nervous strain; high-strung; taut: *a tense person*. 3. characterized by a strain upon the nerves or feelings: *a tense moment*. (*Webster's Encyclopedic Unabridged Dictionary* 1989)

A Tense Moment

That morning, the *batliwala* had come early, calling out for bottles, newspapers, flip-flops, and other recyclables as he pushed his cart along the dirt path behind the building. Zubaida and I were sitting on the floor by the sliding-glass windows in her sparsely furnished living room, drinking tea and watching the pye dogs huddled in the mangroves shrugging sand from their coats. I could hear the resonant clink of the bottles as they slapped and settled on the *batliwala*'s cart.

It was 10 AM, and Iqbal, the sweeper, had not come. So we sat talking, as we often did, about Sind's favorite Sufi poet, Shah Abdul Latif, and his *risalo* (body of work; literally, "message"). Zubaida would recite a verse, at my prompting, and translate it from her native Sindhi into Urdu for me. Presently, there was a knock at the door. Aliya had dropped by to borrow some flour. Aliya, a Punjabi-speaking mother of two, was Zubaida's closest friend in the building. I rose to wait with Aliya in the doorway while Zubaida went to sift flour into a bowl.

As she returned from the kitchen, Zubaida continued our conversation. "For some people," she told me, brushing flour from her tunic, "Latif's *risalo* is their Quran." Aliya gaped at Zubaida, speechless. Zubaida reached across the threshold and handed the bowl to Aliya, repeating the comment: "*Woh log sochte hain ki yeh hamara quran hai*" (Those people think that this is our Quran).

Aliya sputtered, "*Jahalat, kiya jahalat!*" (Ignorance, what ignorance), took the flour, and made a somewhat curt departure. I could feel the tension left behind, like a storm held in abeyance by unseen polarities. Zubaida smiled and shrugged.

We returned to our cushions by the window, but the mood had changed, and our conversation faltered. "See? People say, 'Oh, Sindhis aren't Muslims,'" Zubaida complained. "They just don't understand." She picked up her tea and looked out the window. "Why hasn't Iqbal come?" she sighed. "Today I am very tense."

In the many times that I have considered this event since my return from the field, I have always seemed poised on the brink of an epiphany. Even as the encounter played itself out, I sensed its significance, for here was a way to organically link the seemingly routine and prosaic space of women's informal exchange with the pith of ethnic difference and tension. (This is particularly so, as the exchange was situated in the context of conversations throughout the building about a series of riots involving Sindhi and Jamaati [Islamic activist] students; I will discuss this in detail later in the chapter.) In organizing my field notes for writing, I began to suspect that this event could help me frame my challenge to the tired models of violence and peace handed us by social science—a model in which "tension" plays a somewhat facile role. But it was not until much later that I realized the extent to which the "tension" that I was taking as self-evident was itself deeply in question—that the risks, stakes, and meanings of exchange were going to somehow bring to light the historical play of cultural uncertainty, indeterminacy, and flux through the currency of the striving body.

At its most superficial level, this exchange can highlight for us the tensions at play between a national story that links patriotism with a specifically marked piety and the powerful ethnic imaginaries that it casts out, that can only ever be heretical, as it were. Zubaida's offhand remark about the reverence with which Sindhis hold their patron poet was read by Aliya as shockingly blasphemous, recapitulating the broader way in which ethnic difference is read as the nation's undoing. Much of the tension I perceived hovering in the air (and my somatic participation in the event is far from immaterial) surely centered around this contradiction, the seemingly incommensurable push of the universal, with all its exclusions, and the particular, with all its generalities.

But the social context of the utterance (the cry of "jahalat" and the corresponding shrug) cannot be dismissed as the mere insensate backdrop for more meaningful action. Standing in the doorway, Aliya reached across the threshold and took the flour. She had come to borrow flour, and she left with flour in hand. In her wake, we were faced with the palpable tension of a transaction that has no final action, an open-ended process without resolution. There is, indeed, an elegant homology between the tension of the gift not yet reciprocated and the tension of sociocultural contradiction unresolved.

This is what I find most striking about the exchange—the way in which it sustains, rather than resolves, the tension of contradiction between the national and the ethnic, between the indebted and the generous. And it does so through the medium of a particular subject: one that is willing to participate, somatically, in the life of the local—and a particular body: a body that can bear tension.

This nonresolution of tension—the maintenance of social tension embodied in the tension of the gift not yet returned—is central to the everyday peace sketched out in the previous chapter. In what follows, I draw connections between the transformed conditions of women's informal, local exchange that prevail in buildings like the Shipyard and the emergence of a new kind of peacemaking body. In this distinct context of unprecedented ethnic diversity, relative nuclearization and separation of households from kin and community networks, and a corresponding decline in women's mobility, neighbor exchange takes on greater importance in women's everyday lives. The flow of tension in these relations of exchange—the bodies that bear it and the peace that it enables—is my central concern.

Before I proceed, I want to set up more generally some of the problems with the anthropological approach to peace, in order to frame my own argument about its social production. Following that, I embark on an abbreviated discussion of the literature on exchange (in service to my specific concerns) before returning to the Shipyard.

On Peace and Violence

Ethnic conflict in Pakistan has received much attention from social scientists, and indeed, ethnic and communal violence has had an enormous impact on the lives of Karachi's citizens for the past three decades. But despite the violent interludes, the headlines, and the death counts, despite the proliferation of ethnic grievances and enmities, and despite the ethnic policies of the state, the fact cannot be denied that throughout the city, millions of people have been living together peacefully. What do we make of this?

By posing this question, I am trying to point to ways in which we may get at ethnic conflict and violence by looking at the everyday cultural coordinates of peace and cooperation. The search for resources on peace as a cultural process yields very few results. As Sponsel and Gregor have noted, "In anthropology, until recently, conflict, aggression, and violence have claimed most of our attention; peace, both interpersonal and intergroup, has received relatively short shrift" (1994: xv). War, indeed, has been much more seductive for social scientists, partly because, as Thomas Hardy remarked, it makes "rattling good history," while peace is seen to be "poor reading" (cf. Gregor 1994: 243). But scholarly interest in violence has both followed from and furthered an intransigent notion of innate human aggressiveness that has deep roots, not just in Hobbesian social theory but in the Western Judeo-Christian tradition.

With violence cast as innate, peace can only be defined negatively as the absence of conflict or the curbing or controlling of violence. From this perspective, much of what we call "culture" or "civilization" is merely the sublimated expression of this violence (Freud 1961). Accordingly, many anthropological studies of ritual and carnival have implicitly (if not explicitly) defined peace as sublimation; violent impulses and anxieties are cathartically released through ritual inversions and antistructural ceremonies (Malinowski 1961; Park 1994: 199).

But ethnographic work on "peaceful societies" has prompted anthropologists to ask whether we can understand peace not simply as the absence of violence but as the presence of something else (Sponsel 1994: 6). What this positive presence may be is more difficult to say, as Robarchek warns:

> The image of a peaceful society seems to carry with it a number of associated conceptions: cooperation, communalism, absence of self-interest, and so on. In short, when we hear of a peaceful society, we are likely to envision a society that is somehow the antithesis of the self-absorbed individualism of the modern urban-industrial world. (1989: 32)

Unlike much of social science, peace studies has long recognized the need for a more positive definition of peace. But with its value-explicit approach and its imbrication with liberal politics, this definition largely resembles the modern fantasy described by Robarchek. Peace studies is indeed hobbled by the bringing forward of the Western, universal, rights-bearing individual—integral, without a doubt, to a particularly defined politics, but detrimental to our understanding of the constitutive role of cultural meaning in organizing social life and conflict. Similarly, the language of "conflict resolution" too often assumes that disputes and grievances are objectifiable "problems" in need of a "solution" rather than "mechanisms for negotiating and redefining normative order" (Yngvesson 1993: 8).

Anthropologists seem uniquely positioned to lay bare the cultural notions of self and society that inform violence or peace for the people they study. Several volumes on "the anthropology of peace" (Sponsel and Gregor 1994) and "peaceful societies" (Howell and Willis 1989) have focused on storytelling events, institutions of exchange, witchcraft beliefs, and a host of other cultural phenomena that seem to be practices of peace-making, constructing both, as Gregor labels it, a "sociative" peace, characterized by mutuality and cooperation, and a "separative" peace, marked by sanctions, fears, and avoidance (1994: 245). The nuanced picture of peace that emerges therein is a far cry from the liberal projection of utopian, selfless community; it is edgier, richer, and more persuasive. Briggs writes of Canadian Inuit camps that "peace is also maintained by institutions that generate (and yet contain) fear, anger, and distrust" (1994: 155). For his Xinguaño informants, Gregor writes, "Witches, wild Indians, and blood arouse intense emotions of hatred, disgust, and fear.

Ironically, they also dramatize the values of peace and deter destructive conduct" (1994: 249). What is promising about this literature is its recognition that "opposition and antagonism may coexist with and even help to construct systems of peace and nonviolence" (Briggs 1994: 155). Peace, here, is neither imagined nor experienced as a kind of conformity.

In the anthropological archive, perhaps the closest we come to a rich understanding of positive peace is in studies of exchange (Lévi-Strauss 1969; Malinowski 1961; Mauss 1990; Sahlins 1972). In the absence of centralized states, Mauss argues, exchange is a "total" phenomenon, linking economic activity to legal, religious, and symbolic systems of meaning. Quite explicitly, exchange is represented as a mode of peacemaking:

> Two groups of men who meet can only either draw apart, and, if they show mistrust toward one another or issue a challenge, fight—or they can negotiate. Until legal systems and economies evolved not far removed from our own, it is always with strangers that one "deals," even if allied to them. In the Trobriand Islands, the people of Kiriwina told Malinowski: "The men from Dobu are not good like us; they are cruel, they are cannibals. When we come to Dobu, we are afraid of them. They might kill us. But then I spit out ginger root, and their attitude changes. They lay down their spears and receive us well." Nothing better interprets this unstable state between festival and war. (Mauss 1990: 82)

Despite the Hobbesian implications of the statement—that societies hover on the brink of war, restrained only by king or contract—it provides a felicitous starting point for mobilizing anthropological tools for the study of peace. Speaking of exchange in situations where the state is "nonexistent," Sahlins writes that "peacemaking is not a sporadic intersocietal event, it is a continuous process going on within society itself" (1972: 27). Even in the presence of states—and king or contract—peace as "a mode of social behavior" (Howell and Willis 1989: viii) is a relentless creative process. Furthermore, we do not need to seek out "peaceful societies" in order to see and study peace. There are "islets of peaceability" (Dentan 1994: 70) even in the midst of sensational conflict (see Buckley 1989 for an example from Northern Ireland), and there is an everyday peace that proliferates but goes largely unremarked in the midst of the generalized ethnic antagonism that informs social life in Karachi.

Witnesses to ethnic or communal violence in South Asia have often remarked with surprise on how communities that have long coexisted peacefully can suddenly become bitter enemies—or more pointedly, how "neighbors" can become "killers" (Appadurai 1996: 154). But little attention has been paid to how people "neighbor" in the first place in these cultural contexts. Focusing on the mechanics of neighboring in cities like Karachi enables us to interrogate the possible relationships between peace and everyday exchange. In fact, what we mean by everyday life could actually be understood as something much more substantive, namely, peace. This is not to deny that violence can have an everyday or routinized character (Kleinman 2000; Scheper-Hughes 1992). I am simply suggesting that the "everyday life" we posit as the site of the nonextraordinary, the *not* riot, can be reconceptualized in more positive terms as enabling the presence of something we may choose to call peace.

Exchange

Exchange has long been an anthropological preoccupation, generating scores of monographs, theories, and debates and in some cases defining entire ethnographic "regions" (Melanesian "kula exchange" comes to mind). For a rigorous and varied treatment of this complex topic, the reader must look elsewhere (e.g., Bourdieu 1990; Kapferer 1976; Komter 1996; Malinowski 1961; Mauss 1990; Munn 1986; Raheja 1988; Sahlins 1972; Strathern 1988). My interest in exchange is decidedly more limited.

Anthropologists have frequently noted the way in which exchange can be said to produce hierarchy and difference. To give without receiving is to be superior, *magister*, patron; to receive without reciprocating is, accordingly, to be inferior, *minister*, client (Mauss 1990: 74). Gifting and other forms of prestations have been articulated as challenges (Mauss 1990: 41), agonistic exchanges in and through which rivals compete for "symbolic capital"—honor, prestige, and the like (Bourdieu 1990: 100). Equivalence and delay are critical strategies that players call upon in order to stay in the game and come out on top.

But undue focus on the agonistic dimensions of exchange can lead us to overlook the fundamental anthropological insight about exchange: that it is oriented not simply to individual status but to social relationships,[1] that solidarity is forged in and through the deferral of reciprocity. The quality of this solidarity and the mechanics of deferral that support it require greater consideration.

Even as exchange can be said to (re)produce hierarchies and forge solidary relations, it simultaneously (or, perhaps, as a consequence) operates at another register. According to Munn's (1986) understanding of symbolic value transformation, exchange performs the necessary, symbolic labor of mediating or resolving dangerous (or, at least, disruptive) tensions of sociocultural contradiction (in Gawa, that between ideals of egalitarianism and the realities of hierarchy). The tensions that inhere in the act of exchange itself (between liberty and obligation, debt and expectation) become weighted with the tension of specific sociocultural contradictions; the tension that exchange thus "works out" is far in excess of the act itself.

This is, of course, a simplification, but it does enable us to pose the question: what happens to tension in exchange? It seems to me that the flow of tension in exchange is integral, not epiphenomenal, to the peace it creates. Most ethnographies of exchange characterize this flow as one of discharge. Maschio (1998) cites his New Britain informants as expressing "relief" at the giving of a gift or payment of a debt: "His skin will open, and anger, fear, and resentment will dissipate" (85). Munn (1986) also refers to the symbolic labor of exchange as "resolving" tension, which suggests a release, remission, or completion. But what happens to tension in those moments of deferral, from which peace or solidarity is wrought? If we turn our attention from relief and resolution to deferral and suspense, then how might that change the way we understand peaceful coexistence? This is the question to bear in mind as we turn to consider everyday exchange in the Shipyard.

Neighborly Exchange

In descending the stairs and coming to Zubaida's door to borrow flour, Aliya performed one of the daily exchanges that can be said to structure social relationships in the building. On one level, the term "exchange" is impossibly broad and can be used to refer to almost any social interaction in the neighborhood—from greetings, borrowing, and helping to visits and "sorrow-happiness" exchanges. ("Sorrow-happiness," or *gham shadi/gham khushi*, is the term used to refer to the celebration or mourning of rites of passage, like circumcisions, weddings, and funerals; it can also refer to less landmark joys and sorrows, like birthdays, graduations, and illnesses.) But on another level, "exchange" is a metaphor for, as well as a mode of performing, social relationships. Urdu speakers use the term *lena dena* (take and give) to index the presence or absence of attachment; the phrase *unse koi lena dena nahin* (we have no dealings with them) quite explicitly equates attachment or association with the practice of exchange.

It was not difficult to elicit a kind of metacommentary on neighborly exchange from my informants. When pressed, most women in the Shipyard defined this exchange—or simply "neighborliness"—as a religious duty. In response to my direct questions, women would return with a plethora of *hadith* extolling the virtues, the importance, and the obligation of neighborly regard.[2] "The Prophet said that your neighbor is closer to you than your own kin," my mother-in-law told me, quoting a well-known *hadith*. As Grima (1992: 102) and Barth (1959: 32) have noted, the commitment to local relations of exchange—across class, caste, and other lines of fissure—is an explicit value for their Pathan informants. According to Kulsoom, neighborliness required the niceties of etiquette and nothing more (*salaam dua*—greetings, pleasantries). But for most of my informants, neighborliness was idealized as a greater obligation (and/or opportunity) to provide assistance, to share resources, to exchange sorrow-happiness, and above all to live peaceably with one another. When I asked Parveen what she thought one "owed" one's neighbors, she answered, "First, that there should be no quarrel (*jhagra*)," and she ended with a familiar *hadith:* "He is no believer whose neighbor fears his fist or his tongue."

Routine, informal exchange between neighbors—specifically women—is intensive, even incessant, in the Shipyard. In elicited speech, it is this—the informal exchange of services and resources—that renders neighbors both bane and boon. When we first moved into the Shipyard, my mother-in-law was quick to warn us not to "make relations with neighbors, or it will be '*yeh karo, woh karo, yeh mujhe do, woh mujhe do*' (do this, do that, give me this, give me that)." But in the next breath, she admonished us to stay on good terms with our hallmates. "If you're sick or in trouble in the night, you go to your neighbors for help before anyone else." And indeed, borrowing and helping brought neighbors to each other's doors on a daily basis. Due to the confused plumbing in the Shipyard, one was always negotiating with upstairs and downstairs neighbors over water delivery and storage. As the Shipyard had no connection to the main water line, water was delivered by tankers every morning, pumped up to a holding tank on the roof, and released to the flats twice a day, morning and night. Many residents had installed water tanks in their bathrooms, which filled when the water was released; those without tanks filled buckets.

The problem with this system was that, if a resident failed to open the water valves at delivery time, then the water would not trickle down to the flats below; this precipitated frequent trips by downstairs residents to the upper floors with the plea to *"nari khol den!"* (open the tap).[3] Furthermore, with the serious water shortage facing Karachi as a whole, often the tanker would simply fail to show up. Then people—particularly those without storage tanks—would turn to their neighbors with requests for water.

Stinginess with water was a cause of great resentment. During a particularly dry week, Zubaida had asked Aliya for a gallon of water for cooking. "I can't spare it. I've got my own cooking and cleaning to do," she had replied. Zubaida, who had no storage tanks, was incensed, particularly since only days earlier, Aliya had boasted that, with her three large storage tanks, she was never short of water.

The obligation to share what one has, particularly in times of crisis, is taken very seriously. But at the same time, women in the Shipyard clearly resented those people who appeared at one's door only, as Zubaida remarked, *"jab koi kam ho"* (when there is some work). Zubaida was fed up with neighbors who came only when they needed medical advice from her brother-in-law, who was a doctor, or to borrow kitchen items. The worst offender, she complained, was Kulsoom, who visited once or twice in order to secure Zubaida's promise of Sindhi language tutoring for her daughter Beenish. "People are selfish," she complained. "They never come just to visit."

And yet the invariable dependence of neighbors on one another is often celebrated as an opportunity for social interaction or hospitality. One evening Sheheryar, Faizan, and I had returned to the apartment, but we locked all our keys in the car. While Sheheryar strategized with the *chowkidar* over what to do, Faizan and I went to our neighbor Parveen's flat to wait in comfort. Just as Parveen's husband, Fazal Sahib, was returning home from work, Sheheryar joined us. After explaining the situation, Sheheryar apologized for intruding, and Fazal Sahib waved his hand dismissively, saying, "*Nahin, Bhai, is bahane ap ae,*" invoking a commonly used phrase which translates as "No, Brother, for this excuse/ reason you have come," meaning any excuse that brings you into my home is a good one. Opportunities to host, help, or provide were sought after and relished (at least as often as such requests were lamented or bemoaned), though this was probably more true when the visitor was of high status and where the providing of hospitality conferred obvious prestige on the hosts.

Both types of comments—those that eulogize and those that lament neighbor relations—point to a world in which such sociality is very much a part of ordinary life. But they also bespeak a grave uncertainty as to the norms of reciprocity that are to regulate exchange in this particular space. Behind the seemingly routine comings and goings between neighbors in buildings like the Shipyard lies a mind-boggling quantity of hard labor. "Neighbor," as a category of social relationship, does little to guide Shipyard residents in organizing local life. It is crucial to bear in mind that this kind of dwelling, with its arbitrary and intensive mixing of linguistic/ethnic and sectarian communities under one roof, is experienced as new and as something of a problem. On what basis shall we have dealings with our neighbors? As fellow Sindhis, Shias, or Urdu speakers? As Muslims?

Despite the plethora of *hadith* lauding the expression of neighborly affection, the nature of local exchange clearly answers not simply to a kind of religious humanism but to the quality of civility inherent to the national project. This civility, not surprisingly, constructs its universality as an unmarked, *sharif*, Urdu sensibility. The language of neighboring in the city already problematizes the vernacular. This is nowhere more evident than in community development initiatives in the city's informal settlements. Community activists in Karachi frequently lament what they describe as a refusal or failure of slum dwellers to organize on the basis of "area identity." Rather than forming neighborhood collectives, residents persistently come together as "Gujars," "Jatts," "Christians," "Memons," and so on. Indeed, neighbor identity and neighborhood are central elements in a dominant national imaginary—bringing to mind the voluntary, transcendent features of civic duty and benign pluralism—the triumph of Urdu assimilation and Islamic brotherhood over the "scourge" of parochialism. Discursively and pragmatically, neighborhood and neighborly exchange are an important site where the boundaries of ethnic and national difference get articulated and contested and where the content of this difference gets lived, so to speak.[4]

In the Shipyard, with its pronounced linguistic diversity, Urdu was indeed the language of neighboring: requests for water, greetings, small talk, and social visits were almost invariably conducted in Urdu. Those residents who were not fluent in Urdu—notably Sultan Sahib's wife, who spoke only Pashto, and Ruhi's mother-in-law and Mahvish and Saira's mother, who both spoke only Sindhi—were virtually excluded from this neighboring public. To enter into the very space of neighboring—the hallway, stairwell, portico, doorway, drawing room—was in some ways to concede to this universal, nationalist Urdu "civil."

But there is no simple or automatic way in which exchange in the Shipyard articulates ethnic or national imperatives. On the one hand, there is a pointed disapproval of gifting (or visiting or associating) that is directed only toward one's own people, more narrowly defined (viz. ethnic or linguistic categories). But on the other hand, informants at times expressed the sense that only fellow Sindhis (or fellow Muhajirs, etc.) understood the proper way to be "neighborly," show hospitality, exchange sorrow-happiness, and so on. Consider the following examples.

Parveen and Zubaida distributed Eid sweets to a number of families in the building, including Kulsoom's.[5] Kulsoom never reciprocated. But while Parveen and Zubaida were unfazed by Kulsoom's "failure" to participate in Eid exchanges, they were incensed when they discovered that she had sent me *halim* (a traditional meat dish cooked with whole grains) on the tenth of Moharrum. (Both Kulsoom and my husband's family are Shia, and the tenth of Moharrum is a day of mourning dramatically coded in Pakistan as Shia.)[6] While unilateral gifting at Eid in Karachi is not uncommon and is often explained away as "some people are in the habit of giving, some are not," Kulsoom's prestation of *halim* to a fellow Shia family violated something. It showed that she was, indeed, "in the habit of giving" but only to "her own people."

In a slightly different vein, when our upstairs neighbor, the Baluch customs official, systematically hit up every household for a "loan" of 5,000 rupees, residents began talking about Baluch people as thieves. "Of course, *we* didn't give him the money," Beenish told me. "My mother said, 'Oh, those Baluch people, they're crafty. They'll take your money and then disappear.'" The suspicion of self-interested acquisitiveness— the lack of reciprocity or sacrifice in dealings—was understood not as a random lack of commitment to "the local" but as following from an intransigent identification—Baluchness—that placed him beyond the pale of civility.

While the failure to be "civil" is here an imagined function of residual primordial attachments, at other times it is precisely these attachments which are shown to enable "good citizenship." Thus Zubaida never tired of telling me that Sindhis, more than any other group in Pakistan, were always giving. Their hospitality, she claimed, was famous and unending. "Anyone who has come to Sindh has met with love and generosity, but when we Sindhis come to the city, we meet with hatred (*nafrat*) and disregard." Sindhis, she implied, are good citizens and good neighbors, marked by their unilateral giving as a kind of sacrifice.

The tensions between ethnic difference and civil discourse were also evident in women's discussions of marriage exchange. Marriage exchanges and related affinal systems of gifting are beyond the scope of this project, largely because such exchanges were enacted beyond (and outside) the boundaries of the Shipyard. And indeed, what you owe the people with whom you "exchange women" is different from what you owe neighbors, kin, and friends. But the typology that such practices of exchange were seen to create was central to Shipyard residents' sense of self and community. (Thus *ideas* about marriage exchange as generating value and status were themselves circulated, even if "women" were not.) Consider the following example:

One morning, when I came to visit Zubaida, she was talking on her newly installed phone. I listened with interest to Zubaida's side of the conversation, her lilting Urdu peppered with affectionate phrases and witticisms.

> "I was just talking to my *bhabi* (brother's wife)," Zubaida remarked, as she hung up the phone.
> "But why weren't you speaking in Sindhi?" I asked.
> "Because my *bhabi* is Pathan," she told me. Two of Zubaida's brothers had married girls from "outside" the community. "Oh, yes, we take girls from outside.

But none of our girls has ever married outside. Mine is a very strict family (*bohat sakht khandanwale*)," she said, with a rueful kind of pride.

For Shipyard residents, the loss of status involved in "giving" one's girls outside of the community or *biradari* (clan) was self-evident.[7] At one extreme, to marry one's daughter to a non-Muslim was unthinkable, a loss to the faith, a grave transgression, whereas for a son to marry a non-Muslim strengthened the faith and was broadly recognized as a *sawab ka kam* (an act with divine rewards). Furthermore, my informants assumed that those groups with superior, religious status—like Syeds (descendants of the Prophet)—would allow their daughters to remain forever unmarried before marrying them to a non-Syed.

But the status attached to endogamy was qualified by a discomfort with "clannishness"—a fear that drawing attention to one's commitment to "one's own people," more narrowly defined, threatened or in some way demeaned the civil community of the neighborhood. Thus I encountered assertions and denials of the importance of "marrying-in." Perhaps Zubaida's remark best exemplifies the self-consciousness with which informants crafted these categorizations.

As I discovered early on, Zubaida's household had a long-standing but well-masked conflict with Ruhi's household. The fault, Zubaida claimed, lay with Ilahi Sahib, Ruhi's father-in-law, the building president. Both Zubaida's family (the Channos) and Ruhi's (the Jalbanis) were small-time Sindhi landowners from the interior—the Channos near Khairpur and the Jalbanis near Nawabshah. While Ruhi and Zubaida would often meet and interact politely in the course of any given day, purely social visits were few.

> "They don't like us," Zubaida told me. "They think that they're better. Ilahi Sahib is always walking around like this (puffing up the chest, nose in the air), saying, 'We're Jalbanis! We have so much money!' So Babar and I sometimes joke (mimicking Ilahi Sahib), 'We're Channos! We take girls from outside, but we don't give them (*bahir se le jate hain, laikin nahin dete*). We're Channos!'"

The joke asserts the superior value of endogamy over wealth, but at the same time makes light of it and expresses ambivalence over the way it injects hierarchy and competition into relations that should ideally be egalitarian and solidary.

On a more somber note, women in the Shipyard could be brutally critical when it came to making these distinctions. When a scandal erupted in the building involving Kulsoom's family on the floor above us, her daughter's "love" marriage two years previously to a Sunni (Kulsoom's family is Shia Muhajir) became a topic of renewed criticism. Although the scandal involved Kulsoom's son Raza, it was Kulsoom's acceptance of her daughter Batool's love match that was taken up as proof of both moral laxity and the lack of a redemptive and necessary anger. This moral laxity and lack of anger was evoked to reference not just the individual family but Muhajirs in general, who were said not to "mind" if their girls "married outside."

It is important to recognize that the tensions that exchange generates—those between degrees of belonging (ethnic versus national citizenship) and of intimacy (close, allied, distant, etc.)—are at play not simply in narrative but in everyday practice itself. Consider the following story, in which Mahvish's confusion over the norms of exchange in the Shipyard throws into dramatic relief the uncertain language of reciprocity governing local relations (and hence the uncertain character of these relationships themselves). Specifically, her story reveals how the tensions that are seen to inhere in exchange more generally (that between timeliness and delay, liberty and obligation, etc.) perform, act out, or are overlaid with the tensions of sociocultural contradiction, especially that between universalizing and particularizing claims to identity.

One day, Zubaida and I ventured downstairs to visit Mahvish and Saira, the teenage daughters of a retired Sindhi revenue officer. Both girls (along with their two elder brothers) had grown up in Sann, a village in Dadu district in the Sindhi interior (birthplace of the renowned Sindhi activist G. M. Syed). Mahvish and Saira compared stories with Zubaida about life in the *gaon*, lamenting that Sann, which "used to be filled with love and hospitality," was turning into "a city where no one cares." After living in Hyderabad for a short time, they migrated to Karachi. They had been living in the Shipyard for just over two years.

Mahvish, the elder sister, served us fruit salad and cake and told us of their experience:

"When we moved to Karachi, we thought, 'Oh, what are the neighbors like? Who are they?' Now Bhabi (meaning Zubaida), she's also Sindhi, so our customs (*riwaj*) meet. But the others—well, on Eid, we made all this *mithai* (candy) and we distributed it, and there wasn't even one return. So we thought, 'What is this? Doesn't anybody here do *khushi* (happiness)?' But then we found, well, it's not that. Just that slowly, slowly, you get to know people."

The bewilderment in Mahvish's plea—"doesn't anybody here do *khushi*?"—highlights the many tensions that local exchange in the Shipyard both generates and employs. The indeterminacy of the gift, contingent for its meaning on the return it inspires (Bourdieu 1990: 141), is mirrored in the uncertainty of the social relationship it "encodes" (Strathern 1984: 44). "What are the neighbors like? Who are they?" Mahvish had asked. Surrounded by people who are both unknown (*ghair*) and yet potentially (and ideologically) one's own people (*apne log*), doing *khushi* was a familiar diagnostic of, and prescription for, social intimacy. The failure of the prestation to instigate an exchange was understood, at first, in ethnic terms: "Now Bhabi is also Sindhi, so our *riwaj* meet." The implication, then, is that the other neighbors, with perhaps different and unknown *riwaj*, did not read the gift of *mithai* for what it was—that different and incompatible forms of knowledge rendered the prestation unintelligible and "stripped it retrospectively of its meaning" (Bourdieu 1990: 141). But this explanation—the invocation of irreducible (and epistemological) difference—was later rejected. It's not that the people here don't "do *khushi*," Mahvish found; "just that slowly, slowly, you get to know people." In its rhetorical move to difference and back again, Mahvish's story engages, and in fact generates, tensions between the particularizing language of ethnic affinity and the universalizing terms of civic, or national, community, or "neighborhood." The progression in the tale from country naïveté to urban sophistication is imagined as a shift from the scripted to the improvised, from the convergent to the disjunctive. Mahvish's closing words—"slowly, slowly, you get to know people"—assert a cultivated appreciation for the transformed conditions, terms, and temporalities of "sorrow-happiness" exchange in the city. And in the end, doing *khushi* is restored as a central pragmatic and symbolic mode of forging, marking, and performing social relationships. But the tensions generated therein— between identity and difference, coming together and drawing apart, the paradox of neighbors as at once strangers and one's own people—are necessarily preserved as well.

From Bourdieu's well-known account of Kabyle "challenge" and "riposte" (1990) we can infer that the bulk of the labor of exchange (although Bourdieu himself would more likely use the term "strategy") resides in the nitty-gritty: who to give to; what to give; whether or not to reciprocate; what to reciprocate with, and when. Certainly, women in the Shipyard showed a concern for the principles of reciprocity and associated "strategies," like equivalence:

> "When someone sends me a plate of food," Aliya told me, "I always hold onto the plate for some days; then, when I've made something tasty, I send the plate back with the food I've made on it. I never return an empty plate."

And timing:

> "I don't like it (*mujhe acha nahin lagta*) when you give someone something and then immediately she gives you something in return," Zubaida griped.

Aliya's and Zubaida's words resonate with Bourdieu's understanding of agonistic exchange, in which return and delay are crucial dimensions of both securing honor and staying in the game. An immediate return is a rebuff—a refusal of the debt and obligation that exchange enacts, and failure or refusal to return can mean either snub or dishonor. But this model of agonistic exchange fails to satisfy, for it is not only (or even predominantly) the maximization of private or family honor that women seek in their ongoing local exchanges; the relationships that exchange articulates and forges are ends in themselves. This point became clear to me when I considered the curiously benign figure of Parveen, my next-door neighbor.

Parveen was a Muhajir who taught Urdu and Islamiat at a local grammar school. Her husband was an engineer, and they had two daughters, Shahla, age seven, and Nazu, age six. In all my time in the Shipyard, I never heard a negative word spoken about Parveen or her family. They were uniformly respected. At every Islamic holiday, Parveen made enormous batches of *mithai* and distributed it to each and every neighbor on our hall. It became quite routine to hear a knock on the door and find Shahla or Nazu, holding a covered dish of sweets, saying, "Please, if you can give me back the plate." Moreover, Parveen was scrupulous and prompt with her returns for others' prestations, visibly mindful that they matched in quantity and kind.

But curiously, none of the women in the building, as far as I could tell, were frequent or special visitors at Parveen's flat. When having tea with Zubaida and Aliya, Parveen might drop by to return something borrowed or to inquire after the sweeper. Upon her exit, Zubaida and Aliya would invariably, but gently, mock her. "Don't you like her?" I would press. And both would answer, quite emphatically, "Oh, of course. She's a good person (*woh achi hai*)."

But in fact, as later conversations revealed, Aliya and Zubaida interpreted Parveen's rapid discharge of debt and her indiscriminate prestations as a way of "keeping her distance." And significantly, they linked this "distance," this formality, with Parveen's Muhajir identity and *sharif* sensibilities. Similarly, Aliya and Zubaida gently mocked Parveen's relentless use of formal and deferential terms of address—like *baji*, or sister, and *ap*, the respectful form of "you"—as a stuffy and pretentious Urdu practice. In this, Aliya and Zubaida articulate a widely shared vernacular discomfort with Urdu culture, which is seen as cool and aloof.

Arguably, Parveen's indiscriminate use of food distribution and her exacting reciprocity were read by some as a kind of failure or refusal to *remain in the game* (Bourdieu) or, to use a less agonistic phrase, to remain *engaged*. By giving to everyone, the exchange became meaningless, emptied out, generic (rather like Mahvish's)—hardly worthy of return, and by virtue of her rapid and exacting "discharge" of debt, Parveen was refusing to take on and sustain tension. I would suggest that under these transformed conditions of neighboring, it is precisely such a willingness and capacity to bear tension that marks a commitment to the local (see Appadurai 1996: 193).

Indeed, the central element of informal exchange is that it is disorderly. Neighborly exchange is not the explicit pooling that governs families, households, or other intimate circles, nor is it the exacting, balanced reciprocity of distinct but allied "sides." It is fuzzy, equivalent, and indeterminate—where the expectation of reciprocity is "indefinite" and "weak" (Sahlins 1972: 29). The intimacy of generalized reciprocity necessitates a tolerance for "material imbalance" and "delay." In other words, it requires the willingness—and the capacity—to sustain indefinitely the tension of the not-yet-returned and, by extension, to sustain the tension of the specific social and cultural contradictions that exchange produces in this particular historical circumstance.

Clearly, the tension that figures in this local exchange is governed by a logic not of discharge but of *maintenance*—hence my informants' disapproval of Parveen's too-rapid returns and the refusal of tension that they performed. What we are witness to here is an emergent *ethic of suspense*, in which the moral imperative of reciprocity in this transformed social space demands active irresolution. Mahvish's allusion to these transformed sensibilities of exchange prefigures for us the distinct role that tension is to play in this everyday peace—and the new kind of subject and body that it calls into being. The labor of exchange here can be said to reside not in strategic moves or tactics whereby the player tacks, back and forth, in dog-fight-like fashion (Bourdieu 1977: 11) but rather in the very cords, fibers, nerves, and feelings that must be summoned in order to take on and abide tension.

Because we are deeming tension to be central to exchange and to the peace it creates, we can no longer treat it as a self-evident or transparent category of analysis. In the section that follows, I attempt a limited exegesis of tension, both to unload the baggage with which it is freighted in scholarly discourse on violence and peace and to lay bare its specific history and location in the English language and in the Shipyard.

Violence as Catharsis

What could be more apparent, more facile than the place of "tension" in ethnic violence? The strain of conflicting material or symbolic interests, primordial attachments, or historical enmities leads to mutually opposing movements, creating a tension which, upon reaching its ineffable breaking point, culminates in an "explosion" of violence, an "eruption," a climactic resolution of all that "suspense" and "suppressed excitement" and "anxiety."[8]

That our implicitly psychodynamic language of violence so closely mirrors the sexual act should hardly be surprising, for this commonsensical notion of our violent world owes a debt to the Freudian categories that meld violence and sexual desire in a miasma of "instinctual need," an excitation in the body striving for release—as satisfaction or sublimation (Freud 1961; see also 1965: 72–98). This—the origin of violence—turns out to be the origin of everything: love, cooperation, aesthetics, thought, meaning, and creativity (diffuse, aim-inhibited genital drive and/or sublimated Eros and Thanatos [Freud 1961: 54–55]).

To take seriously the question of tension—its role in collective violence—is to question the model of violence repeatedly handed to us by social science and, even more pressingly, to reject the impoverished model of peace that is its concomitant. But it is also to question the very meaning of tension as a universal, quasi-biological category—to probe its cultural nuances as a historically situated and practically hypothesized articulation.

The obvious problem with a "violence as catharsis" model is that it supports the notion of innate aggressiveness, a notion that has been explicitly condemned but implicitly smuggled into much if not most of the literature on ethnic conflict. Furthermore, Appadurai (1996) has argued against the trope of "explosion" for another reason, namely, that it furthers the notion of primordial difference, the tension of which is ever on the brink of snapping, merely awaiting inevitable triggers. Both of these critiques are sound. But significantly, even those accounts which reject both innate aggressiveness and primordial difference nevertheless retain this model of tension, taking hold of bodies—both individual and collective—and striving for release.

The Freudian model of object relations posits a Subject, driven by psychobiological drives (e.g., hunger, sexual desire), who seeks out a largely inert Object, by virtue of which this need-tension can be "discharged." This model is implicitly applied to collective bodies, so that inevitable tensions—of group differences, competition, or whatever—must find discharge through violent annihilation (war) or sublimation (exchange, ritual, and the like). With violence depicted as the climactic resolution of built-up tension, peace can only be a kind of limp, postorgasmic repose or simply the quietude of the unaroused—not a very inspiring state to champion.

But what if, rather than importing this Freudian metaphor, we were to seek another? The object-relations theories of D. W. Winnicott (1971) and Ernest Schachtel (1984), for example, provide a markedly different way of thinking about the subject, the object, and tension. For both Winnicott and Schachtel, the object is far from inert. Writes Winnicott, "The object, if it is to be used, must necessarily be real in the sense of being part of shared reality, not a bundle of projections" (1971: 88). Like Winnicott, Schachtel challenges Freud's contention that thought is the child of want, and he argues instead that "thought has two ancestors . . . namely, motivating needs *and* a distinctly human capacity, the relatively autonomous capacity for object interest" (1984: 268).

According to Schachtel, the object world is constituted as the child develops the capacity for "focal attention," a way of approaching and perceiving/interpolating the object that exceeds any biological or utilitarian objective: "This object is more than just something which satisfies a particular need; it has aspects other than the one which makes it suitable to satisfy the need. It has an existence of its own" (1984: 266). Thus the object does not simply appear because there is a need that the object may satisfy, nor does it disappear when the need is satisfied. In fact, "primary, biological needs" or "instincts" like hunger or fear *prevent* the emergence/construction of the object. States Schachtel, "The object emerges when the need tension is relaxed" (1984: 266), in a state allowing for "exploratory play."

Schachtel compares the difference between autonomous and need-dominated interest to that between love and sexual desire: "Like love, autonomous object interest is potentially inexhaustible and lasting, while need-dominated interest subsides with the satisfaction of the need, and revives only when the need tension, such as hunger or sexual desire, rises again. Moreover, while need tension, according to Freud, is related to tension discharge, both love and object interest find their fulfillment not in a discharge of tension, but, rather, in the maintenance of it, in sustained and ever renewed acts of relating to the beloved person or to the object of interest" (1984: 274–75).

This is the model of tension that I wish to import (and the relationship of this metaphor to psychic reality is meant to remain merely suggestive)—namely, that peace is an outflow of our distinctly human capacity for sociality; that peace lies in a maintenance of tension, not in its discharge. Violence, accordingly, can be seen as tension refusing—a lack of engagement, a refusal to "subjectify" the object. While total subjectification of the object may be ecstasy, the tension of sustained engagement is actually existing peace.

This, to my mind, is certainly a more persuasive metaphor for understanding peace and violence, but it is by no means timeless or unencumbered, for what are the tools we must summon in order to sustain this tension and achieve peace? What kind of body is it that can take on and bear tension? It is, I suspect, a modern body, with an interiority of nerves and feelings, and it is, above all, a feminine body.

Talking about Tension

According to the *Oxford English Dictionary*, the earliest attested usage of the term "tension" in English can be found in early sixteenth-century medical texts, where it was used to describe any stretching or feeling of tightness in the body. Taken directly from medical Latin, "tension" is a derivative of "tensus," the past participle of the Latin "tendere," to stretch (from which terms like "tendons" emerged). Tension as a physical, external state or force operative in the material world—"A constrained condition of the particles of a body when subjected to forces acting in opposite directions away from each other . . . thus tending to draw them apart, balanced by forces of cohesion holding them together" (*OED*)—can be traced back at least to seventeenth-century physics. For more than two hundred years, the meaning of the word "tension" seems to have been restricted to the tactile, the physical, and the manifest.

By the middle of the eighteenth century, tension had come to acquire new meanings, and it was used to refer to a particular kind of inner experience—that of "a straining, or strained condition, of the mind, feelings, or nerves" (*OED*). This roughly coincides with a broader historical shift in "emotion talk" documented by scholars like Harré and Finlay-Jones (1986) and Paul Heelas (1986). Throughout the Middle Ages, emotions were viewed as external forces, striking one from without. The idea that emotions come from "inside" hardly figures before the seventeenth century, and the introspective, self-psychologizing individual is almost certainly a product of the modern.

The historical emergence of tension as an inner mental or emotional quality is a fascinating phenomenon that I can only touch on here. It seems clear that it is linked to broader developments in literary, political, and technological movements, from modernism to liberal humanism to the industrial revolution, all of which gave rise to particular notions of the individual as autonomous, self-willed, and rights-bearing. But there is another development in the history of tension that is equally striking.

By the mid-nineteenth century, tension had come to accrue a peculiar sense of teleology. The tactility of tension had by this time come to reside not only inside individuals but between them, and what is more, this tension was suddenly progressive and destructive. Citing nineteenth-century writers like Disraeli and Harriet Beecher Stowe, the *OED* defines tension as "a strained condition of feeling or mutual relations which is for the time outwardly calm, but is likely to result in a sudden collapse, or in an outburst of anger or violent action of some kind." It is remarkable that a century after tension becomes defined as an inner mental or emotional experience, it becomes redefined as unbearable.

Not surprisingly, shortly after tension enters the English lexicon as a mental or emotional state with potentially violent consequence, it begins to appear in psychological writings, referring to "a condition of strain produced by anxiety, need, or by a sense of mental, emotional, or physical disequilibrium" (*OED*). In much of this psychological writing from the late nineteenth and early twentieth centuries, tension is less a problem to be therapeutically managed (as it is from the mid-twentieth century onwards, where we find a slew of "tension-relieving" strategies) than it is the very bedrock of the human psyche. As mentioned above, tension is central to Freudian psychology, where innate psychobiological drives are seen to create tensions which must be discharged, either directly (through feeding, mating, or killing) or cathartically (through sublimated activity and ritual, giving rise to all the products of "civilization," from thought and love to literature and metropolises). In theories such as these, the marriage of tension with discharge is not simply potential or "likely" but necessary and inevitable.[9]

These, then, constitute the unreflected roots of our casual adoption of the term "tension" in the analysis of peace and violence. But as this brief discussion of the history of tension suggests, the psychological and everyday association of tension (be it mental/emotional or social/interpersonal) with a kind of inescapable teleology of buildup and discharge is not the only alternative. Schachtel's (1984) distinct framing of the play of tension in object relations is mirrored both in older, more restricted uses of the term and in other trajectories of its etymological origins, for "tension" is related, etymologically, to the variant "tention" and with it "contention," "intention," and "attention"; it is the latter which Schachtel recuperates, and with it, we can envision a "mindful body" (Scheper-

Hughes and Lock 1987) that (willingly) bears tension without outburst or collapse.

That we talk about tension as affecting our nerves or feelings, that we take it on as an inner experience, that we narrativize it, transform it into discourse, psychologize and seek remedy through various therapeutic avenues is very much a reflection of our modern heritage. But what does the use of the terms "tense" and "tension" mean for my Urdu-medium informants?

"Today I Am Very Tense"

At the time, Zubaida's use of the English term "tense" did not strike me as noteworthy. Most Urdu speakers, regardless of social class, have an arsenal of English words they mobilize in innumerable circumstances, a reflection of the transformed social and linguistic conditions begun with British colonialism. But over the course of my fieldwork, a pattern emerged, revealing a whole (almost certainly related) complex of emotion terms for which English was almost invariably favored. These terms include "tense" and "tension," "mind" (as in "don't mind it"), "feel," "like" (as in "I like you"), and "share." That many of the terms have what seem to be close if not exact Urdu equivalents—"mind" (*bura manna*) and "like" (*pasand*)—suggests that the use of English terms is pointing to a broader movement, a practical recognition that something is happening or being constructed that somehow eludes Urdu categories. And indeed, women's invocations of the words "tense" and "tension" often carry with them a sense of trying things out, a struggle for meaning.

Once I turned my attention to the everyday use of "tense" and "tension," I was surprised by its near ubiquity. All the women in the building were "tense"; "tension" was "happening" to everyone. Someone or other was always "feeling" or "getting" tense. Ruhi's is a key example:

Ruhi lived on the first floor with her husband, Wasif, her six-year-old daughter, Sana, her father-in-law, Ilahi Sahib, her mother-in-law, and Wasif's divorced sister, Hajil. Ilahi Sahib had a reputation (not undeserved) as a lecher, and under the pretext of "building management" he would burst into one's apartment without regard for considerations of purdah or privacy. Moreover, he had severely impaired vision (along with a lazy eye) and would often grab onto the arm of any neighbor passing by (male or female), ostensibly to steady himself. Ilahi Sahib and his wife spent six months of every year living with Wasif's younger brother in Canada. During those months, Ruhi "came alive." Female neighbors felt free to visit, and Ruhi could come and go during the day with impunity.

While her in-laws were abroad, I visited Ruhi nearly every afternoon to help her with her English; she had taken a job teaching Urdu at a nearby English-medium grammar school, and she said she felt uncomfortable because the other teachers were all fluent in English, and she was not. One day, Ruhi stopped the lessons and turned to me, concerned.

> "Laura, when my father-in-law (*susr*) comes back, will you still be able to come for lessons? Because he's very clingy (*chipku*), he'll sit and watch and ask me, 'Why is she coming? Why are you seeing her? What are you talking about?'"
>
> "I'm sure it'll be fine," I hedged.
>
> "Oh, my father-in-law is very colorful (*rangila*)," she continued, shaking her head. "While he is in Canada, I am free. I can meet with my friends, go shopping. It is very difficult living with my father-in-law. Everything has to be just so. When he's here, a lot of tension happens to me (*mujhe bohat* tension *ho jati hai*); I feel very tense (*main bohat* tense feel *karti hun*). He's a heart patient. He gets upset. He worries about things. At times I've asked my husband, 'Can't we live separate (*alag*)?' But he says, 'My father is old, a heart patient. I can't leave them.' But one needs to have one's own method of living, waking and sleeping, coming and going."

Ruhi's tacit suggestion that tension both happens to one (*ho jati hai*) and is simultaneously an affective state (tense feel *karti hun*) points to the uncertain quality of somatic knowledge that this mood or posture brings in tow. Does it come from outside or within? The use of the English term "feel" (rather than the available equivalent, *mehsus*) may point to a recognition that a very different body is now involved or being called upon.

When I asked my informants why they chose *tense* or *tension* over Urdu equivalents, most would shrug and say, simply, that it was "appropriate" (*munasib*). Ruhi suggested that the Urdu formulation was too cumbersome. "See, you'd have to say, '*main bohat khichao mehsus karti hun*' (I feel a lot of pull) where you could simply say '*main* tense *hun*' (I am tense)." But according to C. M. Naim, the correct term for tension is not *khichao*, which suggests a pull in which one side is inert or stationary, but *tannao*, which suggests contradictory poles.[10] *Tannao* may be the closest Urdu equivalent to the English "tension," in that it specifically marries physical, material tension—the pull of opposing forces—with social strife, as expressed in the final meaning of the English term "tension," as given in *Webster's Dictionary*: "4. a strained relationship between individuals, groups, nations, etc." Thus one can say, "*Donon bhaiyon se tannao hai*" (There is tension between the two brothers). However, as with *khichao*, one would have to struggle to convey *tannao* as an inner state, through such unlikely formulations as "*zehni tannao*" (mental tension) or, more likely "*uljhan*" (confusion, disturbance). The tension of *tannao* and *khichao* seem resolutely external, out there in the world, in cords and fibers, or strife-ridden social situations. Indeed, there is no small awkwardness in the quest to internalize this concept in Urdu, hence the very common insertion of the English word "tense" to convey something I suspect is comparatively new: the experience of tension as a somatic inner psychobiological fact.

Certainly, there are a host of Urdu terms that can be used to convey inner turmoil, perplexity, or contrariness: *kash, kash-a-kash,* or *kash-ma-kash* are some examples (although these are rarely heard in everyday speech), as are *uljhan* and *fikr* (anxiety or concern). It is a futile exercise to speculate why this or that term is *not* currently standing in for the English tension. Any available Urdu term could certainly be transformed or used in new ways in order to convey new sensibilities that transformed moral and social contexts demand. It could be, however, that the above stated terms for inner turmoil carry a surfeit of meaning that my informants deem inappropriate for the current context. Consider the following example: I had popped next door to borrow cumin. Parveen was standing at the dining table, dividing cubes of goat meat into equal stacks for Eid distribution. The overhead fan was clinking rhythmically, and Parveen lifted a weary arm to wipe the perspiration from her forehead. "Can I help?" I asked, and she declined my offer, but pulled out a chair and asked me to stay and talk while she finished up.

> "It's so difficult, Laura," she told me. "I'm in the school (teaching) until midday, then there's the shopping—and such expenses (*kharcha*)! Then my husband, you know, he's from Lucknow; he wants rice and chapati at every meal, and then two or three dishes. It's so much work. And you see, I wash our clothes myself, because the *masi*, she's Christian, and you know, they don't pray (*namaz nahin parhte*), so they don't worry if the clothes don't come clean. And now it's Eid,

and I've got this meat to get ready, and then I'll give the *mithai*. Oh, these days I get very tense (*main bohat* tense *ho jati hun*)."

For Parveen, the tension that she bore was a burden, but it was also redemptive, a marker of a kind of tireless stoicism that women in the Shipyard openly valued. Declaring this tension was not a form of complaint or lament, but rather a crucial element of its social construction. This tension is not transient, like *uljhan;* it is not something to be shed, evaded, discharged, or lamented (as perhaps *kash* is). This is perhaps why other Urdu terms for inner turmoil, like *kash*, are not seen to suit the mood; the connotation of offense, displeasure, or distraction therein may tip the scales toward complaint and away from burden-well-borne.

When I first began recording women's use of the terms "tense" and "tension," I marveled at the similarities in those situations or contexts which gave rise to these utterances. Zubaida was "tense" in the context of an informal exchange that became loaded with the contradictions of ethnic and national difference; Ruhi "felt tension" from her lack of mobility and restricted visiting/exchange privileges when her father-in-law was in residence; and Parveen "got tense" when contemplating her host of obligations while preparing meat for ritual exchange. Clearly, there is a way in which exchange not only generates and sustains tension but also becomes an occasion for the *articulation* of tension. Talking about tension creates a sensibility of tension borne—along with a normative valuation that this is our lot, this is our life, and it is our duty (*majburi*) to bear it (*bardasht*). Learning to take on and bear tension simultaneously requires that one be able to recognize and articulate "nerves and feelings," and this, in turn, requires a new kind of emotional exchange, or "sharing," by virtue of which these "nerves and feelings" are imagined, narrativized, transformed into discourse.

Arguably, then, it is indeed a modern body that can take on tension—as a mental or emotional burden. *Bearing* it, on the other hand, may require another body altogether. The fact that the patterns of exchange we have been discussing are emphatically gendered—that the labor of exchange in the Shipyard is carried out almost entirely by women—has not escaped our attention. The management of tension therein seems to call not only for a specifically modern subject but also for a feminine—or at least feminized—body.

Women as Maximally Transactive

The intensity of women's local exchange in the Shipyard has historical parallels. According to Gail Minault (1998), Muslim women in precolonial times led rich and active neighborhood lives, moving freely from house to house (via rooftops and other routes that preserved modesty), attending soirees and religious functions, exchanging gifts and visits, in segregated—but far from isolated—female society. Under the scrutiny of nineteenth-century Islamic reformers,[11] this pattern of intense female exchange (and its alarming autonomy from patriarchal control) became the object of censure. Suddenly, long-held practices of ritual and informal exchange between neighbors and relatives were condemned as "corrupt customs," unsanctioned by Islamic law. Notable nineteenth-century social reformer Maulana Ashraf Ali Thanawi pinpointed the sense of obligation inherent in women's often extravagant exchanges of sorrow-happiness as un-Islamic—a "false *shariat*" (religious law). The careful reckoning of exchanges of *mithai* on Islamic holidays, the extravagant "returns" for wedding prestations, and above all, the calculated balancing underpinning such practices was condemned as "evil" as well as "a bother." This "false" sense of obligation is evil, Thanawi contends, because "it is a sin to consider necessary what is not deemed necessary by the *shariat*." Furthermore, "the requirement of exchanging gifts with relatives' children and sending food to relatives' houses—and with this, keeping account of reciprocity and taking loans when you are needy—is foolish and a bother as well." Reformers call on women to "abandon" such customs (Metcalf 1990: 156–57).

For reformers, the problem of exchange—as excessive, burdensome, and falsely binding—is a problem with women. Women's less developed faculty of *aql* (reason) leads them to undisciplined excess: "Women dawdle too long, talk too loud, spend too much, take too much time, and take along too much luggage. They rush in too quickly, they do too much at once, they give too much food, they cry too readily. They are careless with valuables and time" (Metcalf 1990: 318). According to reformist thought and South Asian ethnography, women are "believed to have less controllable propensities for maximal exchange" (Marriott 1976: 137), and so they must discipline and restrict their movements and interactions.

The phrase "maximal exchange" emerges from Marriott's phenomenological account of South Asian transaction, in which subjects are seen to trade in "bodily code-substance": "Persons are generally thought by South Asians to be 'dividual' or divisible. To exist, dividual persons absorb heterogeneous material influences. They must also give out from themselves particles of their own coded substances" (Marriott 1976: 111). Gifts, then, along with services and other transactions, are seen to embody and pass on quasi-material elements of the giver. The strategy of maximal exchange—giving out and absorbing large quantities of bodily code-substance—is associated with masculine qualities of anger, heat, openness, and sexuality. Minimal exchange, conversely, is cool, closed, and restricted. Women who visit too much and make too many prestations contravene the values of *sharm* (shame), which, in effect, eulogize minimal transaction: the closed mouth, the averted gaze, the silent, modest woman.

For this reason, women, even as they accompanied me on visits to other flats, would often qualify their movements with statements like "It doesn't look nice to always be visiting" and "I don't like to be going here and there." "I don't really go out much," Kulsoom told me during an impromptu visit to my apartment. Statements like these—made, as they were, in the context of visiting—were in stark contrast to the sheer intensity of traffic between flats.

Indeed, despite this widely circulated discourse, which valorizes the women who have little contact with neighbors and outsiders, neighboring in the Shipyard was overwhelmingly "women's work" (Papanek 1979). Certainly, men exchanged daily pleasantries, provided assistance, and forged friendships in the building. But due, at least in part, to the sexual division of labor that prevailed, most men were absent from the building during work hours. "Free time" was packed full of meals, prayers, and family obligations that left only minimal opportunities for socializing with the neighbors. (There were, however, several senior men who no longer held jobs, and they, indeed, were more visible players in the dramas of neighborhood life.)

Women—particularly wives—were the key forgers of social links between households. Their responsibilities for household management and the somatic labor of feeding and child care and cleaning necessitated their intense interactions with the local community: sweepers, food vendors, water deliverers, and above all, neighbors—drawing them, on a routine basis, into the communal, semipublic spaces of the hallway, stairwell, gully, and portico. In addition to the informal, everyday exchange of neighborly assistance and affection, women were also the key movers of goods between households. This is as true of more ceremonial giving (like that associated with affinal exchange [Eglar 1960] and sorrow-happiness [Werbner 1990]) as it is of routine borrowing and lending.

There is more, however, to women's strategy of "maximal exchange" than simple exigency. For one thing, women construct their labors of visiting and managing and borrowing as pleasurable practices. Grima, writing of her Pathan informants, notes that "women who express any wish at all for a better life frame it in terms of having a husband or in-laws who grant them more visiting rights" (1992: 44). As I discuss in chapter 5, yearnings for intimacy, attachment, and pleasure play out intensely in this homosocial "public," vying with both the household and the increasingly available "companionate couple" as the site for "having a life" (Berlant 1998).

But in addition to the pleasure that local exchange makes possible, there is also a sense that it is a necessary labor. People in the Shipyard about whom one knows little—with whom one has few or no dealings—remain dangerous strangers, potential ill doers. When women warned me about this or that flat and this or that family, it was almost invariably a household with whom they had no relationship. Thus Zubaida would caution me about the downstairs corner flat: "Don't let Faizan play there; they have MQM connections." Ruhi, who lived on the first floor, spoke in a similar fashion about the upper floors: "I don't let Sana play up there. There are too many boys hanging around." Exchange, in a sense, domesticates what is potentially an antagonistic, violence-inviting space. Indeed, the interstitial spaces of the apartment building—the stairwells, hallways, and balconies—are the source of some anxiety. Being neither clearly inside nor outside, "common" or "possessed" (Hull 1995), they are seen as inadequately inhabited and vulnerable to the invasion of supernatural forces (like djinns, witches, or ghosts). They are also seen to invite conflict.

Not only is local exchange considered a necessary labor. It is also construed as one which women alone are capable of performing. Women suggest that men are simply not equipped to handle the vicissitudes of balance in exchange, due to their vulnerability to sudden, explosive anger.

For this reason, women frequently keep the details of their local dealings hidden from husbands and male in-laws. Zubaida kept a pile of clothes that she was stitching for Aliya hidden in a closet, taking it out to work on only when her husband and brother-in-law were away. "They'd just get mad at Aliya and say, 'Doesn't she know you have your own work to do?'" Zubaida explained, adding, "Aliya helps me, too, when I need it." It is also common for a husband to chastise his wife for visiting too often, demanding that she wait for others to visit "in return." Women's words suggest that it is precisely the willingness to tolerate "material imbalance and delay" (Sahlins 1972: 29)—so central to generalized reciprocity— that men lack. In slightly different terms, we could say that men are viewed as intolerant of *tension*—that this masculinity is deemed "tension-refusing," if you will.

It is significant that the labor of neighborly exchange in the Shipyard is carried out almost exclusively by women. It is also remarkable that this labor takes place largely in the *absence* of men. When men are in residence, the individuation of household and family unit prevails (in contrast to the more fluid and open character of neighboring that applies when they are away). This raises a host of questions about the gendered, embodied, and spatiotemporal conditions of peacemaking in buildings like the Shipyard; about the specific femininities and masculinities emerging therein; and about how we may envision—however provisionally—the connection between everyday peace in the apartment building and ethnic violence in the city (and the street) more generally.

To further address these questions, I wish to return to the opening anecdote, that "tense moment" in which the neighborly exchange of flour engaged a trove of sociocultural tensions that have thus far passed largely unremarked. The immediate sociopolitical context of the exchange gives substance to the tensions we perceive as being "managed" therein and provides an opportunity to compare, however tentatively, the current of peaceful exchange with that of violent action.

Jahalat and Riots

When Zubaida, in passing the flour to Aliya, remarked in an offhand manner that some Sindhis consider Latif's magnum opus to be their Quran, Aliya replied: "*Jahalat, kiya jahalat.*" Literally, *jahalat* means "imperfect knowledge, ignorance, barbarism, brutality." In this context, the connotations of religious failings are clear: the roots of the word are shared with *jahiliat*, as in *aiyam-i-jahiliat*, the days of ignorance and paganism prior to the coming of Islam. Both Zubaida's offhand (blasphemous?) remark and Aliya's brusque (pious?) response must be understood in the exchange's more immediate context, in which residents were absorbed in news reports and rumors surrounding a series of riots that shook Karachi's Dow Medical College that summer of 1997.

One morning in July, Zubaida called to me breathlessly as we passed one another in the hallway: "Some Sindhi students were beaten yesterday."

"What?" I stammered. "Who? Where?"

"At Dow Medical College," she said and hurried off. I turned back to my apartment and picked up the day's newspaper. The story was on the front page. Apparently, a riot involving two student groups had left eleven people injured and two hospitalized (and three days later, one dead). I followed the story with dismay and interest, along with my neighbors, who had much to say about the event and its political significance.

Earlier, in June, a number of Sindhi Muslim students at Dow Medical College—members of the Sindhi Medicos Association—had celebrated their exam results with a kind of Hindu *Holi* festival, throwing paint on one another and their fellow classmates. Workers of the Islami Jamiat-e Taliba (IJT)—the student wing of the well-known Islamic political/activist group Jamaat-e Islami—protested, and fighting broke out. For the next month, there were sporadic clashes between the two groups, culminating in a full-scale riot in July.

The event made headlines for days, as Karachi's various ethnic and religious parties struggled to interpret the riot and claim it, so to speak, for their own cultural and political projects. According to Sindhi groups, the "Dow incident" had nothing to do with religion and everything to do with the political, social, and cultural disenfranchisement of Sindhis and their aggrieved minority status in Karachi. The officers of the Sindhi Medicos Association demanded that the government take steps to protect Sindhi students in the educational institutions of the city. Strikes broke out in hospitals and universities throughout Sindh; classes were boy-cotted, demonstrations were staged, and Dow Medical College remained closed for over a month.

Meanwhile, IJT leaders claimed that Sindhi groups were distorting the facts by giving the riot an "ethnic color." The Sindhi students were to blame, they contended, for holding an "immoral *Holi* programme in the college." From this perspective, the riot was about the threat that heterodoxy poses to the sanctity and integrity of the nation. Jamiat leader Hafiz Naeemur Rehman was quoted in the July 11, 1997, edition of *Dawn* as saying: "Pakistan, which came into existence in the name of Islam, is celebrating its golden jubilee, while a handful group is promoting un-Islamic culture and distorting the Islamic identity of the educational institutions." Indeed, he added, "The Sindhi medicos and the Sindhi nationalist organizations have nothing to do with Islam."

In order to understand these events and the public response to them, we need to bear in mind the relationship between "nationalism" and "ethnicity" in Karachi—the compelling association of the national with Islam and the particular saga and legacy of Karachi's Muhajirs. We need to consider the problematic relationship between Karachi and the Sindhi interior, its historical roots as well as spatial, and how this translates into a Sindhi struggle for a piece of the urban pie (as well as a stab at defining an indigenous urbane). It is instructive to consider what this event is not about: it is not about religious minorities and their rights. IJT condemnations of the Sindhi students' celebration of "a kind of *Holi*" were not framed as an attack on the rights of Hindu students; the students involved were, in fact, Muslim. Similarly, Sindhi condemnations of intolerance were not made in defense of their Hindu compatriots. Rather, what was at issue was the place of religion vis-à-vis local or regional culture in a Pakistani and/or Sindhi national imaginary. The specific anxiety and ambivalence surrounding "local custom" in the ongoing struggle for national identity in Pakistan points to the broader sense in which official nationalism becomes elided with Islam and, correspondingly, how "ethnicity" itself becomes a kind of "heresy." In what follows, I will try to unpack the discursive intersections that the riot lays bare, before returning to its everyday treatment in the building.

In October 1997, several international cultural institutes and a local news group sponsored a seminar on migration in Karachi, pulling in speakers from three European countries to present papers alongside local Pakistani scholars. During a panel discussion, the moderator remarked on the curious fact that British colonialism, while pivotal to social and literary criticism in Indian scholarship, had failed to produce the same critical and theoretical response in the Pakistani academy. A member of the audience sardonically suggested that the explanation was quite simple: "See, the Indians got rid of the British; but we got rid of the Hindus."

Indeed, any survey of scholarly literature emerging from Pakistan would immediately recognize the centrality of communal religious identity in the construction of national consciousness; the Islamic character of the state and the specific character of this Islam have been a matter of literary preoccupation and political contest at least since partition. Pakistani nationalism, having its origins in the "two-nation theory," obsessively furthers this duality—what it is: a nation of and for Muslims, and what it is not: Hindu.

The national anxiety surrounding Hinduism—that which has been expunged—has little to do with the presence and practices of Pakistan's remaining Hindus (estimated to be less than 3 percent of the national population), the majority of whom reside in Sindh, eking out livings as landless cultivators or unskilled laborers. Rather, this anxiety is internal to official, or *sharif*, nationalism—that narrative which translates the experience of Urdu-speaking Indian Muslims and their *hijrat* (migration) into a kind of Oedipal origin story of the nation. Herein, the enabling factor—Hinduism—can never truly be absent, and indeed it threatens to return, like the repressed, in all efforts at self-constitution. The problem is daunting. A South Asian Islam free of (or untainted by) Hindu influence is laboriously conjured up and transported into the past. The natural spokespeople for, or subjects of, this discourse then become Muhajirs; exogenous-identified, tracing their origins to Arab, Persian, and Central Asian Muslim settlers and conquerors, none of the viscera of autochthony need complicate their reconstituted memories.

The state thus has a kind of natural body in Muhajirs. Naturalizing the territory of the nation, however, is a little trickier. The area that is now Pakistan became so because of its demographics; before partition, the majority of the inhabitants were certainly Muslim. Baluchistan and the Northwest Frontier Province with its majority Pathan population had long histories of Islamic practice and strong historical ties with Central

Asian empires. Punjab, being more divided, was itself partitioned. It is in Sindh, however, that the state finds its most complex and contradictory space, and it is here that its efforts at naturalization/nationalization are most conflicted.

The Muslim character of Sindh could be said to have its origins in Mohammed Bin Qasim's conquest of its capital, Alor, in AD 713. Arab explorers from this period clearly differentiate "Sind" from "Hind"—the former being viewed as an enlightened entrepôt of Islamic culture, the latter hopelessly Vedic. However, while Sindh remained under Muslim (though not singularly Arab) rule for centuries, this rule was generally remote, and in many ways it left little impression on the local population. Indeed, it was not until the twelfth century, which brought scores of Persian and Arab Sufi missions to Sindh, that wide-scale conversion to Islam occurred. Islamic mysticism found ready acceptance in Sindh, and even where conversion did not take place, there was a marked degree of syncretic practice, blending Hindu and Sufi devotional ritual.

For the majority of Muslim Sindhis, then, Islam enters genealogical memory as a story of conversion—a gradual, benevolently syncretic conversion at that. For the state, the indigenous body, consequently, is already heretical: Sindhis are "ethnic," where *ethnic* can only mean "Hindu convert" and thus suspect. (Just as Indian Muslims are suspected of being sympathetic to Pakistan, so Muslim Sindhis are viewed as "incompletely converted.")

Thus, despite centuries of religious syncretism in Sindh, there is a pronounced difficulty on the part of the state in recognizing the materiality of a Hindu past, which in fact is not finished and therefore not "the past." It makes sense, then, that when the Sindhi Muslim students at Dow Medical College celebrated their exam results by throwing paint in a manner reminiscent of Hindu *Holi* ceremonies, college administrators promptly decried it as "culture invasion" (*Dawn*, 8 July 1997)—something foreign, outside, and irreducibly other. The metaphor of boundaries being breached, "invaded," is appropriately corporeal (and martial), considering the violence that followed, ultimately restoring a clear separation between impenetrably "national" bodies and flimsy, vulnerable, heretical ones.

Furthermore, as the Dow incident makes clear, it is not just the student body but the Islamic character of public space that must be protected. IJT leaders invoke the fiftieth jubilee of Pakistan, reminding that the nation "came into existence in the name of Islam," rendering all the more blasphemous the promotion of "un-Islamic culture" in the college. Not the presence of religious minorities but the improperly converted indigenes were "distorting the Islamic identity of [Pakistan's] educational institutions" (*Dawn*, 11 July 1997).

This effort to nationalize public space—to imbue the public with a necessarily Islamic, and arguably immigrant, non-indigenous character—is similarly apparent in historic preservation efforts in Karachi. When nongovernmental organizations rallied for the restoration of the Hindu Gymkhana (a former recreational club/resort) and its return to "the people," disputes arose over how the space should be used and who the people were, exactly, to whom it should be returned. Since its designation as "evacuee property" in 1947, the Hindu Gymkhana has been occupied by a succession of government agencies including the Ministry of Law, police, and paramilitary rangers. Built in the early twentieth century by local Hindu societies, the palatial structure—a landmark of Indo-Saracenic architecture, originally served as a public recreational space for Karachi's elite Hindu population. During Benazir Bhutto's tenure in the early 1990s, the Sindh Culture Department took over the building, proposing to fully renovate it and install a fine arts institute, specializing in Sindhi handicrafts. This, apparently, was not what preservation activists had in mind. Proposals were put forward instead to secure the Gymkhana for a natural history museum, a research institute, a press club—all more acceptably "national" spaces for "national" audiences. Notably silenced in this debate were local Hindu associations, which claimed to possess the deed to the property and were demanding that the building be restored to its original purpose for its originally intended consumers.

Whereas Hindu Gymkhana—with its civic connotations of sport, recreation, and exclusive fraternity—was found to be redeemable (once purged of its offending difference), other historical "Hindu" buildings have faced more dire fates. Consider the island of Manora, a combination naval fort and public beach resort. Preservationists have drafted plans to restore many of the island's colonial-era (and older) buildings—the officers' mess, a lighthouse, two Christian churches, one Sufi shrine, and two Sikh temples. A Hindu temple on the island was not included in restoration plans; it had been so badly desecrated as to be unsalvageable, and visitors to the island who come to enjoy the white, sandy beaches have taken to using the temple as a lavatory.

Even more striking, though, is the treatment of Hindu sculptures and artwork in the National Museum in Karachi. One cannot help but notice that all the Buddhist artifacts, as well as those from the archaeological sites of Taxila and Mohenjo-daro, are clearly labeled as to date and where in Pakistan they were discovered. The Hindu sculptures, however, remain undated, with their site of discovery unmarked. Clearly, there is a reluctance here to articulate a historical and spatial legacy of Hinduism in a nation that thinks itself into being through the language of Islam.

My point here is not simply to identify the Islamicizing tenor of a dominant Pakistani imaginary, which is so obvious as to be banal. In the scholarly corpus on Pakistan, much has been written on what the Pakistani nation is, or should be, or "was meant to be"; what "Islamic state" means; what the relationship between nationalism and religious discourse is understood to be. But there is very little discussion of what has had to happen to get here, on what has been denied, repressed, refused, and reviled—a pressing question, when one considers the way in which this floating signifier (the cast-off) gets attached to particular bodies, rendering them heretical in the sense of antinational *and* un-Islamic.

After the Dow Medical College incident, IJT leaders dismissed Sindhi political identity with the simple statement "Sindhi nationalism has nothing to do with Islam" (*Dawn*, 11 July 1997). This viewpoint is entirely consistent with dominant Pakistani nationalism and conjures up the history of a complex and troubled relationship between the Sindh province and its major city, Karachi, and, since independence, between Sindh and the nation of Pakistan. The disparagement of regional identity has been part of state policy practically since its inception; with ordinances like One Unit, which abolished provincial boundaries, outlawed vernacular education, and generally stifled local cultural expression, government leaders hoped to present a unified front (West Pakistan) to its suddenly adversarial neighbor, India. This also had much to do with the remote presence of its companion wing, East Pakistan, and its increasingly separate character. The threat of repeated, internal partition rendered cultural difference dangerous, and Islam became a favored rallying point for national unity. Grumbles were heard in response to One Unit, but nowhere more dramatically than in Sindh.

The situation in Sindh was complicated by two factors. First, due to the syncretic nature of religious and everyday practice in the province—particularly in the rural areas—Hindu and Muslim Sindhi pasts, traditions, and literatures were deeply interwoven. Untangling what is Muslim from what is Hindu in Sindhi practice was in many ways impossible. Consequently, rejecting "what is Hindu" amounts to rejecting all that is local. As president of the Jiye Sindh Qaumi Mahaz remarked, when Sindhis pressed government leaders to preserve and promote the rich heritage of Sindhi literature as a national treasure, they were told, "That? That's all Hindu literature," meaning it has nothing to do with Islam and, accordingly, Pakistan. The second complicating factor in Sindh emerges not from the links between Muslim and Hindu Sindhis but from their differences: before partition, the dominant Sindhi presence in the urban areas was Hindu; Sindhi Muslims were largely farmers, and they participated only very minimally in the mercantile development of colonial Karachi. Thus, at partition, when Sindh passed undivided to Pakistan, the dramatic exodus of Sindhi Hindus amounted to an erasure of a local Sindhi urbane; the local practitioners of urban identities, Hindu Sindhis, were replaced not by Sindhi Muslims but by immigrants from across the border. Sindhis continue to be dramatically underrepresented in Karachi, and the character of the city reflects this, particularly in terms of its antagonistic relationship with the rural hinterland. Thus Sindhi literature, even the lexicon of a Sindhi urbane, is problematic in the face of dominant nationalism.

At the same time, the very absence of Sindhis in the city renders them all the more suspect. Historically a state based on feudal holdings and agricultural power, Pakistan's financial and political power has gradually shifted to the urban industrial sector. However, there has been significant continuity in the transfer of power from landed to urban industrial wealth, meaning the landed elite eventually became the urban industrial elite. Symbolically, the urban is more powerful and moral. Echoes of "moral city, heretical wilderness" are apparent in the way that the rural hinterland with its cast of characters, Sindhis, is envisioned: an illiterate, un-Islamic, decadent, impenetrable, criminal frontier. With its bandits and its shrines with saints and masses of followers, the interior represents a site of illicit authority, parallel relations of power that the state cannot seem to harness.

Following the July riot, neighbors and friends offered me unsolicited opinions about the event. "That *Holi* those boys did," said Aliya, "it's forbidden; it's not our custom." Sadiq, a Muhajir neighbor, pulled me aside and confided, "You have to watch out for these Sindhis. They're not really Muslims. They'll do *Holi*, and they'll do *Diwali* (the Hindu Festival of Lights). They don't go to the mosque, they go to the *mazar* (shrine), and there they do bad things: hashish, male prostitution, dancing girls. They're not religious people."[12] When discussing the riot with a group of my husband's English-medium, upper-middle-class acquaintances, Riaz, who nourished particular antipathy toward Sindhis, complained, "What did the Sindhis ever do for Pakistan? All they want to do is break it. They might as well be Hindus. Or Indians."

Zubaida, Ruhi, and Mahvish—all Sindhi—were at times visibly resentful of the reputation of Sindhis as "Hindus." But they were also inclined to laugh it off and interpret it as an urban affectation. "See," explained Zubaida, "we've lived with Hindus for so long that we're using many Hindu customs. In the village, everyone does this."

I spent an afternoon with a member of the Sindhi press and her Sindhi activist husband, and we discussed the Dow riot:

> "People say of Sindhis, oh, they're Hindus," the activist explained. "But Sindhi culture has developed as a mixture of Buddhism and Arab Islam. Indian Islam is a mix of Hinduism and Turkish and Persian Islam. So that explains the differences in our values, namely, our tolerance. People are shocked when they come to Sindh and see how tolerant we are of other religions. If you read our poetry, it is always denying the ability to claim knowledge of the one truth, denying that there is only one true religion. This is how Hindus and Muslims are going to the same shrines and how we are using certain Hindu customs and greetings."

Sindhi nationalists repeatedly state that Sindhi Islam is no less Islamic but is, in fact, morally superior in its tolerance—a tolerance manifest in the syncretism of shared shrines, symbols, and customs. Sindhi nationalists make much of the plethora of "shared shrines" in the interior. Actually, the *mazar*, Sufi music and poetry, and the social relationship of *pir* and *murid* (saint and devotee) are extremely significant elements of rural Sindhi life. Shah Abdul Latif, the seventeenth-century Sufi poet of whom Zubaida spoke, is particularly revered, his contribution to Sindhi literature reckoned on a par with English's Shakespeare. Historically, Sufism, as doctrine and practice, has stood in antagonistic relationship to state power and Islamic orthodoxy (Ansari 1992). The kinship of Latif's *kafi* or *vai* verse with Hindu *Bhakti* devotionals—alongside the marked participation of Hindus at Latif's and other Sindhi shrines—renders Sindhi spirituality/religiosity itself dangerously heretical. Sindhi literature professor Durre Shawar Syed talked to me about the ideally noncommunal character of Sufism in Sindh, meaning that it attracts and embraces both Hindu and Muslim devotees:

> Followers of Shah Latif preached love for mankind. For the Sufis of Sindh, they never allowed religion to interfere with that. The relationship doesn't belong to external things, but to inner; the *mandir* (temple), the mosque, doesn't matter.

I remarked that when I visited Latif's shrine in Bhitshah, the *mazar* steps were crowded with obviously Hindu as well as Muslim devotees and mystics. I even asked a *rakhwala* (caretaker), who pointed out for me resident Hindu and Muslim *faqirs* and *mastanis* (religious ecstatics). Nodding in agreement, Professor Syed told me this story:

> There is a shrine of Uderolal, near Tando Adam, that is an extraordinary sight. On one side of the mausoleum is a mosque, and on the other is a *mandir*. Hindus and Muslims would come to visit the mausoleum. During the saint's lifetime, the two groups got along very well. After he died, a crisis arose; the Hindus wanted to cremate him, as is their custom, and the Muslims wanted to bury him. And there was some tension—people who were so united when he was alive—but it grew violent. And then a miracle happened. They had put a sheet over the body, and when they removed it, there was a bunch of flowers on the bed. The body had disappeared! So they took half of the flowers and burned them, and the other half they buried.

As this story demonstrates, the communal harmony that shared devotion enables is itself the miracle that sanctifies the saint.

The specific context of ethnic and national conflict that I have laid out here clearly figures in both the riot and the *jahalat* exchange. Both events generate and engage historically meaningful tensions, but the trajectory of these tensions—the bodies and spaces that they create—are dramatically different. In attempting to compare the two, I am cognizant of the difficulties—the wealth of variables (not to mention methodological inadequacies) that render them apples and oranges, so to speak. I beg the reader's indulgence that we may view this comparison as a heuristic exercise, designed to raise questions rather than to answer them.

Zubaida's assertion of unassimilated ethnic difference and Aliya's invocation of national imperatives took place in both a physical and metaphorical threshold. The screen door linking Zubaida's living room to the hallway marks a boundary either side of which remains ambiguous. Home, private property (particular opinion), and common space (national discourse) are loose constructions that achieve more force when men return home and outer doors close. That the exchange of flour—and the verbal exchange that overlaid it—took place along this threshold serves to localize for a moment the tensions that they generated. I could feel the tension there, hanging in the air.

That the casual request for flour signals a broader pattern of "generalized reciprocity" further ensures the maintenance of this tension. It is in the nature of this exchange that one is never clear whether this transfer of flour is a gift or a return. It carries with it the promise, however vague, of future action. In the absence of definitive and concluding "returns," the tension of this form of exchange can remain forever unresolved. Tense moments, however, pass.

Aliya's curt receipt of the flour, Zubaida's shrug, and, above all, Zubaida's declaration, "I am tense," track for us the movement of this tension from an external, interpersonal contradiction to a psychic, bodily burden. Zubaida's narrativization of her "tension" furthers its production as an inner emotional state—a "strain upon the nerves and feelings." It also signals the emergence of this new and peculiar embodied subject that is willing and able to bear tension. Indeed, this "bearing" lies in the guarantee of repetition. This exchange was singular only to me. For Aliya and Zubaida, as for the other women in the building, it was simply one of many, before and to come.

The flow of tension, we can imagine, was very different in the oft-discussed riot. In newspaper accounts of the event, tension plays an expected role; Sindhi students perform a controversial *Holi* festival, causing tension to develop with Jamaati students who deem it "un-Islamic." The tension "builds" over weeks, punctuated by occasional scuffles, and it finally culminates or "resolves" in an explosive riot.

It seems to me, however, that tension is not resolved here but refused. One can discern a kind of clarity, finality, or certainty (Appadurai 1998) in the riot that signals a submersion of ambiguity.[13] That the students involved are already "Sindhis" and "Jamaatis" is taken as a given. The paradox of Sindhi students as both "ethnic" others and "national" (cum "religious") selves is negated through a kind of expulsion. Violence simultaneously creates a national space (the civic, Islamic educational sphere) and a heretical body (the Sindhi) which can then be cast out. The riot signifies not a resolution of tension but a failure of its engagement. It is only in the aftermath of riot, when civic organizations, political parties, and religious groups begin demonstrating and debating in response, that these tensions are reengaged, a necessary process if alternative visions of the nation—and truer "subjectifications of objects"—are to abide.

Do campus politics promote the refusal of sustained self-other engagement? Do models of youthful masculinity generate an intolerance to tension? Do popular understandings of tension-discharge create their own reality? This I do not know. Obviously, I lack the ethnographic material to place the riot in its everyday context of campus politics, spatialities, associations, gathering, walking, arguing, etc. Indeed, one may ask how it is possible to compare the *jahalat* exchange with the riot when they differ so markedly—two women/two groups of male students; a living room doorway/a campus common space. I anticipate that some will complain that naturally the *jahalat* exchange ends peacefully, for it occurred in the intimacy of the home, the neighborhood, the private sphere, and not in the street or on campus, where (collective) violence "usually" happens. Women's peacemaking practices, some may protest, cannot help us understand violence (or imagine peace) in such places. I would argue, however, that it is precisely this labor of exchange—this work of managing and sustaining tension, as a somatic and psychic burden—which enables "home" or local spaces to be so "naturally" or "obviously" peaceful. There is much we can learn from it.

The alternative model of tension vis-à-vis peace and violence that I have proposed seems to me to account better for the everyday peace that was characteristic of life in the Shipyard. I must stop short, however, of championing this peacemaking as a blueprint for progressive politics, for this particular peace has a psychic cost—bought, as it is, at the price of male dominance and women's sacrifice. The extent to which women's labors of emotional regulation and management dictate their activities (nay, write their very bodies and subjectivities if you will) is overwhelming, particularly when we consider that it is not simply their own "tension" (or, as we will see, other emotions) that they must manage, but that of their men.

We must also remember the rather more insidious cost of this peace, which rests on the production of gendered subjects for its efficacy and intelligibility. As we will see in the next chapter, these embodied, feminine labors of peace are caught up in a web of discursive and affective cultural formations that promote, or make possible, masculine violence—thus paradoxically generating that which they aim to contain.

Finally, it is clear that we need not view women's relationship to peace through the singular (naturalizing and celebratory) lens of maternalist politics. While gender difference is a condition of these exchange practices and the peace it generates in the Shipyard, this difference is resolutely culturally constructed. Indeed, the ethic of suspense that can be said to govern women's local relations in the building refers to neither the naturalized body (as in maternalist peace politics) nor an enduring psyche (as in Carol Gilligan's "ethic of care" [1982]). Contingent and contested, this ethic emerges, rather, within the specific set of complex social and historical circumstances in which women like my informants find themselves.

4

Anger

Throughout my days in the Shipyard, from my first awkward meetings with neighbors to our final, warm good-byes, women would spontaneously—and, it often seemed to me, inexplicably—tell me stories. The question *"ek qissa sunaun?"* (Shall I tell you a story?) punctuated many a hallway and drawing room conversation. Informants' tales are of great interest to anthropologists because of the way they point to local genres, discourses, and cultural preoccupations less caught up in, or elicited by, the ethnographer's questioning. In the Shipyard, there was one such "genre" of stories that women never seemed to tire of telling: stories of angry men and victimized women.

Zubaida's is a more or less representative example:

"In a village near ours, there lived a beautiful woman. She was so pretty and so simple (*sidhi*) and innocent. Her parents married her to her first cousin, and he took her away to his own house, where they lived apart from his family. She was so good. She spent her time reading the Quran and taking care of the house and the food. She never went outside unless it was in full *burqa*.

"But her husband was very jealous, and whenever he would come home, he would be angry, and ask her, 'Did you see anyone today?' She would always answer, 'No, no one,' and it was the truth.

"If he took his wife out with him, even in *burqa*, her beauty would shine through—her hands, her feet, her eyes—and men would look her way. But she kept her eyes down, never flirted. Still her husband would get so angry. And finally one day he killed her. He left her body lying in the courtyard and ran away. It was many days later that her family came to ask after her, and they had to find her there like that."

This was the first of what I initially labeled the "honor killing stories" that I was to hear. Zubaida told it to me at my doorstep one afternoon when she had come looking for her children, Meher and Zain. In the months that followed, I heard many more like it—most so similar as to warrant little more than a scribble in my field notes: "Another honor killing story today." Ruhi told me one at our second meeting, as we sat drinking tea in her drawing room. Hers was about a woman in a *gaon* near Ruhi's natal town of Nawabshah. The woman's husband was gone for several weeks looking for work, and while he was away, his wife was ordered to deliver some fruit to the landlord's *haveli* (mansion). When the husband returned and came to hear of her errand, he was overcome with anger. Convinced that she had been unfaithful (*us ne ghalat kam kiya*),[1] he bombarded her with questions and accusations. This story, too, ended in violence, with the man killing his wife, chopping her up in pieces, and depositing them in front of the *haveli*.

Variations in the stories of this kind were remarkably minor, having to do with details about the woman (she was rich or poor, beautiful or plain, veiled, childless, etc.) or the degree of violence visited upon her (beating, burning, maiming, but usually murder). Some were drawn out, detailed, and well told, like Zubaida's. Many were mere headlines, terse and epigrammatic, like Hina's mother's comment: "A woman was killed by her husband in my village last week for no reason, no reason at all." All the stories took place in villages, and all of them were represented as "true" (*sach*)—a story, but not a fairy tale (*kahani*).

The more "honor killing" stories I heard, the more I struggled to ascertain their meaning. Set, as they invariably were, in the *gaon*, could they have something to do with "the city" and migration? Were these tales simply cenotaphs for the backward, ignorant village—experiments with crafting an "indigenous urbane"? In fact, I believe these stories do have something to do with "the city" and "the village," but not in the way I initially imagined. What about the relational character of the tellings? Were these grim tales of victimized women specifically directed at me? Did they say something about my "structural" relationship with my neighbors? Were their narrators asserting a kind of "parity of modernity" or, conversely, claiming a preponderance of suffering—a "look at what we have to deal with" kind of statement? I believe these stories have something to do with me and my relationship with my neighbors, but not in the manner, or even in the direction, that I first supposed.

The closer I looked at the content of these accounts, the more I began to question my casual label "honor killing story," for who had said anything about honor? Certainly not the women narrators. In contrast to the spellbinding nature of these stories—for narrator and audience alike—discussions of infidelity or dishonor and their accompanying punishment were largely matter-of-fact. Zubaida often shared gossip with me of friends who had "gone bad" and had affairs, remarking in wonder that "if a woman in my family did that, our men would kill her (*usko qatil kar dete*)." Zubaida, Aliya, and Ruhi all told me tales of women who mischievously invited attention—defied purdah, showed their curves, made flirtatious signs with their eyes—and incurred their husband's or kinsmen's wrath.

But the striking common factor in this particular "genre" of tales I am describing is the unimpeachable fact of women's innocence. These are women wrongfully accused. Indeed, the murdered woman's moral probity is so pivotal to the tale that it forces a reconfiguration of the truth as always apocryphal—or, rather, the story's necessary truth is accomplished only *through* apocrypha. These stories are invariably told in the "third person all knowing" tense. The teller and the audience are obligated to "know" what is in the woman's heart; hence she tells her husband she has seen no one, "and it is the truth"; she was killed "for no reason, no reason at all." It is the senselessness of the husband's anger and its limitless consequences that makes the story so compelling.

On reflection, it was clear to me that these were not familiar tales of "honor" and its violation. Honor was not the star of the show at all. On the contrary, these were stories about anger—male anger—as a force in women's lives.

As many anthropologists have noted, "honor" has long been an object of fascination for researchers of so-called circum-Mediterranean societies. This, of course, is not without empirical justification, although Wikan (1984) is right to question the anthropologist's investment in preserving an all-too-familiar, romantic vision of honorable men controlling their women, avenging slights, and jockeying for power. But more to the point, the tendency to posit "honor" as *the* dominant, organizing cultural principle in such societies has blinded us both to the multiplicity of cultural ends that subjects pursue and to the narratives and practices of those subjects who reside on the other side of honor, namely, women.

Feminist anthropologists like Abu-Lughod, Grima, and Wikan have helped focus attention on the different ways in which women become authors and subjects of a discourse of honor. Despite these strides, however, there remains a tendency to ascribe an almost ontological salience to honor that is denied other cultural discourses. Purdah, for example, becomes simply a "sign" that honor is at stake, and anger is simply a "sign" that honor has been lost.

It is significant that, while "honor" and its oft-quoted handmaiden "shame" have undergone increasingly careful ethnographic treatment, the same cannot be said of anger, which is largely represented as an intelligible response to any perceived loss of honor. Indeed, the anthropologist is often complicit in identifying with—and legitimizing—this anger as rational and moral (even if condemned as excessive).

This is quite different from the understanding of (male) anger expressed in women's stories (which we can no longer comfortably label "honor killing stories" and must rename "stories of angry men"). Therein, male anger is invariably represented as irrational—separate from thought and separate from moral evaluation, reasoning, and judgment. This anger is unpredictable and uncontrollable. It is also represented as exerting a defining influence on women's lives—regulating social relations and practices on an everyday basis and, at its extreme, suffering life or bringing death.

In the previous chapter, we saw women laboring to take on and bear the tension of sociocultural contradiction manifest in interpersonal exchange. In this chapter, I detail women's understandings of male anger and the labor they exert to manage and regulate it. As we will see, these efforts at managing male anger are viewed as critical to the maintenance of local exchange relations and, by extension, to the possibility of peace itself.

Anthropology of Emotion

The study of emotions by anthropologists is relatively popular, judging from several review essays which have attempted to locate such study in the history of the discipline (Abu-Lughod and Lutz 1990; Lutz and White 1986). One of the most emphatic and eloquent proponents of a cultural approach to affect was Michelle Rosaldo, who, emboldened by a Geertzian perspective, declared "affects" to be "no less cultural and no more private than beliefs" (1984: 141). While an earlier anthropology had been content to relativize the *interpretation* or *management* of emotion (e.g., Briggs 1970), Rosaldo's intervention was to posit the affect itself as wholly culturally constructed. Emotions thus were not universal raw feelings, impulses, or drives which were then subjected to cultural treatment (hypo- or hypercognition [Levy 1984], elaboration or repression, etc.). Rather, it was the very corporeality of affect that was to become the subject of anthropological inquiry.

To illustrate, Rosaldo contrasted Western notions of anger with those of her Ilongot informants. According to a Western "folk theory" of emotion, labeled the "hydraulic metaphor" by Solomon (1984) and, less self-consciously, "drive theory" by Freudians, anger felt is either expressed and vented or repressed and bottled up. It is an internal energy whose denial is dangerous and destructive to the self. But among the Ilongots, Rosaldo contends, offenders can "pay off" victims' anger or angry people can simply "forget" their anger for the greater social good. According to the "drive theory" of emotion, anger repressed simmers and grows until it explodes as violence. Ilongots, however, neither make nor perform a connection between violence and pent-up anger.

Rosaldo's definition of emotions as "embodied thoughts" promised to go far in challenging the mind-body dichotomy that is, among other things, one of the abiding legacies of the European Enlightenment. It is this dichotomy which has enabled social scientists to pass over the body—and emotion—as irrelevant to (or inaccessible for) studies of cultural, historical, or political processes. For Rosaldo, the concept of "embodied thoughts" was a way to get at the subjective salience of culture—a way of understanding how cultural meaning has power for subjects beyond reason and beyond calculation. "Through embodiment," she writes, "collective symbols acquire the power, tension, relevance, and sense emerging from our individuated histories" (1984: 141). For others, however, the term "embodied thoughts" has been an invitation to reduce affect to cognition, a move which resembles an Enlightenment fantasy of eliminating the body, of doing away with any troubling, excessive, and uncontrollable alien agency that challenges or hinders reason and self-will. Thus, while a Western folk theory casts affect as irrational, involuntary, uncontrolled, natural, subjective, the anthropologist can turn this on its head, reconfiguring affect as rational, voluntary, controlled, learned, objective.

More encouraging are those ethnographic studies of emotions that focus on the discursive dimensions of affective life. Rather than crafting alternative master theories of emotion, such studies pay attention to local "emotion discourses" and public, affective performances: "We have to take indigenous theories of emotion seriously," Abu-Lughod and Lutz contend, "because they inform emotional performances" (1990: 14). It is with this understanding that I looked more closely at women's stories of "angry men" and at the practical and narrative treatment of male anger in everyday life. In the stories they tell, as well as in the routine practices of child rearing, gossiping, visiting, cooking, and shopping, women construct and negotiate a culturally specific discourse and praxis of male anger. It is this discourse and the practical sensibilities it engenders that I wish to explore.

Anger in the Shipyard

One dry and windless February morning, I stood with Zubaida in her kitchen while milky tea boiled on the stove. Meher, Zubaida's six-year-old daughter, and Zain, her five-year-old son, were home sick with colds. The two sat together quietly on the wicker sofa, watching a Hindi film on satellite TV. Suddenly, for no apparent reason, Zain turned angrily and began kicking Meher. She started to cry in loud, choking sobs, and Zubaida turned to address her. "Sit somewhere else, Meher," she said, adding to me, "Zain's health is not good." Zubaida said nothing to reprimand Zain, but as Meher continued to cry, Zubaida scolded her, chiding: "Oh, you cry like this? (*Aise roti ho?*) Eh! Eh! Eh! And the birds outside are laughing at you like this: Ha! Ha! Ha!"

Like the stories of "angry men," this exchange highlights a notion of male anger that is wholly naturalized, irrational, unpredictable in direction as well as timing. Zain's anger is not viewed as juridical—a rational response to the transgression of a norm; but neither is it viewed as something one could control or intervene on. Significantly, it is Meher's *crying*—not Zain's violence—that is censured. It occurred to me that there was something didactic about the encounter, that it was a lesson for Meher on how to defer to male anger, to manage it and accommodate it. It is in this sense that women's stories of "angry men" were, indeed, directed at me. They, too, were didactic—cautionary tales, meant to let me in on a logic of practice. I will return to this point later.

When women talk about male anger, they use the Urdu term *ghussa*, which Grima translates as "anger mixed with cruelty" (1992: 36). *Ghussa* has an implicit connection with violence and passion that gentler terms for anger or displeasure do not (e.g., *naraz hona*, to be annoyed; *bura manna*, to take badly or take offense; *"mind" karna*, to mind). In linguistic terms, anger is represented predominantly as an external impulse, something that "happens" to one (Brenneis 1990: 119). One finds oneself having "arrived at anger" (*ghusse men a jana*); anger "strikes" one (*lagna*); anger "comes" to one (*a jana*). But one also "becomes" angry (*ghussa ho jana*) or "shows" anger (*ghussa dikhana*). Thus there is some ambiguity about the agency involved.

Anger holds a special place in *sharif* discourse. In *sharif* thought, anger is a vice, a base impulse rooted in the lower soul (*nafs*) that must be controlled and conquered by *aql* (wisdom). *Nafs* is the site of undisciplined, uncontrolled will, the source of all "impulses"; *aql* is reason, discrimination, the instrument through which impulses are controlled or channeled into socially desired dispositions and moral habits. In religious thought, anger is condemned as the loss of reason. Social reformer Maulana Thanawi writes forcefully on "The Evil of Anger and Its Cure": "In anger, sense disappears. No one can think through an outcome. Your mouth speaks words that are out of place, and your hands commit acts that are violent" (Metcalf 1990: 188). Moreover, there are innumerable *hadith* which associate the lack of anger with piety. For example, "'The strong,' said Mohammad, 'is not he who overcomes others. The strong is he who overcomes himself. A man must learn to control his anger'" (Burton 1994: 103).[2]

In women's narratives and practices, however, men are rarely cast as capable of controlling or conquering anger. Male anger is seen as immune to discipline or reform. Because of its boundless destructive potential, this anger is to be tactically avoided as far as possible—and failing that, it must be endured. Women's anger, on the other hand, is represented as a qualitatively different thing.

In the middle of a conversation about "Eve-teasing" (roughly, the local term for catcalls or street/sexual harassment), I described for Zubaida and Aliya an incident that had occurred earlier in the day. My husband and I were stepping into our car when a servant standing on a west-open balcony called out to me. I looked up, and he started making kissing sounds and suggestive gestures.

> "Can you believe that guy?" I said to Sheheryar, and furious, he stepped out of the car.
> "Look with care at people!" he berated the man. "Next time, I won't speak so lovingly to you."
> Zubaida and Aliya were horrified.
> "How could you tell your husband?" they asked me.
> "No, Laura," Aliya said. "You should have waited until your husband wasn't with you. Then you should have called the boy down lovingly: 'Yes, oh, come down here.' And when he came, you should have beaten him."
> "Yes," Zubaida agreed. "You have to handle these things by yourself. Spit at him; beat him; go to his house later, call him out, and beat him. But don't tell your husband. That's dangerous."
> "That's right," Aliya added. "He'll call his friends, the other will call his, and people can get hurt. Blood will be shed (*khun kharaba ho jaega*). If *you* beat him, it's better."

Zubaida and Aliya's comments reveal an intimate association of male anger with the transgression of limits—in particular, the breaching of bodily boundaries. "*Khun kharaba*" means blood feud or bloodshed. Another phrase used when talking about male anger is the similarly corporal "*khun sar pe le lena*"—roughly, taking blood on the head. A popular Urdu song from the mid-1990s, "Chief Sahib," featured the line "*Ghussa dikhaoge to khun sar pe le lega*": Show anger, and I'll take the blood on my head, meaning I will return your anger, an eye for an eye. Anger between males (where no bonds of deference exist such as that between fathers and sons, masters and servants) is a dangerous currency, a challenge that must be reciprocated.

Aliya continued:

"One time, I was walking through Bhori Bazaar with my sister, and a man touched my waist (*kammar*) and my bra. So I got ready. I opened my shopping bag and took out a big wooden spoon I had just bought. Then, when I was looking at bangles, and I felt this hand on my shoulder, I grabbed it and starting slapping him. Then my sister said, 'What are you doing? You've got a wooden spoon in your hand!' And I said, 'You're right.' So I started beating him with the spoon. Oh, I beat him so much, and a crowd gathered, and they asked, 'What happened? What did he do?' and I said, 'He was snatching my purse!' See, if I told them that he put his hand on me (*us ne mujhpar hath lagaya*), then the insult would also be on me. And the crowd just beat this man so hard!"

While men's anger is dangerous and uncontainable, something to be avoided and feared, women's anger is necessary and tactical. Women's anger and its expression through violence (spitting and beating) are represented as intelligent, reasoning, directed, controllable, and restrained. Women's anger is moral and productive. It is, in fact, a tactic of containment. The danger of invoking male anger is the risk of an escalation of conflict and violence ("He'll call his friends, the other will call his"; "blood will be shed"). The utility of cultivating women's anger lies in its ability to restrain conflict. The corporal imagery of male versus female anger is also striking. Male anger is present as a kind of immediate physicality—the mindless pulse of fists flying and blood spilling. Women's anger, on the other hand, speaks of a cooler bodily discipline—the hand holding the spoon, poised and waiting.

While male anger is "a provocation to reply," women's anger is a punishment, a moral judgment that concludes a transaction. Thus Aliya and Zubaida encouraged me to feel anger and to "handle it myself."

"If someone grabs you, then you should beat him. And everyone will rush to support you because you are a woman," Aliya told me.

"But," Zubaida warned, "some men, if this happens, will blame their wives—'Oh, you must have given him a look or a sign.'"

This is another danger of invoking male anger. The anger of one's men, even in one's own defense, is unpredictable in direction and can quickly turn from "Eve-teaser" to "Eve."

The implication in these remarks is that women's anger garners unconditional community support (in situations where male anger does not) precisely because it is not construed as base "impulse," "out of place," or beyond "sense." On the contrary, it is discerning, the product—not the failure—of reason and wisdom (*aql*). When they appealed to me to feel anger and handle it myself, I complained that it just didn't come naturally to me—that getting angry and yelling at or slapping a strange man (rather than feeling wounded and escaping the situation only to brood about it later) was not my first instinct. "But it was the same for us at first," Aliya said. "You just have to do it two or three times. It's a matter of habit (*adat*)."

The idea that one can "learn" to feel anger is in complete accordance with local and Islamic theories of emotion. Affects, in general, are seen to be both unwilled and cultivated—inner states as well as performances. Morally valued emotions, like shame (*sharm*), are understood to be the product of repeated disciplining practice. Shame (like women's anger) is a habit, "learned like [a] physical skill." Indeed, according to reformist thought, "correct external behavior is the first step toward creating inner virtues." Aliya had assured me that, after "showing anger" two or three times, I would naturally "feel" angry. It is actions that make affects. Hence the Prophet's exhortation to pretend to cry at funerals if tears do not come naturally, for from this "similitude" will come "verity" (Metcalf 1990: 168).

This rationale presents us with something of a paradox, for if affect (appropriate affect) is a matter of discipline—the making of virtues into habits—then why, according to women, can't men learn to control their anger? What is different about male anger (or male reason)? What is different, we can conclude, is the ambivalence and contestation surrounding the designation of male anger as virtue or vice. Consider the following exchange:

While standing in the first floor hallway chatting with Ruhi and Mahvish, I related to them an unpleasant experience from that same afternoon. Sheheryar, Faizan, and I were driving down Zamzama Boulevard when an impatient driver behind us began blowing his horn and swerving erratically in an attempt to get by. The car drove up on the sidewalk to pass us, then pulled in front of us and swerved to park diagonally, blocking the road. The driver, a man in his late twenties clad in jeans and *kurta*, jumped out. He ran up to our car, pulled open Sheheryar's door, and punched him repeatedly in the face before dashing off again.

The two women looked at me expectantly.

> "Didn't Sheheryar Bhai beat him?" Mahvish insisted.
> "No," I answered.
> "Why not?" Ruhi asked, in surprise.
> "It all happened so fast," I said, lamely.
> Shaking her head and clicking her tongue, Ruhi admonished, "*Sheheryar Bhai ko usko marna chahie tha* (Brother Sheheryar should have beaten him)."

When telling this story to other neighbors, it met with the same refrain: "Sheheryar should have beaten that man." It was inconceivable, even suspicious, that my husband's first response to such provocation and abuse was not anger and violence. At that moment, it became clear to me that male anger was not just unwilled. Like shame and other virtues, it was also a matter of performance. Anger was viewed not just as an *inevitable* facet of masculinity but as a *necessary*, even foundational, one. Indeed, while women avoid and lament male anger in their everyday lives, they nonetheless celebrate—and cultivate—angry men.

With this insight, I reconsidered Zubaida's response to her son's angry outburst. The fact that children are viewed as having "small brains" and lacking the necessary *aql* for self-control and reason does not explain why Meher's crying is viewed as an appropriate matter for rebuke and intervention, while Zain's violence is not. Clearly, Zain's anger was not only tolerated but also indulged or even fostered. This is reminiscent of Abu-Lughod's (1986) observation that Bedouin women seek to discipline girls so they do not become willful and they indulge boys so they do not become fearful. Boys in the Shipyard, similarly, had to be reared into their anger.

Thus, alongside *sharif* discourse—with its dogged objection to anger and its celebration of *aql*, moderation "in all things," and "unfailing self-control" (Metcalf 1990: 9)—there is another moral code. Like Bourdieu's "sense of honor," Abu-Lughod's "ideology of honor," and Grima's "*badal*" (exchange/revenge), this "regional" discourse—the code of the "periphery," if you will—celebrates a specific vision of masculine agency. Herein, the failure to "take revenge"—to avenge slights or punish abuses—is "weak and dishonorable" (Grima 1992: 4), evil and emasculating (Abu-Lughod 1986: 90). There is a Punjabi proverb that sums up this sentiment concisely: "'Now this is only a footpath, but it may open onto a wide road'" (Eglar 1960: 79). Only angry men can vigilantly monitor and punish the smallest of insults which, left unretaliated, grow into gaping affronts.

Far from being disruptive, anger articulates a kind of order. Of her Pathan informants, Grima writes: "[Anger] is tolerated and excused in relations of inequality where the person of superior status exercises it toward a person of inferior status. A woman will say in a parenthetical whisper not suggesting any reproach, for instance, that her husband is *ghossanak* (angry, harsh, and even physically abusive)" (Grima 1992: 36). Indeed, women suggest, it is natural for men to get angry at women, parents at children, masters at servants. Anger is part of a sensibility of power and the privileges and responsibilities (of discipline and maintaining the correct order of things) it confers. Likewise, relations or postures of deference are characterized by the absence of anger. It is abhorrent and unnatural to get angry at those to whom you owe respect (*izzat karni chahie*). The affect of deference, one could argue, is *sharm*, and anger is a clear contravention of *sharm*.

Who can get angry at whom, while not uncontested, is normatively prescribed by kinship, generational, and class/caste systems. Servants cannot get angry at masters; children cannot get angry at parents or elders. Men cannot get angry at superordinate male kin, neither affinal nor consanguinal (but, while owing respect to elder affinal and consanguinal *female* kin, they nonetheless maintain penal authority over *all* consanguinal female kin and their wives in matters of honor). Women cannot get angry at superordinate male *or* female affines or cognates, and it "doesn't look nice" (*acha nahin lagta*) for women to get angry at all.[3] Anger expressed toward "inferiors" is not viewed as a challenge that must be "returned," but anger between equals, or toward superiors, must be either reciprocated (in the former instance) or punished (in the latter). Of course, the meaning of anger—as punishment and/or provocation, legitimate and/or subversive, juridical and/or performative—is contingent upon the response it receives (Bourdieu 1977: 12). Anger is relationally produced and constitutive of hierarchies, even as it is constituted by them. Consider the following example:

During Ramzan (the month of fasting; in 1997, it fell in January), a conflict developed between my household and our neighbors two floors below us. Our water heater (which stood in one of our eastern balconies) was leaking, and at water delivery time, water would spill out from our balcony onto the terrace garden of Sultan Sahib's flat. We thought little of it, as overflow from the water tank on the roof habitually rained down on the ground floor gardens twice a day. Sultan Sahib, however, asked Sheheryar mildly if he could fix it. So we attempted a makeshift repair, which consisted of stuffing rags in the drainpipe and bailing out the pooling water by hand each day. This proved to be imperfect, and some water would still drain from our balcony to the ground below.

One morning at water delivery time, Sultan Sahib stood in the field beyond his garden wall with Ilahi Sahib at his side. Shaking his fist at the trickle of water falling onto his terrace, Sultan Sahib shouted, "Turn off your water heater! You're ruining my garden!" Sheheryar and I stepped out onto the balcony, and Sultan Sahib repeated his angry words. "Don't shout at me!" Sheheryar shot back, annoyed, and Sultan Sahib again demanded that Sheheryar fix the water heater. Growing angry himself, Sheheryar retorted, "Sultan Sahib, I don't even talk to people like you." Sultan Sahib blustered, "Well, I don't even spit on people like you!" At that, we stepped back inside.

Eager to end this negativity and avoid future confrontations, I convinced Sheheryar that we should get the water heater repaired. Relations with Sultan Sahib, however, remained strained. Then, at sunrise on the morning of Eid-ul Fitr (the holiday that celebrates the end of Ramzan), Sheheryar left the flat to join his father for Eid prayers at the Shia mosque across town. He was stopped in the gully by Ilahi Sahib, who was standing with several other senior men, among them Sultan Sahib. "Look, Sheheryar, it's Eid," Ilahi Sahib said, grabbing hold of Sheheryar's arm. "You must end this quarrel (*jhagra*). You shouldn't speak that way. Sultan Sahib is your elder." And turning to Sultan Sahib, Ilahi Sahib said, gesturing at Sheheryar: "Look, he's a child. Forgive him." Goaded and pushed by the circle of men around them, Sheheryar and Sultan Sahib smiled and then, as is customary between men on Eid, they embraced. In this instance, the dangerous and disruptive exchange of male anger displayed in the scene on the balcony weeks previously was neutralized as a result of a reconfiguration of Sheheryar and Sultan's relationship from one of male equals to one of child/son and elder, although Sultan could not have been more than ten years Sheheryar's senior. Accordingly, the anger was transformed from challenge to childish behavior—transgressive but forgivable.

The centrality of anger as marking order and its transgression—in performing hierarchies, if you will—was also made clear to me through the circulation of gossip about our upstairs neighbors, the Baluch customs official, his wife, and two children. Everyone in the building knew that the husband was abusive. Night after night, one could hear his angry shouting and his wife's plaintive cries. The husband was universally disliked in the building, condemned as a fraud, a bribe-taker, and a con artist. The wife and children were pitied and almost never seen.

One morning, Iqbal—the young Punjabi Christian sweeper who cleaned for a number of families in the building—came to my flat an hour early, obviously distressed. She had come from her service with the flat above us.

> "Oh, such fighting," she told me. "He was slapping the wife, like this, and then he had his hands around her throat, like this. And his elder daughter, she was screaming at him, "*Ulu ka patha! Ulu ka patha!*" (Son of an owl!) So I said, 'I've got to go.' The wife said, 'No, it's nothing,' but I left. I won't go there again, not even to get my pay. Can you believe it? *Ulu ka patha!*"

By the time morning chores were finished, the story had spread throughout the hallway. When I visited Zubaida and Aliya later that day, they were still talking about it. But while the beating was seen as tragic and condemned as cruel, it was the specter of the daughter's anger at her father and her shouts of "*Ulu ka patha*" that struck the women as taleworthy; it, and not the husband's anger, was disorderly, out of place. While no one *explicitly* condemned the daughter's response as morally wrong or shameful, her anger was clearly seen as a sign of the greater intrinsic chaos and perversity of the entire situation.

Anger and Ethnic Discourse

While women cast men as subject to uncontrollable, irrational anger, and while women see themselves as tactically managing and avoiding male anger in their everyday lives, women nevertheless celebrate and promote male anger in general, and they do so to announce not just individual virility but the virility, status, and piety of the entire corporate group. Consider Zubaida's remarks:

> "Sometimes I think I should get out. Take a job, be a teacher like your *sathwali* (next-door neighbor—Parveen, a Muhajir). But our Sindhi men get very angry (*hamare Sindhi mard bohat ghusse ho jate hain*). Our Sindhi men are very strict (*sakht*). They don't like their women going out or marrying outside (of the *biradari*). Muhajir men are not so angry. They let their wives go out, have jobs. They're free."

For Zubaida, the greater anger of Sindhi men is a matter of both exigency and pride, for anger is a hallmark not just of masculine efficacy and power but also of ethnic identity and boundary. Anger, so perceived, is both performative and totemic.[4] To deny the anger of Muhajir men is to emasculate them. Carroll Pastner notes, in a similar fashion, that "the most cogent form of the derogation of Baluch culture is in terms of the honor of the Baluch; hence the claim that Baluch 'don't get upset' about adultery" (1982: 179). Thus, to return to the gossip surrounding the Baluch family who lived above us, it is likely that the daughter's cries of "*Ulu ka patha*" were read not just as a random perversion but as a confirmation of an already circulating stereotype: that Baluch men are not angry enough, not men at all; their women and their daughters are shameless, and their men are ineffectual.

Anger is a powerful lexicon of difference and is deeply imbricated in the specific symbolic content of ethnic enmity in Karachi. The two dominant and competing discourses of anger—one that values reason, moderation, and the control of anger, and one that values anger itself as central to masculinity—are directly associated with particular ethnic groups. Thus the former, *sharif* discourse, is associated with "the culture symbolized by Urdu," its "natural" body being that of the Muhajir, and the latter (which I will gloss as "anger as masculinity") is associated with everything else: the vernacular, rural, tribal, and regional cultures.[5]

In *sharif* discourse, angry men are barbaric—weak because they are not in control of their impulses. Indeed, Metcalf notes, "the regional culture" as a whole is often "equated with *nafs*, as a dark unruly world, less disciplined and less ordered than the principles represented by Islam" (1990: 15). Thus a Muhajir neighbor, Sadiq, claims he avoids Sindhi men because "they're crazy. One little thing and they'll kill you." The very terms "tribal," "feudal," and "rural" are often used, pejoratively, to connote backward, irrational, violent, crass *intemperance*. Anger is anathema to a *sharif*, urbane, civilized, modern identity.

In the "anger as masculinity" discourse, however, the terms "rural" and "tribal," along with "patrilineage" (*zat*), "extended family" (*biradari*), and "family" (*khandan*), connote moral groundedness, people in their proper place. The urbane, temperate culture that Urdu represents is weak and flabby, a world unanchored. It is in this sense, then, that women's "stories of angry men" do have something to do with "the city" and "the village." Village men are seen as angrier, more protective of hierarchy, more deeply rooted, and grounded in the right and natural order of things.

With this insight, we can reconsider Mahvish and Ruhi's responses to my husband's "failed" anger in the face of violent provocation. As my neighbors were well aware, Sheheryar is the product of the union between a *sharif*, Urdu-speaking Muhajir father and a local Sindhi mother. The absence of (performative) anger marks the debilitating (or, from another perspective, ennobling) influence of Urdu gentility, further confirmed by my husband's lack of Sindhi fluency. Sheheryar's repeated alignment with Urdu culture was particularly disappointing for my Sindhi neighbors (like Mahvish, Ruhi, and Zubaida), who perpetually tried to emphasize the affinity that our common Sindhi link afforded. Thus Zubaida would often tease, "*Sheheryar Bhai ko Sindhi ani chahie*"—figuratively, "Sheheryar Brother should be able to speak/know/do Sindhi," but literally, "Sindhi should come to Sheheryar Brother." This linguistic form gives a felicitous sense of "Sindhi" as something that you both speak and perform; showing anger is a way of performing Sindhi-ness.

It is possible to read the history of colonial and national struggle in Karachi (or Sindh more broadly) as a contest between "center" and "periphery" over the meaning and deployment of anger. Indeed, we could begin with the colonial intervention on penal authority in Sindh, which, not coincidentally, focused pointedly on "honor killings." Colonial administrators like Charles Napier bemoaned the widespread incidence of murder (or "execution") of women in the region at the hands of husbands, fathers, brothers, and other male relatives. In precolonial Sindh, "A man was not considered guilty of a capital offense if he killed a wife or female relative suspected of adultery" (Khuhro 1978: 26). Soon after the 1843 conquest of Sindh, Napier drafted a proclamation criminalizing such "honor killings" and instituting exile and death as punishments.

It is critical to note, for our purposes, that the colonial state's arrogation of penal authority is simultaneously an arrogation of male anger. The association of anger with penal authority has deep roots in Western civilization, from ancient Greek notions of punishment as the "angry defense of family honor" (Allen 2000: 50) to modern efforts to submit a fundamentally moral and juridical anger to the cool-headed, disembodied, and disembedded reason of a neutral justice (Benhabib 1992: 3). This liberal Enlightenment project of "legislative reason" is carried on by the Pakistani state, which, in an effort to intervene on rogue, "tribal," and "feudal" justice, has cast itself as the angry punisher of adulterous women. Under the *hudud* laws—religious "limits" promulgated under Zia's Islamization program—women (and men) convicted of adultery or fornication (*zina*) can be put to death. But to this date, such a punishment has never been carried out, and the number of "honor killings" per year, as reported by the Human Rights Commission of Pakistan, certainly rivals the number of *zina* convictions.

This is probably due to the fact that women's "virtue" (or men's "honor") is not a problem in need of a solution but a symbolic site of struggle between competing modes of authority, expressed around discordant notions of anger. Like the colonial government before it, the Pakistani state has misidentified the anger which it has tried to arrogate—as strictly juridical. Rather, as women in the Shipyard suggest, this anger is itself a form of value. Its power rests not in the fact of punishment but in performance, not in what it effects but in what it communicates about the actor and his community.

If we are to understand the place of anger in national and ethnic struggle in Pakistan, we need to revisit the symbolic tensions of this national story and the others it imagines into being. This begins as a story of Indian Muslim unity, forged in dialectic with a Hindu majority. The two-nation theory, which underpinned the call for partition, held that Indian Muslims were a nation because they were "one." But once Pakistan came into being, this "theory" set the stage for an intransigent ideological struggle between an ideal "Islamic unity" and ethnic, linguistic, and cultural diversity.

The nature of this "unity," we will recall, was very specific; it was to be the continuation of *sharif* culture—that glorified conglomerate of Urdu and etiquette, nobility and faith, so central to Muslim reform and anticolonial movements. Urdu was installed and vigorously promoted as the national language, while regional, provincial, and ethnic identities, languages, and literatures were disparaged (and, for a decade and a half, outlawed). Claiming an ethnic position was condemned as antinational and thus un-Islamic. The culture that Urdu represents, in contrast, came to represent all that is patriotic, noble, and devout. This is how Muhajirs, despite their practical disenfranchisement, became cast as the natural and rightful inheritors of the nation.

Clearly, *sharif* nationalism continues the reform project of progress, faith, reason, and moderation in the making of a "modern" democratic polity. The only space that regional culture can occupy herein is that of prehistory: backward, tribal, rural, superstitious, immoderate, irrational ignorance. Undoubtedly, Muhajirs have a very different relationship to the cultural capital of Urdu, as well as to the "taint" of the vernacular, than do Pakistan's other ethno-linguistic groups. Very crudely, there is a sense in which what Muhajirs get for free, others must acquire through social and economic privilege (for example, several generations of Urdu—or English—education). Furthermore, for a Punjabi or Sindhi (or other "ethnic") to be *sharif*, the vernacular must reside simply as a quaint folk-loric heritage and not as necessity.

How does anger fit into this dialectic? Anger is a key symbol in the discursive distinction between citizen and savage, between a national, *sharif* temperament and a backward, "tribal" mentality. Anger symbolizes the excess that is at the heart of hegemony's failure—the failure of the nation to contain difference, to assimilate it, to render it a matter of benign heritage rather than living, dynamic dissent.

Angry men are constructed as transgressing the boundaries of state authority and national community. In Karachi, anger figures implicitly in public discourse about who belongs in the city and who does not. In February 1998, Pathans and Muhajirs rioted in Karachi over the elope-ment of a young Pathan woman with a Muhajir man. Threats were made on the lives of both bride and groom, and the groom was shot on the steps of a Karachi courthouse by members of the bride's family. Ethnic party leaders were ambivalent in their response to the incident. (Before the shooting, Pakistan People's Party leader Benazir Bhutto—then deposed—had demanded that the girl be returned to her family; the Muhajir Qaumi Movement remained silent.) But the national intelligentsia expressed horror at the shooting—horror that such a thing could happen, not in the tribal hinterland, the backward villages or towns of the provinces, but in the cosmopolitan city of Karachi. The anger of the bride's male relatives signaled a kind of trespass; it did not "belong" in the city—and neither, by extension, did Pathans.

The city, while not the "moral city" of Islamic antiquity, is nevertheless the imagined site of fulfillment of a specifically modern Islamic reason in service to religious law and national goals. While the literal opposite to *sharif* may be *zaif* (weak, slave, low-born), in practical use its opposite is *jahil* (ignorant person). The fact that the epithet *jahil* is often used with *ganwar*—giving the meaning "ignorant villager"—is indicative of the symbolic convergence of national categories with spatial and ethnic coordinates. Muhajirs—who are only ever urban—are cast as *sharif*: modern, rational, temperate citizens. Pathans, Sindhis, Baluch, and even the power-wielding majority, Punjabis, cannot escape their association with all things rural, provincial, tribal, and feudal; they are considered *jahil ganwar*s: ignorant, irrational, and intemperate. They are angry, and it is their anger that marks them as beyond the pale.

More tentatively, while it is crucial to historicize the construction of anger in nationalist discourse, one can perhaps historicize the anger itself. For if, as women in the Shipyard suggest, "our men are angry," should we not look to the recent origin of the community and its boundaries that the pronoun "our" indexes? Briefly, with the postpartition growth of ethnic politics (following the sudden ethnic asymmetry brought about by the creation of Pakistan), we can suggest that there has been an increase in male anger[6]—not because anger is juridical, a natural, rational response to political disempowerment or inequality but because anger is a cultural currency that procures status or, rather, makes claims to parity. It is a familiar form of cultural capital that signifies masculine power, efficacy, and superiority. Anger is an intelligible posture in situations of political inequality, not because of a possible future effect (e.g., violence leading to political transformation) but because of its own inherently redemptive character.

To reiterate, anger evokes the limits of national community, separating barbaric, angry men from *sharif* male citizens. But anger also separates respectable women from not-so-respectable ones. In reformist and *sharif* discourse, anger is certainly discouraged for both genders, but in men, it is simply a vice. As noted, women's anger toward superordinate kin is clearly forbidden. But even toward non-kin, equals and inferiors, it is condemned. Women's anger is ugly: a contravention of the beautiful and ennobling qualities of shame, modesty, and reticence with which women, in particular, are most associated. Beyond aesthetics, women's anger is seen as socially disruptive. Brenneis notes that women's anger and the in-fighting between sisters-in-law is often blamed for the breakup of joint family households (1990: 122). Indeed, in *sharif* discourse, there is very little that is redemptive about women's anger.

What, then, do we make of the women in the Shipyard and their traffic in anger as value? Who are these women who spit and beat and fight? Which women are promoting the totemic anger of their men and arrogating juridical anger for themselves? They are women who reside on the margins of respectability—ethnic, rural, and not-quite-comfortably middle-class. Aliya, a Punjabi-speaker, and Zubaida, Ruhi, and Mahvish, all Sindhi-speakers, universalized their specific "structural" experience in their stories and conversations. Aliya's claim is particularly telling: "If someone grabs you, then you should beat him. And everyone will rush to support you because you are a woman." In order to warrant public support from the men around her, a woman has to be seen as respectable, which is a matter of both moral conduct and social standing. But the very act of drawing attention to the offense—particularly (but not only) if it is sexual—can cast doubt on a woman's respectability. (This is the reasoning behind Aliya's subterfuge in which she recast a sexual assault as a purse-snatching.) Public support is always uncertain and ambivalent, challenging respectability even as it affirms it.

While middle- to upper-class women are more likely to get support in such circumstances, they are also perhaps less likely to demonstrate affront. Showing anger (however moral) is not *sharif*. The women, then, who get angry and fight are the same women who tell these stories of angry men. They are ambiguously positioned between competing discourses of anger, one celebratory, one reproving, and they are already distanced from the kind of respectability that a surrender of anger would index and achieve.

Managing Male Anger

While women in the Shipyard "structurally" differ in the extent to which they glorify their angry men and cultivate their own (moral) anger, all women seemed to share an appreciation for the dangerous nature of male anger. Thus, while male anger can be mobilized as a discourse of difference and boundary, it is much more immediately present as a principle that links women to one another. Women's understanding of male anger engenders a specific sensibility or praxis of peace, where women labor to protect each other, themselves, and their own "angry men" from *ghussa*'s destructive potential. In the Shipyard, women were vigilantly mindful of the potential anger of their own and their neighbors' husbands. Zubaida, who disliked leaving the building alone, would often ask me to accompany her for shopping and other errands. Each time, despite my demurral, she would insist that I first clear it with my husband so that he would not "take it badly" [*bura na mane(n)*] were he to come home and find me gone. Similarly, when Parveen would ask for rides to work with me, she would always ask, concerned, *"Bhai to 'mind' na karenge?"* (Brother won't mind, will he?)

It is significant that, in instances like these, women almost invariably used gentler terms for anger than *ghussa*—terms like *bura manna*, *"mind" karna*, and *naraz hona*. The unwillingness to ascribe *ghussa* to someone else's man speaks to the ambivalence around its social valuation. To suggest that so-and-so's husband is angry could be read as an affront, for cool-headed reason is publicly praised and admired, particularly in civil (or extrafamilial) sites of community, like neighborhood, mosque, and marketplace. For this reason, women are more likely to use *ghussa* when talking about their own husbands or male kin or when speaking generally or telling stories. The use of the English term "mind" is also telling, for concepts that are emotionally weighty and fraught with ambivalence are often translated into a more neutral English term in routine speech.

Because women view male anger as largely irrational, separate from thought and judgment (or, to put it another way, as performative rather than juridical), women recognize that it is not enough to "obey norms" and avoid even the appearance of impropriety. There are a whole range of preemptive moves that women make in order to ward off male anger. Indeed, women's tactics are often more akin to Zubaida's demand that

Meher "sit somewhere else." Avoiding men in certain circumstances, and excluding them from certain routine practices, are key examples. Referring to Pathan women, Grima writes that "when a man comes home angry, women may pass the word in whispers among themselves that *khapa day*, implying a warning that he is sensitive and irritable and they should keep out of his way or he may become abusive" (1992: 38). The strategy of "handling things" on their own is another example; to bring conflicts to a husband's or male relative's attention is seen as dangerous and unwise and is thus a court of last resort. This is why, as we have seen, women refrain from drawing male relatives into conflicts over "Eve-teasing," relying, instead, on their own moral anger to intelligently manage the situation.

The same goes for conflicts in the apartment building. Zubaida fumed for days over a neighbor's uncivil behavior—her refusals to return greetings and her backhanded criticisms of Zubaida's children's clothing. Despite her growing indignation, Zubaida kept the conflict a secret from her husband, Babar, explaining that, were he to get "in the middle" of this predicament (*bich men ata*), it would "never be solved" (*hal nahin hota*). More specifically, Zubaida simply saw herself as better able to handle the problem and other problems of its kind. For this reason, in part, men are largely excluded from the daily reckoning of reciprocity in exchange. Women in the Shipyard suggest that men are simply not equipped to handle the vicissitudes of balance in exchange, due to their vulnerability to sudden irrational anger.

In their desire to preserve social relations of exchange in the building, women take great care not to get other women in "trouble" (*taklif*). Social visits, for example, are usually conducted when husbands and male in-laws are at work. Similarly, women often conceal from their husbands and other relatives the details of their informal exchanges with neighbors. Thus, as mentioned in chapter 3, when Aliya brought Zubaida a pile of clothing that needed to be tailored, Zubaida kept it hidden in the corner of a closet, bringing it out to work on only when her husband and brother-in-law were out of the apartment. "They'd just get mad at Aliya and say, 'Doesn't she know you've got your own work to do?'" Zubaida explained. Moreover, women are extremely judicious with potentially damaging information and gossip about other Shipyard wives, for the disrepute of a single neighbor vastly decreases women's theater of action. (I will have more to say about this in chapter 5.) Visiting or associating with such a neighbor is seen as an invitation to male ire.

Women's efforts to avoid and manage male anger necessitate a kind of public, creative, collective labor. This "public" may indeed constitute a site of construction of women's agency and political efficacy—with reference to both gendered power relations within the household and relations of ethnic peace and enmity in the neighborhood. But there is also a sense in which male anger marks the very boundaries of the possible, setting limits on this very public by governing women's participation in local relations of exchange. Take the following example:

In a squatter settlement along the southern side of the building, there lived a young Afghani woman whom Zubaida had befriended. Qauser had a nine-month-old daughter and lived with her husband, his parents, and his siblings. Qauser and her family had fled war-torn Kabul and had been living as refugees in various parts of Pakistan for several years. Qauser spoke Pashto, but her Urdu was passable, and Zubaida would often stand on her balcony and chat with her while hanging laundry on the line. Sometimes Zubaida would lower bread or other leftovers down to Qauser in a basket tied to a rope (this was also a common system for collecting produce purchased from the *thailawala*, who made daily stops at the Shipyard). At other times, Qauser would make and send up a tasty, extra large Afghani *nan* (leavened flatbread), cooked over hot coals in her clay oven.

One day, the normally robust Zubaida was feeling under the weather, and when her husband returned home from work, she asked him if she could forgo making *chapati*s for the evening meal. Could he, instead, purchase *roti*s from the nearby Pathan hotel? "I don't work all day to come home and eat food from outside," he had angrily retorted. "You make the *chapati*s. There's nothing wrong with you." With sundown approaching, Zubaida stepped out onto the balcony to collect the laundry (dew deposits on clothes at dusk), and Qauser greeted her warmly. Seeing that Zubaida was unwell, Qauser offered to send up some fresh *nan* for her. But when Zubaida went to the kitchen for the basket and rope, Babar stopped her. "We're not taking *nan* from her," he said. "How low are we that we're taking bread from beggars?"

Reluctantly, Zubaida returned to the balcony and declined Qauser's offer. But Qauser was hurt. "What's wrong with my *roti*?" she asked. "Is it not clean? Are my hands dirty?"

Zubaida told me of this incident the following day, and she was visibly upset about the rift her husband's anger had caused in her relationship with Qauser. Zubaida's inability to accept Qauser's hospitality created a situation of unbalanced reciprocity and effectively terminated (though perhaps not irretrievably) their exchange relationship. Babar's anger had reconfigured the space of friendship into one of charity, and it drew boundaries around the space of Zubaida's future dealings in the neighborhood.

I end with this account because it forbids a reading of anger as simply a "correlate" of honor (Papanek 1982: 39). Male anger, in women's narratives, is bigger than honor, meaning it is about everything and nothing; it is wanting *chapatis* and governing chastity; it is inexplicable kicking and groundless homicidal rage. As women's stories suggest, the wages of male anger are death, and the condition of women's public or "extradomestic" social life and attachment is male sufferance.

Ironically, the central problem in a masculine and academic discourse of honor is the control and management of women's sexuality/passions. Women are viewed, even in the comparatively gender egalitarian language of reform, as less capable of *aql*, more in danger of "moving out of control, of displaying excess, of spilling over" (Metcalf 1990: 14). But in women's narratives, men are rarely granted superior *aql*. On the contrary, far from a story of men managing women's sexuality, this is a story of women managing men's anger. It is men who are subject to uncontrollable (violent) urges, and women, with their superior *aql*, who are called upon to manage this unruly masculinity, with its tendency toward agentless excess.

Parenthetically, while my research is specifically concerned with women's practice, my routine if fleeting interactions with men led me to believe that they share women's appreciation for the volatile and excessive qualities of male anger. For example, I have observed that when a difference of opinion is stated in men's casual discussions about political matters, the speaker will often finish with the plea " *'mind' na kare(n)*"— don't mind it, don't take offense. Lindholm goes so far as to claim that the reputedly bellicose Pathans are more pacifistic in their everyday public encounters than other South Asians, because of the recognition that anger expressed will lead to a blood feud, "a feud which implicates all of one's lineage mates" (1996: 205, 194). Both Grima and Lindholm contend that such anger, restrained in public encounters between male equals, finds legitimate expression at home, directed toward women and social inferiors.

But as their stories reveal, women grant male anger a kind of life of its own. Even this "natural," "legitimate" (however senseless) anger can lose its way and end up in public, extradomestic spaces, bringing bloodshed in its wake. In this sense, women in the Shipyard unwittingly share the opinion of certain contemporary theorists of collective violence that culturally sanctioned or "legitimate" violence/anger can "spill over" into "other spheres where it may not be approved" (Kakar 1996: 31). Indeed, the labor of managing male anger does not simply lie in calculation—in determining those paths which best evade an angry response. As we have seen, women view male anger not as rationally linked to external (transgressive) events but rather as internal to masculine virility itself. Men's choleric temperaments require careful handling: heightened sensitivity to emotional signals, anticipatory labors of distraction and derailment—but above all, of containment: women labor (and teach their daughters) to absorb, receive, and tolerate male anger in the containable space of "home," lest it "get away."

Male anger does not figure merely as a hindrance to women's local exchange; it is part of exchange's raison d'être. We will recall that women view local exchange as a necessary labor that men are ill-equipped to perform because they cannot tolerate tension (tension being pivotal to this particular peace). Male anger, similarly, is a threat to the maintenance of this tension; with its specific teleology of challenge, offense, and retaliation/resolution, male anger is seen as a form of exchange that is anathema to peaceful coexistence. This anger already marks, or effects, the refusal (or remission) of tension. The labor of maintaining tension through exchange—thus staying engaged—is contingent on, but also coterminous with, the avoidance, management, or containment of male anger.

Women's notions of—and efforts to manage—male anger, like their efforts at sustaining social/cultural tension through exchange, are pivotal logics and praxes of everyday peacemaking in buildings like the Shipyard.

But again, it is impossible simply to champion this labor. Clearly, women are complicit in reproducing a discourse that links anger with masculinity and group status, thus generating the very emotions they must labor to manage and buttressing the system of gender difference and male dominance that ultimately constrains them.

"Staying in the game"—the routine visiting, borrowing, returning, and helping that characterizes local exchange in the Shipyard—is a high stakes endeavor for women. Managing and avoiding the anger of their men and their neighbors' men, bearing the tension of social contradiction as a psychic and somatic event—these are purchased at considerable psychic cost. What inspires women to take on this labor, to feel the pain, to risk so much? What makes bearing this tension and negotiating this anger worthwhile?

Women in the Shipyard frame their routine practices of exchange as pleasurable and satisfying activities. More than this, the specific conditions of sociality in buildings like the Shipyard, with their extrafamilial focus, provide women with new opportunities and transformed idioms for intimacy. It is to this intimacy and its historic, contested, political, discursive, and affective contexts that I now turn.

Clifton Beach, a Popular Holiday Spot for City Dwellers

Children on Their Way to School

College Students and Vendors near Burns Road

Women Attending a Drama Performance Sponsored by a Nongovernmental
Development Agency

Paramilitary Rangers on Patrol in Clifton

Police Stopping Motorcyclists near the Clifton Bridge

Urban Shepherds Watching Their Flock

A Market—A Typical Sight throughout Karachi

A High-end Shopping Mall in Clifton

Women Crowd around a Meeting Hall in Rehri, a Fishing Village on Karachi's Outermost Borders

Women at a Family Gathering in Old Clifton

5

Intimacy

In addition to the wealth of "angry men" stories with which I was regaled, stories drawing explicitly on *hadith* and other religious themes were legion. One topic in particular stood out as a perpetual favorite. I will shorthand it, roughly, as "the moral deed justly rewarded." Typically, tales with this theme featured a good and modest woman who, due to extreme poverty, is forced to commit immoral and illegal acts, like consuming *haram* (forbidden) food, stealing, or engaging in prostitution. Through a self-sacrificing act—like feeding a *faqir* or tending a wounded animal—the woman's sins are erased. A messenger of God comes to inform her that this "good deed" is "her Hajj."

So ubiquitous was this type of story that my husband and I laughingly referred to them as "'This is your Hajj' story #306," "#307," and so on. But as I was to discover, the intriguing tensions that these stories engage, between performative morality or duty and an inner goodness, between signs of piety and the pious soul, serve to dramatize a powerful, ongoing theme in women's local relationships: the coherence, or lack thereof, between one's "insides" and one's "outsides."

The leitmotif of these stories is that external circumstances (generally poverty) prevent the protagonist's "outsides" from matching her "insides." The appearance of the messenger enables or secures a longed-for transparency, where the truth of the woman's insides, her inner goodness, is readable—by the woman herself and the world at large. Significantly, resolution does not lie in a transformation of material conditions, such that the protagonist's outward comportment may, at last, reflect her inner state. On the contrary, the reward for her good deed is a kind of divine intimacy, a "being known" by God. To know and be known is an end in itself.

But there is another truth that unfolds in these tales—a warning of sorts. For just as exigent circumstance may obscure the truth of a noble heart, the reverse is also true: outward signs of piety, solicitude, or friendship can mask evil or malevolent hearts. There is a saying I heard repeated many times in the Shipyard: *dost hota nahin, har hath milanewala:* Not everyone who shakes your hand is your friend.[1]

As the stories foretell, women's everyday reflections on intimacy are fraught with paradox. There are expressions of deep longing—for transparency, access to the insides, the inner life of self and others; on the other hand, there are clear and oft repeated interdictions on being open, violable, exposed. In this chapter, I consider women's understanding of intimacy as it emerges through a kind of labor of attachment—both licit and covert—performed in the civic, homosocial space of the apartment building. This is an intimacy that refers neither to the modern figure of the romantic couple (which, though increasingly ideologically available for my informants, remains markedly suspect) nor to the idiom of kinship. The possibility of intimacy in this new space may go far in explaining women's commitment to the intense daily labor of individual and collective emotional regulation on which everyday peace rests. But as I will demonstrate, the specific terms of this intimate female sociality—this knowing and being known—may be rather more complexly related to the emergence of the peacemaking subject.

Before I proceed, I wish to remind the reader of the specificity of this site, a form of dwelling that, to an unprecedented degree (both historically and biographically for my informants) brings together strangers—people from a diversity of ethnic, linguistic, and sectarian backgrounds—under one roof. Furthermore, as a result of both financial constraints and concerns about modesty and gender segregation, women in the Shipyard (and I'm talking specifically about married women) were not mobile. Without cars or money for cabs (or, for that matter, permission from husbands or in-laws), they were unable to visit, with any regularity, their affinal or consanguinal kin (or old schoolmates) who lived in other parts of the city or beyond. The point of this is that this local space is both unprecedentedly foreign for most of these women, meaning they are surrounded by *ghair log* (outsiders) and at the same time it defines, more than ever, women's theater of action. Except for special occasion visits to family and sporadic weekend outings with husbands and children, women literally spent their day-to-day lives at home.

In more ways than one, women's social relationships in the Shipyard—and Karachi more generally—are regulated by the sociocultural institution, or discourse, of purdah. Purdah is no doubt familiar to most Western readers as a system of veiling and the segregation of women in the *zenana*, or women's space. But perhaps more important, purdah is a key site of regulation of social intimacy, articulating the complex, shifting, and contested relationships between variously defined "insides" and "outsides." Before I turn to the construction of intimacy vis-à-vis female sociality in the Shipyard, I offer a very selective reading of purdah, one which can help explain my informants' ambivalent orientation toward both the conjugal couple and the family as sites of affective attachment.

Purdah in Discourse and Practice

If one were to consult a nineteenth-century Urdu text devoted to women's moral education, one would come away with at least two conclusions: first, that purdah hinders women's moral and religious refinement and hence, through domestic influence, holds an entire nation of husbands and sons hostage to backward, superstitious custom; and second, that a large number of Muslim women in Pakistan and India today have, indeed, "come out" of purdah. But the history and the definition of purdah in South Asia is and perhaps always has been a more complicated affair.

Purdah held a central place in nineteenth-century anticolonial Islamic reform movements, which were inseparable from local processes of embourgoisement—the development of a middle class which opposed itself both to the masses and to the decadent, aristocratic elite. For this emergent service gentry class, purdah—specifically veiling and the seclusion of women—was seen to hinder the uplift of the entire Muslim community. The relatively autonomous, feminine world of the *zenana* enabled the promulgation of "foolish" and "unnecessary" customs, "wasteful" practices, and general backwardness.

At the same time, however, purdah was fiercely defended by these same reformers (and their detractors) as central to religious law (*shariat*). Due to Hindu influence, reformers argued, the religious dictates of purdah—simple exhortations for modesty—had been corrupted into an unthinkably draconian institution. While Hindu women were compelled to veil in front of senior male affines as a gesture of avoidance and deference, Islamic law dictated modesty in the face of non-kin males. In South Asia, there was often little distinction between the way purdah was practiced by both groups; religious reform aimed at inserting a nominally Islamic brand of purdah as a way of distinguishing the community from Western and Hindu culture.

"Coming out of purdah," for reformers, specifically meant leaving the *zenana*—abandoning the veil and mixing with non-kin men. The biggest problem with this, according to concerned parents and ambivalent reformers, was that once out of purdah, women might "choose" their own mates. (Before reform, women were largely prevented from learning how to write because of the fear that, once enabled, they would write letters to strange men; see Minault 1998; Naim 1987.) Reformers retorted that proper religious and moral education could take the place of veiling and seclusion; that properly educated, enlightened, and "Islamicized" women would be able to take moral responsibility for their actions. Indeed, reform set in motion the transformation of purdah from an external institution to an internalized norm, envisioning a shift from collective policing and control to individual moral responsibility.

But one has to question the extent to which purdah has ever meant only veiling and seclusion and whether the subtler, embodied, and affective practices of purdah in evidence today are entirely new. To begin, we need to question the dominant narrative of purdah, the well-worn story of male honor garnered through the control over women's sexuality. From this perspective, purdah—both the spatial and sartorial standards of female modesty or "shame" embodied in veiling and seclusion, and the more behavioral and gestural forms of deference and reticence informing everyday interaction—serves to protect women's virginity, a central sign in a system of marriage exchange that underpins and secures male patrilineal solidarity. Women "choosing" their own husbands clearly threatens both generational power relations and the priority of the male patriline (and, at times, the purity of the community), and premarital sex presumably threatens the foundation of exchange (in which virginity is a central commodity). However, there is more to the story.

A growing body of literature on purdah in South Asia (Minault 1998; Papanek and Minault 1982; Raheja and Gold 1994) demonstrates that if we are to understand the social meanings and uses of purdah, then it must be studied as it emerges in everyday contexts. For example, it is generally accepted that Muslim women, beginning at puberty, veil for non-kin males, and Hindu women veil for senior affines, and that for Muslims, purdah is all about sexuality and the protection of the afore-mentioned "male patriline," whereas for Hindus, purdah articulates women's marginal and ambivalent position in the marital household and thus begins only at marriage. The problem with this ideological scenario is that it misses one of the most notable elements of purdah as it emerges in daily practice: that purdah is as much about status and self-fashioning as it is about sexuality and that it articulates relations *among* women as much as it does relations between women and men.

Purdah has been seen to articulate social class; disenfranchised groups throughout South Asia have historically taken up veiling as a claim to bourgeois status, for only middle-class families can afford to segregate their women from the mixed company of field or workplace. Purdah can also figure dramatically in ethnic nationalist discourse, where *other* groups are labeled inferior, effete, and immoral because their women don't do purdah (Pastner 1990) (or, conversely, barbaric and retrograde because they *do*). In the Shipyard, veiling was a matter of sometimes vehement, but often simply comic, dispute, as the following example demonstrates.

In the month after Ramzan, there was a wedding in the building, and many neighbors were invited (though my husband and I were not). The wedding took place on the penthouse terrace (apparently without the permission of the penthouse owner-tenants, who were away visiting rel-atives at the time). The day after the event, Zubaida gave me all the details.

"We were up on the penthouse, and all the ladies were sitting with *dupatta*s on their shoulders. Well, the wind was blowing my hair around, so I covered it with my *dupatta*, like this. And it's my custom, anyway. At one-dish parties, or when-ever there are men at the table, I cover my head, and I don't look around like this and that or laugh with mouth open wide.

"So later, Aliya came to my house and said, 'Stupid! Why were you sitting like this, with *dupatta* on your head?'

"'Why?' I asked her.

"'My husband scolded me,' she said, 'saying, "Look how nicely Bhabi is sitting there, so *sharif*." You got me in trouble!'"

At that point, Zubaida laughed, making fun of herself, wrapping the *dupatta* tightly around her head leaving only her face exposed, nodding her head side to side comically. In this instance, Zubaida was laughing at the inadvertent glory she had secured by virtue of her cosmetic effort to keep her hair in place. In other instances, the not infrequent laughter directed at what is deemed inappropriate or indiscriminate veiling signals something more.

As Papanek and Minault have noted, purdah is a central mode of practicing and indexing deference relations. In other words, you veil (or act shy) for those who have authority over you, or, for many Muslim women, you veil in front of non-kin men if you are in the presence of authority figures (or, in some cases, simply people who will "talk").[2] This explains why Muslim women, in the absence of any Quranic injunction, will frequently veil or at least act shy around senior affines, just as Hindu women are said to be enjoined to do. And this is also why few women in the Shipyard could be seen to veil for everyone.

One day when Aliya and I were visiting Zubaida, the *thailawala* stopped by, calling out his wares. "Come, let's get some vegetables," Zubaida said, and the three of us stepped out onto the balcony. As we stepped out, I, and I alone, put my *dupatta* on my head. Zubaida noticed and turned to Aliya, saying, "Look at that. She's even better than we are. We never bother when we're stepping out here."

With her somewhat surprised compliment, Zubaida was informing me in a kind and subtle way that I had misread the *praxis*, if you will, of purdah. For, while the balcony may indeed be a semipublic space, visible by non-kin men, neither Zubaida nor Aliya constructed the men one meets there—the *thailawala*, the Afghan refugees and squatters—as worthy of veiling *for*. By refusing to veil, in effect they were saying: these are not marriageable men; they have no imaginable claim to my interest or my deference, and no one could possibly say or think otherwise.[3]

While I, being a foreigner in need of education and condescension, was excused for failing to make social use of purdah, others were not.

Roqaya, the owner of our flat, had never actually lived in the Shipyard, but she was a frequent visitor to the building nonetheless. Thus all my friends knew her. Roqaya habitually wore *hijab*—a headscarf completely covering her hair and shoulders, rather like a nun's habit. The Shipyard women found her enormously funny; they called her the *hijabwali* (one who wears *hijab*) and skillfully mimicked her dress and manners whenever her name came up. At first I assumed that this had more to do with Roqaya's perceived snobbery than the donning of *hijab*—she was, by her own admission, "too good" to live in the Shipyard, being of noble, Lucknowi, Shia *nawabi* (royal) blood. But they had a similar if much less biting and more tolerant response to our neighbor, Parveen.

When walking down the halls, or coming to mine or another neighbor's flat for errands, Parveen kept her *dupatta* on her head. Most of the women I knew in the Shipyard, especially those with whom I was friends, did not veil for Sheheryar, nor did I for their spouses. Veiling seemed to imply something, not just about the relative status of the parties but also about the perceived degree of "risk" involved in the encounter (viz. reputations in jeopardy). Veiling for one's friend's spouse could signify a lack of trust, sexualize relations that were struggling to achieve "fictive kin" status, or inject hierarchy in relations that are ideally egalitarian. It was a tricky business. One needed to veil enough, for the right people, to demonstrate an appropriate degree of *sharm* (if you are shameless, no one will dare associate with you). But one needed to tactically eschew veiling in order to assert status and to affirm a closer, less formal social relationship (between women, via their husbands).

Because Parveen veiled indiscriminately, she missed the opportunity to use purdah as a sign of status and intimacy. This had consequences for her social relations with neighbors, who never seemed to warm up to her. Women found her odd, out of it, dowdy, even—but certainly pious (*nek*) and good (*achi*). It is significant that both Roqaya and Parveen were Urdu speakers, while their critics in the building represented the vernacular. As I discuss later, one of the identifying features of *sharif* discourse as it emerged in reform and later nationalist narratives was the attempt to sever purdah and *sharm* from their social, relational context, turning them inwards, as a kind of ideal attribute or personality trait. According to this logic, one does indeed "veil" (in one way or another) for everyone, because one *is* (rather than *acts* or *feels*) shy.

These last few examples point to what I hold to be the most significant dimension of purdah for women in the Shipyard: its role in regulating social intimacy. To fully understand the way in which purdah articulates (and challenges) boundaries between selves and others and both enables and sets limits on self and other knowledge, we need to move beyond purdah as veiling and seclusion and explore its more subtle, embodied, and affective forms. We also need to understand the cultural models of intimacy in relation to which Shipyard residents come to expect and seek certain kinds of lives while rejecting or avoiding others.

The Shame of True Love

One morning, Aliya and I were visiting at Zubaida's flat. Zubaida was helping me read through some Sindhi language materials, while she was plucking Aliya's eyebrows through a process known as threading. Zubaida and I were laughing and chatting, but Aliya was in a hurry.

> "Come on, do my threading. I want to go back upstairs," Aliya complained.
> "Why?" Zubaida asked, annoyed, "So you can go and sit in your husband's lap?"
> "Yes," Aliya joked. "I've been so busy all morning that I haven't had a chance (*moqa nahin mila*)."
> Shaking her head, Zubaida muttered, "She's rushing off just for that *haddi* (bone)."
> Aliya turned to me with a grin. "See, a *haddi* is a very small thing," she said. "*Hadda!*"
> "Allah!" Zubaida shrieked, and we all burst out laughing.

In order to get the joke, one needs to understand some of the details of the Urdu language, namely, that feminine and diminutive objects generally, but not always, end in *i*, whereas masculine and large objects generally end in *a*. But in order to understand the significance of the exchange, one must appreciate the somewhat ambivalent character of conjugality in Pakistan. The nuance of Aliya and Zubaida's interaction suggests that "rushing home to your husband" is funny, something to laugh about. Indeed, according to my informants' banter, the whole business of sex and marital love in general was something of a joke, something immensely comical and trivial. Zubaida's invocation of "the husband" is illuminating. Aliya was more than likely rushing home to finish her morning chores. In fact, it is the possibility of choosing the company of your husband over a more exclusive female sociality that is at issue, for where is intimacy, the pleasure of attachment, the very site of "having a life" seen to lie? Where exactly do husbands fit in?

When I first arrived in Pakistan, I was prepared for the fact that the conjugal couple would have a different salience for my informants than for Western observers, for whom the couple is the much worshipped, ideological, and structural center of a normative version of the family and discourses of romantic love. Ethnographic literature on Pakistan and North India has well documented the ambivalent character of the marital couple—and the bride in particular—as potentially disruptive of male, patrilineal solidarity. A plethora of structural and narrative practices seem to serve to distance husbands from wives, beginning with the competing interests of the joint family household, in which the married couple is but one unit answering to the broader authority of the older generation, and extending to a host of interdictions on the expression of conjugal affection. The Punjabi proverb—directed at men and cited by Kakar (1990: 19)—is apropos here: "A woman who shows more love for you than your mother is a slut" (cf. Raheja and Gold 1994: 124).

But as other anthropologists have noted, this dominant ethnographic discourse on conjugality as subordinate to the interests and attachments of the agnatic line fails to account for the experience and desires of the bride. While the public expression of indifference and distance vis-à-vis one's spouse is an expected moral performance (one aimed at least in part at keeping the peace in the joint family household), a tender and loving relationship between husband and wife is nevertheless both a covert and an explicit goal. A host of proverbs, rituals, and wedding songs sung at *mehndi* ceremonies poignantly express the hope that love between bride and groom will quickly follow.[4] In the Shipyard, expressions of hope or celebration for conjugal solidarity would surface, often implicitly, in women's conversations. For example, when I complained to Zubaida that my mother-in-law was unhappy with my research-related sojourns into different parts of the city, Zubaida asked, "Well, what does Sheheryar Bhai say?" When I replied that he didn't mind, she said, "Then it's okay. If *he* likes it, then it's okay." Indeed, women quite explicitly seek to forge loving and supportive bonds with their husbands, often precisely to mitigate against the influence of a hostile mother-in-law, who may view the bride as competition for her son's love and loyalty. (The position of the mother-in-law is understandable; mother-son relationships are one of the few culturally legitimate sites of intimacy for women, and women look forward to depending on their sons for emotional and financial support in their old age; see Luhrmann 1996.)

At the same time, "the couple" as a practical unit of sociality and action was clearly associated with the modern. Ruhi attended weekly Quran classes with her husband, and Zubaida and Aliya found this to be a surprising and "ultramodern" practice. In fact, Ruhi's father-in-law encouraged the couple to socialize together because he was distrustful of the character (or perhaps the autonomy) of female sociality in the apartment building.

Despite a marked ambivalence toward the modern figure of the romantic couple, my informants would nevertheless praise, give thanks for, or covet conjugal solidarity and tenderness. But implying that a woman was pining for her husband—that her marital relationship was characterized by dependency, deep longing, and emotional vulnerability—was dismissed as laughable. This discomfited laughter plugs into a central anxiety surrounding selfhood, an anxiety nowhere more evident than in women's oft-told stories of true love (*ishq*).[5]

My women neighbors knew, or at least suspected, that in many ways my marriage was not like theirs. But it was different in a familiar way: mine was a love match. In the early days of research, women in the building would hesitate to comment to me on my marriage or question me about it directly (this changed as time went by). But one day Zubaida told me a very telling story. In some ways, it was identical to so many of the love stories one comes across in folk tales, dime novels, television dramas, and film, containing a stock plot which resonates throughout much of South Asia and the Islamic world. In other ways, of course, it spoke rather specifically to my situation:

> "I'll tell you a true story of something that happened in a village near mine many years ago. My mother told me this story; it happened when she was small. A British girl named Bali came for some work in Sindh—I don't know what kind, maybe with the government. She came and stayed in a village near ours and lived with a family for a long time. She fell in love with our ways. She even spoke Sindhi. She did all the things that the village women would do. When they would

go to get the water from the well, filling those big jars (*matkas*) and putting them on their heads, she would say, 'Put the water on me, too! Let me carry the water, too!' (*Mujhe bhi pani laga do*).

"There was a Sindhi boy who had been away at university. When he came back to the village, they saw each other and fell in love. He forgot about his schooling; he forgot everything. She also forgot her work, all of it, and she became ill. Bali went back home to her family in London, and some time later, people in the village came to know that she had died. The young man who loved her had gone crazy. He became a wanderer (*avaragard*), like a *faqir* (religious mendicant). Everyone in the village remembered her, how she would say, 'Put the water on me,' how she loved all things Sindhi. The boy never became right again."

The elements of this story that are singular are, of course, of interest. A foreign girl—not unlike an anthropologist—comes to Sindh and falls in love with "all things Sindhi." Adaptive and open-minded, she eagerly participates in local life, showing genuine affection for the people and the customs of the land, a fact which saves her from being simply an antihero, a dangerous, immoral temptress who leads a local boy astray. But despite this narrative recuperation of Bali, she remains nonetheless an agent in her own tragic downfall—and that of her Beloved. For, singularities aside, it is in the juggernaut of true or mad love and its inevitable denouement that the story's moral lies. It is a story that begins with visibility, which leads to vision and then to invasion; it ends with self-effacement, erasure, insanity, or death.

Preventing visibility is one of the central objectives of purdah—indeed, to hide a woman's "ornaments" from the illicit or unintentional gaze of potential lovers is a Quranic injunction. Mixing freely with the men and women of the village, Bali is hypervisible, her enchanting manner noticed and remembered by "everyone." But with Bali's visibility comes a kind of violability. Her open, simple (*sadi sidhi*), guileless ways and her easy rapprochement with villagers and village customs bespeak a certain accessibility of self—a dangerous and negligent breach in psychic boundaries.

Precisely because the self is seen to be vulnerable to invasion by alien agencies—supernatural, divine, human, and/or fated—rigid boundaries around the self are a central dimension of purdah. In a cosmos where human senses are not passive receivers of information but materialities, forces which take effect in the world, the gestural elements of purdah—keeping one's eyes down—take on specific meaning. Visibility is problematic precisely because it enables vision. *Nazar* (look) is understood as a force that can "stick" to one (*lagna*), causing any manner of misfortune.[6] Indeed, as Bouhdiba (1998) reminds us, vision is immensely fraught for Muslims; citing the famous *sura* (verse) which declares, "Say to the believers that they cast down their eyes," he argues that to look is already to begin to transgress the limits set by God (and thus to court damnation).

When Bali and the unnamed Sindhi boy "see" one another, they are struck with love; it is an act of neither will nor choice but of recognition. The risk of visibility and vision inheres in the possibility that violate selves and intemperate or unmasked senses will inadvertently recognize a destined beloved. Fated lovers and beloveds (*ashiq* and *mashuq*) are seen to roam the earth. When they recognize one another, there is no willful thwarting of convention in order to secure union; there is only submission or, more accurately, a replacement of self by the external agency of *ishq*. Purdah, then—restriction on visibility and vision, but also the prevention of self-exposure through reticence, silence, downcast eyes, and closed mouth—is aimed in part at protecting and preserving those most human (read: culturally valued) of faculties: reason, will, agency. The dangers of *ishq* lie in the erasure of will, the loss of self set in motion by the sufferance of entry of this alien agency.

Significantly, it is the erasure of self and will that *ishq* enacts that is problematic; notice in Bali's story that the insanity and illness and "forgetting" of one's real life happens before the couple's separation. It is not the thwarting of young love that instigates tragedy; rather, it is love itself. If fated lovers and beloveds populate the earth, the divine goal of human existence is not to locate and unite; in contrast to the familiar Western romantic tenet, such a vision of idealized completion of the self in romantic oneness is not, for Pakistanis, the hegemonic, fantasized ideal nor the routinized site of "having a life." The high cultural premium placed on reason—deemed the most human of qualities—dramatically conflicts with such romantic merging.

At the end of Bali's story, the young man—the Lover—becomes a wanderer, "like a *faqir*." There is a striking similarity between tales of the tragic and transformative power of excessive romantic love and tales of the transformative power of Sufi shrines. Consider the following story. Ruhi recounted it one afternoon in her drawing room while I was helping her with her English studies:

> "One time, my father's friend was getting ready to go to the *urs* (death anniversary) of Moinuddin Chishti in India. He was a very religious man, and he had been talking about this for a long time. He worked for Karachi Metropolitan Corporation. His daughter, who was studying to be a doctor, wanted to go with him. She wasn't in the habit of going to the *mazar* (shrine), but still she wanted to go, and after a lot of convincing, her father agreed.
>
> "So they went, and they arrived a few days before the *urs* began. That first night, they went to the shrine, and the building was locked, so the father asked the *rakhwala* (caretaker) if he would open the door so he and his daughter could go in. They went in, and after circling the tomb, something happened: his daughter fainted. The man called for the *rakhwala*, and they put some water on her face. When she woke up, she turned to her father and said, 'I will never leave here.' She had become a *mastani* (one who is devoid of sense; drunk with the love of God). Her father begged her to come home, but it was no use. So she lived there from then on."

The similarities between this and Bali's story are readily apparent, although here, the daughter's "visibility" is less of a moral problem than Bali's, unless we consider that for mainstream Pakistani society, and in orthodox Islamic discourse, visiting shrines is frowned upon as a superstitious, heterodox practice. The juxtaposition between earthly, human love (*ishq-e majazi*) and divine love (*ishq-e haqiqi*) is a central feature of Sufi devotional practice and narrative traditions (Devji 1991). In popular literature and everyday storytelling, Sufi saints and *faqir*s are often said to turn to spiritual devotion after an earthly romance has rendered them senseless. States and Islamic orthodoxies have long been antagonistic to Sufis for political and ideological reasons, not the least of which concerns their divergent valuations of individual reason and self-will versus self-transcendence and merging. But both agree that *ishq*—human or divine—equals a loss of self that negates the exercise of will and that the only protection against *ishq* lies in the social (or, according to reformers, individual) control over visibility and vision, or in the restriction of access, suffered or sought, to the inner life—the hidden, authentic inside of selves and others.

That purdah in some way protected not simply sexual chastity but an inner, authentic "self" was not immediately apparent to me. In my many discussions with my neighbors about the comparative moral character of American and Pakistani women, I would repeatedly assert the relatively puritanical stance much of American society holds toward premarital sex (and sex in general). In her effort to fully identify and correct my misunderstandings, Ruhi at one point burst out, "Yes, yes, Laura, but where we come from, it's not just 'sex.' *Love* before marriage is wrong." Sex, in general, seemed to be much less morally complicated for my neighbors than it was for me. Virginity was an *amanat* (something held in trust) that belonged to your future husband. But once delivered, my neighbors suggested, it was not at all uncommon for women to engage in extramarital affairs (although this is publicly condemned as sinful, not to mention illegal). The risks associated with infidelity were largely identified as public censure and punishment, whereas the risks associated with love lay in revealing, devaluing, or losing that which is most authentically "inner."

The dichotomy between the inner life and the external world—*batin* and *zahir* (also *andar* and *bahir* in more colloquial speech)—is deeply linked with Karachiites' understandings of the duality of personhood. Composed of both angelic and animal properties, humans are made up of spirit (*ruh*) and body (*jism*). Their actions are guided by similarly dualistic forces: *aql* (cool-headed reason) and *nafs* (hot, psychobiological energy or passion). The cool spirituality of *ruh* is associated with the inner, the authentic, and the divine; the hot, animalistic intemperance of *nafs* is associated with the outer, the illusory, the temporal. Just as reason (*aql*) is valued as the most sublime of human characteristics, so that which is inner (*batin*) is treasured as something transcendent and true. But this inner, authentic core is represented by my informants as something ever at risk—both of being overpowered by the hot and mindless forces of *nafs* and of being sullied, evacuated, or lost through the profligacy of the human senses.

One afternoon Parveen and I had a long conversation about these concepts of *batin* and the inner life. Parveen, of all my informants, was the most adept at explaining to me the nuance of particularly recondite cultural notions. At one point, I asked her what harm there could be in expressing one's feelings, in telling a friend or husband what you felt "inside." Nonplussed, she protested, "But, Laura, if I tell these things, then there'll be nothing left inside. It'll become empty." The very word for inner—*batin*—also means that which is hidden (versus *zahir*, which means not only the outer but also the manifest, the known, the visible). It follows, then, that if something is no longer hidden—in the sense of *batin*—then it is simultaneously no longer inner. The idea that revealing one's inner life effects an irremediable transformation—or evacuation— goes far in explaining this sense of vulnerability and a corresponding desire for the protection of purdah.

Inasmuch as these ideas about *ishq*, the inner life, and purdah make up a rich and intricate web of moral and philosophical cultural discourses, it should come as no surprise that they are also contested, subverted, and reconfigured in everyday practice and narrative. A number of anthropologists have pointed to the heady romances that characterize youth culture in much of South Asia (e.g., Lukose 2001), and the desire for open-hearted conversation was a key—if necessarily somewhat covert— element of neighboring in the Shipyard. But I suspect that these concepts of *batin* and self-boundaries are nevertheless still powerfully at play. A Pakistani friend questioned my argument by asking why, if purdah is seen to protect women from the dangerous, invasive, and self-effacing forces of romantic love, were *purdah nashin*s (women wearing purdah) the most outrageous flirts? In one sense, veiled women are in the perfect position to exercise vision without visibility, to look without being looked at— which surely mitigates against the risks of "recognition." But more generally, flirting seems to be about mastery as opposed to merging—mastery over the boundaries of self, a confidence that such boundaries can be teased and explored without being invaded. Perhaps youthful romance is less about a desire for the self-transcendence that *ishq* inserts than about a kind of confidence that one truly is inviolate—that the boundaries will hold.

In this regard, the situational character of these discussions on purdah must be considered. Without exception, the women with whom I discussed these specific matters were married mothers of daughters. While they themselves may have been convinced of their own self-mastery when they were schoolgirls (and there are indications that this is the case), they are now in the position of enforcing or preaching purdah, and they genuinely fear for their daughters' futures. Subject to the authority and the often oppressive demands of husbands and senior affines, my

informants viewed agency and the exercise of will as the ultimate fantasized ideal, and they wished as much for their own daughters. The cautionary tales about the dangers of visibility, vision, and invasion were
aimed at daughters: young women who, in the relative freedom of premarital girlhood, were perhaps less alarmed by the prospects of romantic
self-effacement and at the same time foolishly bold in their boundary-
teasing experiments with self-mastery.

Having said this, I want to emphasize that women in the Shipyard
regard mad, romantic love and love matches with neither undying envy
nor scathing reproach. There is, in fact, a kind of quiet fascination with
love matches, just as there is with women who have become *mastani*s or
with anyone who has chosen or fallen into a path dramatically different
from that which was prescribed. But in conversation after conversation,
love (*ishq*) emerged as a dangerous force, one fearful to women because
it was seen to foreclose options, to embroil one in an inevitable plot that
erases agency and self-will. In addition to the loss of will—indeed, a kind
of possession—that love is seen to insert, it also sets in motion a series
of likely events that most women would be loathe to pursue: defiance of
family (for love, or even simply "self-chosen" marriages are dramatically
subversive of generational and patriarchal authority) and a corresponding
social ostracism. The loss of community that would accompany such an
act is abhorrent to my informants, for it is largely within the extended
family and local neighborhood networks that women find material and
emotional support, solidarity, pleasure, and purpose.

Intimacy and the Family

It is clear that the figure of the conjugal couple as a potential
site of emotional support and intimacy is problematic for women in the
Shipyard, both because of notions of *ishq* and the violability of the self
and because of the often divisive actions of the extended family. But in
this regard there are also limits to what a married woman can expect
from her affinal kin or even from her natal family. Some households in
the Shipyard were essentially "nuclearized," consisting simply of the marital couple and their children. This was the case for Parveen, Aliya, Qazi
Sahib's wife, and Sultan Sahib's wife. Kulsoom and Mrs. Habib were

nuclear families without their husbands in residence. Kulsoom was a co-wife whose husband resided with his younger bride. Mrs. Habib's husband was a sailor who was at sea for nine months out of every year. Due to their limited mobility, daily interaction with their affines (especially sisters-in-law) was impractical.[7] The same is true with natal kin, although, even when natal kin reside nearby, frequent visits by a married woman to her natal family are frowned upon as threatening the transfer of the bride's loyalty to her affinal home. Early in my research, my neighbor, Hina's mother, introduced me to Seema, her *devrani* (husband's younger brother's wife). Seema lived with her husband and eighteen-month-old daughter in an apartment building several blocks away. Coincidentally, Seema's parents and siblings all lived in the Shipyard. Her parents and a brother with his wife and children lived in a flat on the first floor, and another brother lived with his wife and children and his two unmarried brothers in a flat on the second floor, right next to Zubaida. Thus on Seema's frequent trips to the Shipyard to visit Hina's mother, she would routinely stop by to see her natal relatives. Toward the end of my research, Hina's mother's family vacated their apartment and moved to Peshawar. A few weeks before the move, Seema stopped by to see me and expressed some sadness that we would probably not see much of each other in the future.

> "But why not?" I asked, confused.
> "Because my *jethani* (husband's older brother's wife) won't be here, and I won't be able to come and visit as often."

Seema's frequent ventures to the Shipyard to visit her *jethani* were liberally allowed, but traversing the same distance explicitly to visit her natal kin was another matter. Thus even in "nuclearized" situations where the extended family is absent, women's socialization with those kinswomen who would have made up the joint family household is nevertheless promoted over other forms of sociality.

Even when a woman can maintain close spatial ties with affinal or natal kin, the complex, interwoven, and hierarchical nature of these bonds often mitigates against particular forms of familiarity or intimacy. Take the following example. One morning, I went to visit Zubaida and found her considerably shaken and upset.

"Babar fought with me. Yesterday I was unwell. I had fever and aches. I asked my *devar* if he would bring medicines from his office for me. When he came home, he had forgotten, so when Babar came home, I asked him to get some. We were low on rations—bread, milk—so he went shopping. When he came back, I asked him for the medicines, and he told me that he hadn't bought them—that I didn't need them. He said, 'It's just a virus. Medicine won't work. Why should we waste the money?' I was so upset that 'hysteria' happened to me. I fainted. Then Babar and my *devar* felt bad.

"But this happened before, when we were in the village. My mother-in-law was fighting with me, and I was so upset that I became unconscious. Later, when I was better, my mother asked, 'What happened? Were they fighting with you?' And I said, 'No, Ammi, everything's fine. It was just heat stroke.' See, if I tell them, 'Oh, Babar fights with me' or 'My in-laws are mean to me,' then they'll get mad. Maybe my brothers will feel hatred for Babar, or try to take me away from here, and I don't want that. This is my house, my children. Am I going to leave that?"

As this story reveals, Zubaida's self-expression is restricted in many ways. She is constrained (by purdah and codes of deference) from expressing anger at her in-laws or fighting back, which leaves her few options other than "hysteria." But she is also constrained by the agonistic relationship between her affinal and natal families, such that seeking support from one side poses a threat to the other. It is in this sort of context, then, that women's local relationships in the building—this homosocial, neighboring public—become the site of potential fulfillment of somewhat covert longings for intimacy.

Civic Intimacy

Once I became a regular visitor at Zubaida's flat, she confided in me that she had been looking for a friend ever since she moved to the Shipyard.

"My brother always told me, 'Make good friends. Don't tell your troubles to relatives, don't complain to them, don't answer back. Stay quiet, or your troubles will increase. Make some good friends outside of the family that you can share your true feelings with.' Since I came here, I've been looking for a good friend. I met with two or three ladies, but they didn't let me into their hearts (*dil ke andar jane nahin diya*). So I prayed to God to send me a good friend, and there was Aliya, and there was you."

Like Zubaida, women in the Shipyard almost invariably used the English word "share" to convey a kind of emotional exchange, or intimacy,
for which local Urdu categories were deemed inappropriate. Significantly, the English word "feelings" is also preferred over Urdu near-
equivalents (*mehsus*), pointing to a recognition that the moods, sentiments, and bodies involved in this desire are somehow problematic and
in transition.

At the time, women's tentative and halting expressions of longing for
someone to "share with" seemed surprising to me, particularly considering the aforementioned premium placed on self-boundaries—on the
protection and concealment of that which is inner (*batin*). Anthropologist
Lila Abu-Lughod (1986) has argued that for Muslims, speaking of the
inner life is expressly forbidden, and even my informants suggested that
to do so was a contravention of purdah. Aliya insisted that "open," "honest" conversation was a rarity in Pakistan. "No one will tell you the truth
about their lives, what they truly feel (*sachi* feel *karti hain*)," she said.
"We observe purdah. We don't speak freely." When Zubaida related to
me the details of her sister's difficult life, I asked if her sister was unhappy
or dissatisfied in her marriage. "I don't know," Zubaida said. "At times
I've thought maybe she's sad, maybe she wanted to marry someone else.
But she hasn't told me, and I haven't asked. We keep such purdah that
we don't tell such things."

It must be noted that this is not an interdiction on physical intimacy,
or talk about sorrowful events and certain kinds of suffering, which can
have quite express and ritualized forms in Pakistan (see Grima 1992).
Rather, this refers specifically to talk about one's feelings. Not only does
such talk risk the sullying or evacuation of one's inner authentic core,
but it is also seen to announce to the world a kind of moral laxity. There
is a homology that women express between sexual incontinence and an
open mouth, careless words, and emotional displays—and no one can
decide which is a worse transgression. Thus Ruhi said, with pride, "It is
not my custom to be free with everyone, to laugh with mouth wide open,
to move my body like this (swaying her hips and chest)."

Indeed, girls, and especially brides, are praised for their reticence,
their closed aspect. This is why three servant girls at a wedding I attended
mocked the South American bride, saying, "Oh, look at her, looking here
and there, laughing with mouth open like this, and eating with such

gusto!" Then in a soft voice, one of them began singing a popular Hindi film song that declared, "In weddings, we have lost all sense of shame."

Patently, the modest woman is one who keeps her eyes down, her mouth closed, open neither to the invasive forces of sex or love nor to the potentially corrupting influence of others. While nineteenth-century Islamic reform narratives sought to transform purdah from an external institution (of veiling and seclusion) to an internalized norm (of deferential and privacy practices), they also fundamentally dislodged these practices of shame from their relational moorings. Reform—and *sharif*—discourse lifts *sharm*, with its habitus of modesty and deference, from the concrete relations between women and potential mates, on the one hand, and between superiors and inferiors, on the other. What was once reserved for the expression of bonds of authority and respect became generalized as an ideal temperament for men and women, at all times, and in whatever company—including the neighboring *zenana*. Thus, even in this gender-segregated space of equals, free and familiar speech and unguarded emotions can be seen as transgressive or "shameless."

To reiterate: Women view the routine, gestural, and behavioral practices of purdah as protecting one's inner authentic self and simultaneously as a kind of moral performance. But most important for our purposes is the way in which the labor of purdah and *sharm* gets reconfigured vis-à-vis the imperatives and longings of neighboring.

The central problematic of neighbors, of course, is that they are unknown and unplaced; unlike kin, neighbors (in buildings like the Shipyard) are strangers whose lot and good name are not linked with one's own. As Zubaida's brother's advice suggests, outsiders—inasmuch as they are disinterested equals—make better friends than do family members. That this notion has broader resonance is suggested by the fact that the closer the friendship between two women in the building, the less likely they are to use kin terms of address for one another. Social distance, formal manners, or deference and the hierarchical elevation of the addressee promoted the widespread use of titles ("Mrs. Habib," "Nafisa Begum"—sometimes even, to my amusement, "Mrs. Sheheryar"), teknonymics (Hina's mother), and kin terms of address (*baji* [sister]; *bhabi* [brother's wife]; Auntie). Referring to a woman neighbor by her first name could connote several things: a "modern" sensibility, the assumption of seniority or hierarchy vis-à-vis the addressee, or, most likely, the assertion of social equality and intimacy. That the use of first names alludes most dramatically to social intimacy is evident in the fact that women almost never refer to or address male neighbors by their first names alone; they are almost always appended with titles or kin terms, e.g., Sheheryar Bhai; Sultan Sahib; Fazal Sahib. Otherwise, the implication of familiarity would be ill received. Similarly, women are generally reluctant to refer to their own husbands by their first names and will often use the term "that one," "so-and-so's father," or—if the addressee is a friend—"my husband" (*shauhar*). The abandonment of kin terms in close friendships in the building recapitulates the idealized remove of such relationships from the hierarchies (and sentiments and disciplines) of family organization.

Neighbors, then, are attractive to women as potential intimates precisely because they are outsiders. On the other hand, meeting with outsiders, and thereby becoming associated with them, has risks. As Zubaida warned me,

> "Women can wear the veil, but still flirt with their eyes. Usually people you meet, including people in this building, they deceive you (*woh dhoka dete hain*). Sometimes they just come because my brother-in-law is a doctor, or they want medicine, or something. They never come for no reason. And some people, their habits are not good, and their inside is different from their outside, so it's not good to spend too much time with them."

The dangers of meeting people whose "habits are not good" lie in the risk of transgression, scandal, and guilt by association. And because people are not transparent, because their insides may be different from their outsides, women must call upon sharply honed skills of reading—reading for the insides of others.

This discipline of reading the character, intent, and inner orientation of others is complicated, women suggest, by the workings of a pernicious modernity that acts on those urban residents who lack firm and intensive grounding in moral (usually equated with rural) communities. On numerous occasions, Ruhi, Parveen, Aliya, and Zubaida would complain to me about the deleterious effect of satellite TV on their vulnerable children. "See?" Aliya said, pointing to a dance sequence from a Hindi film on satellite TV. "Our children watch this, and it affects them (*asr parta hai*). They understand so much, more so than we did. Their brains have become very big." The city, with its intemperate images, is seen as a kind of corrupting modernity that opens bodies to desire—desire for commodities, sex, freedom—and at the same time increases brains. Those who have been reshaped by this modernity possess the cleverness to dissimulate, to mask the looseness, intemperance, and wild desires of their insides. This is particularly troubling in a place like Karachi, women claim, because external constraint—the punitive presence of extended family (*biradari*)—is seen to be minimal or even absent. Reading the insides of others, then, is viewed as both more important and more difficult in buildings like the Shipyard. This was nowhere more evident than in the aftermath of scandal, which I describe in detail below.

In the enervating heat of midsummer, Sheheryar, Faizan, and I fled Karachi for Pakistan's northern areas. After two weeks of exploring Swat and Kalam (the foothills of the Hindu Kush), we returned refreshed to our damp and sandy apartment by the sea. I spent the next day zipping feverishly from one flat to the next, telling neighbors about my trip and inquiring as to *Karachi ki halat* (Karachi's state) in our absence, not to mention borrowing water and chasing down Faizan, who was busy renewing the acquaintance of neighborhood children. Every moment of rest we grabbed for ourselves in the "privacy" of our apartment was fractured by the doorbell: the *chowkidar* dropping off the gas bill; neighbors welcoming us home; the newspaper seller requesting payment.

Finally, by 9 PM, after putting Faizan to bed, we had settled down to an escapist Hollywood video and cold drinks when again the doorbell rang. Sheheryar, exasperated, went to the door. I could hear his softly puzzled, polite Urdu from where I sat, and I rose to investigate. It was a middle-aged couple, perhaps early forties, the woman slightly heavyset in *shalwar kameez*, the man in shirt and trousers. They were complete strangers. "Well, won't you come in," Sheheryar offered, and I headed into the kitchen for *nimko* (snacks) and cold drinks.

They had come to ask about Raza, the twenty-year-old son of our upstairs neighbor Kulsoom. Raza was their daughter's classmate at Government College, and Raza's family had sent a proposal of marriage for her (*rishta bheja*). Apparently, this couple had spent the day going from neighbor to neighbor "making inquiries" about Raza's family. Did we know them?

As a matter of fact, Raza's family was one of the first we met when we moved into the Shipyard. Twelve-year-old Beenish was fond of Faizan, and she would frequently stop by to entertain him or to bring him to play with the third-floor children. (Children played quite freely in the hallways on their own floors, but there was a degree of territoriality about these semipublic spaces. "Go play on your own floor" was the general rule, unless the play was led by an older kid, like Beenish, who commanded greater mobility in the building.) Raza's family, like my husband's, was Shia and Muhajir, thus we knew some people in common, had a similar itinerary for Moharrum *majlis* and *kunda* "hopping," and so on.[8] Moreover, Kulsoom was well acquainted with the owner of our flat, Roqaya.

Early on, I noticed that this family mixed much less with neighbors than seemed to be the norm. As is often the case in Pakistan, their social class was somewhat difficult to pin down. I had assumed they were more elite than the majority of residents because, while Kulsoom and her older daughter, Batool, spoke only Urdu, both Raza and Beenish were fluent in English. (Zubaida, however, rather scathingly informed me that Kulsoom was "just" a co-wife, whose husband spent all his money and time on his younger bride.) Beenish had told me when we first met that her mother was very strict and wouldn't let her play with many of the children in the building "because they're rude and badly behaved." It was her mother's opinion that there were "not very many nice people" living in this building.

So did we know them? the couple was asking. "Oh, yes, we know them quite well," and the conversation bifurcated, as it so often does, with Sheheryar talking to the concerned father, and me to the mother. What was the family like?

"They're very *sharif* and sober," I ventured, and received a pleased nod. "I don't let my son go into just anyone's home, but I freely send him there."

But what of Raza's mother? A more difficult question: was she *tez* (cunning, manipulative, sharp)? In all honesty, I had found Kulsoom to be a rather intimidating, hard, and quite probably *tez* woman—indeed, a potentially tyrannical mother-in-law. "Well," I hesitated, "she's very serious. But pious." I found it difficult to give a straight answer, which perhaps conveyed my ambivalence.

The woman asked me about the elder sister and brother. I told her I hadn't met the brother but that he wasn't married. The sister, Batool, was married to a Sunni physician. Settled in Gulshan Iqbal, Batool would come to see me whenever she was visiting at her mother's flat, so I knew the whole story of her love match: the young doctor's knock on the wrong door, her offer of tea, their growing friendship, and finally marriage.

Meanwhile, I could make out the progression of the *mardana* conversation, which focused more on the broader context—how kids these days mingle at college; it's not the same as it used to be; Sheheryar asking the man about his job with Karachi Metropolitan Corporation, answering questions about Raza's character ("He seems honest, gentle, good-humored") and the reputation of the family more generally ("We've never heard anything bad about them, and we have only good things to say"). After a good hour of conversation, the couple thanked us, extended invitations for us to visit "anytime," and went on their way.

I was absolutely riveted to have been included so organically in this process of bringing and investigating *rishta*. The business of "making inquiries"—be it about the bride and her family or the groom and his—is not at all uncommon, although it is perhaps a distinctly urban phenomenon. Marriages in the *gaon* tend to be more *khandan*- or *biradari*-endogamous, which means either that the family is one or so well known that inquiries are not necessary. Furthermore, within the context of *biradari*, a bride's relatives can offer *zamanat* (surety) to vouch for her chastity, which is the main issue of reputation from the perspective of the groom's side. In the city, where marriages are so often *khandan*-exogamous, where *biradari* is weak or not applicable, and where community is so large, "scouts" are often sent to neighbors and/or the university of the potential bride or groom to ascertain the concerned party's reputation and character. The less known about the girl, the better. As for the groom, it is generally expected that his reputation will be bad (though not the good name of his *khandan*). It was somewhat atypical for the actual parents of the potential bride to be making such direct inquiries, but not unheard of. It seemed to me that, besides a more general concern with reputation, the parents (the mother in particular) were anxious to know what kind of home they would be sending their daughter into, what kind of mother-in-law she would have to face, and how her life would change should the match indeed be made.

I pumped my husband for more information.

"Isn't Raza awfully young to be getting married?" I asked. "He's only twenty."

"It's only a *mangni* (engagement)," Sheheryar chided, reminding me that engagements can stretch on for many years, a fact I'd gleaned from my conversations with industrial home students in Lyari, a large Baluch slum in the inner city. There, most of the girls had been betrothed since childhood, but to cousins—a very different matter.

My mind spinning, I stumbled off to bed, to the reassuring click of the overhead fan and the flutter of the tattered mosquito net. I resolved to seek out Beenish and ask her for the whole story first thing in the morning.

But it was not to be. After climbing the stairs to Beenish's flat, I found no one at home. The front door was shut and padlocked from the outside. I turned and headed instead for Zubaida's flat, where I found her chatting happily with Aliya while helping Iqbal sort laundry.

> "Did someone come last night and ask you about Raza's family?" I asked them, breathlessly.
>
> "Yes," they told me, and they leaned forward with interest. "What did the couple ask you?"
>
> "What's the mother like, what's the family like."
>
> "And what did you say?" Zubaida pressed.
>
> "I said that they're refined people, good people" (*woh sharif log hain, ache log hain*).
>
> Zubaida and Aliya exchanged knowing glances. "*Nahin*, Laura, *woh ache log nahin hain*," Zubaida told me: "They are *not* good people."

Then they told me the whole story. Apparently, Raza had been having a sexual affair with a woman who lived two floors above us—Aliya's *ham divar* (next-door neighbor). This woman was the wife of a Sindhi *daku* (bandit), who was in jail in Khairpur for having committed a robbery in which someone was shot and killed. Zubaida said that they hid the money on the roof of this building, and when her husband was imprisoned, the wife bought a 20 lakh (2 million rupees) house and shifted all of their furniture there. The wife would spend her days in the new house and her nights here in the empty flat with Raza. "Raza is a flirt," Aliya told me, "and this woman always came to the door in such flimsy 'nighties,' no bra; you could see everything!"

Finally, some of the incarcerated husband's relatives came to check on the apartment, and they saw all the furniture gone, and they discovered the wife with Raza. The next day, the police came and arrested them both for *zina* (adultery and fornication). After one night in jail, Raza was released (no one seemed to know what happened to the *daku*'s wife), and within a matter of days Beenish's family had packed up and moved out of the Shipyard.

This scandal—involving, as it did, the Sindhi wife of an imprisoned *daku* (Sindhi stereotype par excellence) and a middle-class Muhajir youth (the stuff that the MQM is made of) prompted the telling of numerous "ethnic stories." For Aliya and Zubaida, this *ghalat kam* (bad deed) was possible in part because Muhajirs are loose and uncontained; their bodies are open, unrestrained, visible, and migratory. In the wake of the scandal, Aliya and Zubaida were quick to tell me about the misdeeds of Raza's entire family, especially his twelve-year-old sister.

> "Beenish used to do a lot of mischief (*bohat shararat karti thi*)," Aliya confided. "The fifth floor is always empty, and she would be up there with boys. And she wouldn't wear a bra or vest or use a *dupatta*. She used to come to my house, and I would tell her, 'Please, dress up better when you come to my house.' 'Yes, they are getting big, aren't they,' she told me! And one time, Anam (Aliya's five-year-old daughter) said to me, 'Ammi, when I get big, will my hair be this long (pointing to her waist), like Beenish's?' 'Yes,' I answered, and Anam said, 'Good! Then I, too, can do *yun, yun*' (like this, like this), tossing her hair and sticking out her chest. So the next time Beenish came over, I asked her to go home, and her mother got very angry. She asked me, 'Why did you send my daughter away?' I said, 'Because I also have a daughter, and yes, she's little, so she can wear frocks and such. But please dress your daughter up nicely before sending her out.'"

The spectacle of the daughter's lack of bodily containment and the perversity of her mother's lack of concern were seen to be mirrored in a more fundamental breakdown of the "right order of things."

> "Those kids answer their parents back," Aliya said, incredulous. "One daughter, Batool, would fight with her mother like this, pulling at her hair! Even to this day I don't answer back my elder siblings."
>
> "And Batool's marriage," Zubaida added, breaking in, "I'm sure that there was something up," at which point they both muttered something about "pregnancy" and "misdeeds."

Ironically, while Parveen and Roqaya had been ridiculed for what other women in the Shipyard viewed as a stuffy and vacuous "Muhajir" (or urban bourgeois) interpretation of purdah, Raza and Beenish's family was viewed as emblematic of the wild, *be pardah* (immodest, uncovered), and degenerative modernity that Urdu culture simultaneously represents. Here, Muhajir bodies are violable, uncontained, unplaced, and undisciplined. Sindhi and Punjabi bodies, in contrast, are viewed as tight, covered, restrained, and fixed.

The difference between the groups, however, is read as a function of urbanity. To explain the adulterous behavior of the Sindhi *daku's* wife, Zubaida asserted that "when Sindhis come to the city, their minds become bad." In Zubaida's words, it is the absence of a self-sanctioning community that makes urban citizens so morally bankrupt: "In the village, you can't do bad things and then flee. In Karachi, they do that." Urbanites like Muhajirs, who lack rural roots, are unbound and thus uncontrolled. Sindhis and Punjabis, on the other hand, are properly "placed"; they are mindful of generational differences; they don't "answer back to their elders"; they are not *tez* or *chalak* (clever); they are innocent as children, modest as sexualized adults, and strict or angry as parents and husbands.

Among my neighbors—Sindhi, Punjabi, and Muhajir—there was a pronounced anxiety about one's children as status-demonstrators of group identity and as vulnerable targets of a baneful, transformative modernity. "See, in your society, it's different," Aliya said. "In ours, we don't want our daughters to be ultramodern. And nowadays their brains are so much bigger than ours were." At this point, Zubaida and Aliya conversed briefly about the dangers of television, with its provocative images. "Today's children are very clever," Zubaida concurred.

But there was more going on here than a fear of the corrupting influence of satellite television, with its Hindi films and American soap operas. One afternoon, Zubaida and Aliya were talking about Urdu and their children's language skills. While the adults in her household spoke to one another in Sindhi, Zubaida spoke almost exclusively to her children in Urdu, in a self-conscious effort to prepare them for Urdu-medium schools. "But," she insisted, "they both understand Sindhi, and when we go to the *gaon*, they are speaking it after two or three days."

"What about your daughter?" I asked Aliya. "Is she learning Punjabi?" Aliya is a native Punjabi speaker.

"Anam?" Aliya laughed. "She's a Muhajir!"

Aliya's response points to an anxiety over the lost identity and rootedness that is expressed in her daughter's alienation from the vernacular. Indeed, if Urdu is her mother tongue, then is Anam not a Muhajir, her body loose and uncontained, her hair and chest swaying freely, her character and her place migratory and self-willed?

As is clear, the scandal surrounding Raza's indiscretion, his family's sudden departure, and the appearance of the couple investigating *rishta* set in motion an intriguing explosion of discourse—about neighbors, about living in the city, about strangers and one's own people. There was an urgent tenor to the (often evasive) talk, for no one needed reminding that events such as this—an adulterous, interethnic affair—were the sparks from which ethnic riots flared. Nevertheless, what was immediately striking to me in the aftermath of scandal was the proliferation of what seemed to be direct acts of peacekeeping: the judicious containment of gossip; the disavowal of knowledge or association; a refusal to take sides. All in all, it seemed as if "peace" were resting on a kind of disengagement or emotional distancing—a denial of self-relevance. But as the days passed, I realized that, far from a disengagement, I was witnessing a dramatic *intensification* of emotional labor: the avoidance of male anger; the willing embodiment of tension in exchange practices that had become suddenly fraught with danger; and most poignantly, the ambivalent highstakes labor of reading for the insides of others.

Huddled on the floor in Zubaida's living room, Aliya, Zubaida, and I speculated about the meaning behind the couple's visit and their inquiries about Raza. Perhaps Raza's family was responding to the crisis by trying to marry him off quickly—that is, finding a legitimate site for his suddenly obvious sexuality. The couple's visit in itself was intriguing for what it suggested about the nature of neighborhood or "neighborness" as a kind of civic identity that must share space with more primordial-claiming ones (like community, or *biradari*) in its ability to place or locate subjects or to provide self-knowledge.

"I feel terrible," I said, "for having given that couple the wrong impression. I told them they were good people."

"Oh, but we all did that," Zubaida remarked.

"What?"

"Of course. We just smiled, and said, 'Oh, yes, we don't know them well, but they're good.'"

"But why didn't you tell them what you knew?"

"It wouldn't look nice (*acha nahin lagta*). And I can assure you that no one they talked to in the building spoke the truth to them. It's a matter of shame (*sharm ki bat hai*)."

Momentarily nonplussed, I kept muttering how "stupid" I felt, having misjudged the family so entirely.

"But we didn't know in the beginning, either," Zubaida assured me. "We were all deceived. I gave Beenish tuitions," she added, "and Aliya, you're the most stupid; you were friends with that *daku*'s wife!"

At this, they laughed heartily, and after a few moments, Aliya left. Zubaida turned to me, suddenly somber:

"The thing is, some people say that Aliya is bad, too, because she knew that woman. And my husband has forbidden me to visit her, so I'm scared to go to her house, lest people think that I'm not good, either. We meet, she comes if there's *kam* (business) or the children. But I don't meet with her much anymore. I think she also took some money from that woman to hold on to. See, she may have some involvement. I don't know."

As Zubaida's words suggest, women like Aliya, who had been friends with the arrested woman, were suddenly tainted by mere association, and *their* friends had to struggle to regroup in the face of transformed moral circumstances. But to fully grasp what is at stake when a friend or neighbor goes astray, one needs to know more about the nature (and the corresponding dangers) of female friendship in the Shipyard. Within the wider network of female sociality and exchange in the building, there was a great deal of tolerance among women for the development of particular friendships—a kind of pairing up. These friendships were characterized by daily visits, fierce loyalty, and an almost transubstantiated association. Thus, when the electrical fire in the building drove all residents outside, a woman I had never met turned to introduce herself to me and exclaimed, in recognition, "Oh, yes. You meet with the woman in the corner flat," meaning Zubaida.

That a woman can become so inextricably associated with her friend is a source of both pleasure and danger. Indeed, this is the reasoning behind husbands' and senior affines' disapproval of such relationships and their frequent exhortations to "visit less." This is also why women are so fervently solicitous of one another's reputations and why scandalous behavior on the part of a neighbor or friend is so devastating and unforgivable. Zubaida told me once of a friend with whom she used to go walking in a nearby park. To Zubaida's surprise, the woman took to reciting love poems during their walks, and Zubaida wondered, "Why, after all these years of marriage, is she interested in this?" Later, Zubaida learned that the husband had "gone bad"—started taking bribes, drinking, frequenting prostitutes. For revenge, Zubaida's friend took a lover. Now, she told me, whenever she sees this woman at the park, she tells Babar, "Let's go, for what if she comes and talks to me? She's such a bad woman, and people will think, oh, I'm bad, too—*ki, ek jaise hain*—they're just alike."

I asked what she would do if this woman came to her door.

"I'd say, 'What are you doing here? Go away! I hate you!'" Clearly, a friend's "bad deeds" are experienced as a personal betrayal.

The next morning, when I went to visit Zubaida, she was rushing around busily working. "A family boy has come from the *gaon*," she told me. "Babar's mother's sister's son" (*Babar ki khala ka beta*). The events and discussions of the day before were spinning through my mind, but our conversation seemed to skirt the issue. We talked about her *gaon* and how she misses it:

> "All the houses in the *mohalla* are connected," Zubaida reminisced, "so that women can find a path through them without ever going outside. There was no purdah except when we left the *mohalla*. And if we go to my *gaon*, you'll see that everyone will come to meet me. But Karachi, it is not like that. Here I feel I'm living where very dangerous people are living! I am afraid, and Babar has frightened me (*Babar ne mujhe daraya*). He told me, 'Zubaida, you have to be careful; think and understand before meeting with people. People are one way on the outside and another on the inside.' Even people we thought were our friends turned out to be bad people. That's why Babar has told me to meet less with Aliya. Because people think that she is not a good woman (*log samajhte hain ki woh achi aurat nahin*)."
>
> "Why?" I asked.

"Because she was friends with that woman, those criminals. And one day, Babar was going for prayers, and a neighbor man said to him, 'Your wife meets with that woman. She shouldn't; she's not *sharif.*' Babar said to me, 'You are not so wise, not clever; Aliya is very clever' (*tum itni aqlmand to nahin, chalak nahin; woh bohat chalak hai*)."

As Babar's words imply, women in general are viewed as less capable of reading the character, intent, and inner truth of people, and it is a view that women themselves cultivate. To say, "I'm not that wise" is to take up the protective idiom of childhood; my mistakes are the result of childish incompetence rather than deliberate wrongdoing. To be *chalak*, or clever, moreover, is to be smart (big brained) in a negatively valued way—to possess the power to manipulate, dissimulate, evade, and fool.

Despite this notion that women lack the necessary *aql* to successfully read the "hearts" of others, it is a labor that they perform all the time. As mothers, they read the character of potential brides and affines, looking to reject the *tez* (the cunning dissemblers) and keep the *sidhi* (the simple, the guileless, the transparent). It is a labor that they perform in the building as well: first, as they build networks of sociality within which the labor of coexistence, neighboring, and exchange can be safely (if not seamlessly) enacted; and next, as they seek out friends who will "share" with them, let them into their hearts (*dil ke andar jane dena*). This is the trickiest labor of all, for the very signs of sharing—an open heart, feelings expressed, secret truths revealed—can also allude to the one thing that must be avoided: loose morals.

This, I think, points to what is specific, and perhaps new, about the language of insides and outsides in buildings like the Shipyard. The discipline of reading others and making judgments about their character, status, and authority is not at all new; it has long been central to both moral and aesthetic practices of deference, in their various historical incarnations, and to the requisites of matchmaking. But the demand for—the possibility of—intimacy within this new space changes the terms, risks, and ends of this labor.

Her spirits low, Zubaida moved about the room, picking up clutter. "In the village, people can't do bad things and then flee. In Karachi, they do that. Oh," she sighed, "how people can live without a friend I just don't know. It's as if you can't get any peace (*sakun*)." Zubaida's words strikingly show that this labor of reading the insides of others—so necessary for protecting reputation, for "thinking and understanding before meeting with people"—has become an end in itself. The "sharing" of one's inner life, the reciprocal exchange of affective resources, contents, and truths, is both the means to social life and its somewhat illicit purpose. Indeed, what begins as a labor of purdah—a necessary skill to enable social congress without dishonor—then becomes a challenge to purdah by encouraging openness and the breaching of self-other boundaries. This explains women's contradictory responses to the emotional displays of others. Thus women who show weakness by crying or complaining are told to "be brave" (*bahadur bano*), to "be strong" (*mazbut*). But at the same time, women are clearly riveted by such displays and try to extend them, coaxing the distraught woman to say more, explain, reveal, even as they softly admonish her not to cry. Women are drawn to these guileless expressions of emotion and eagerly seek out the company of those with whom they have "shared" such breaches of self-boundaries.

Zubaida confided that she was in a quandary. Earlier that morning, Aliya had dropped off a stack of clothes to be sewn. Zubaida kept the clothing in a closet, taking it out to work on it only when her husband and brother-in-law were away.

> "I have no time for this, but I won't say no. She comes to my house when it's time for me to cook stew, and my *devar* sees her, and he gets angry and tells Babar. But she helps me, too," Zubaida added, in Aliya's defense.

Unwilling to sever exchange relations and desperately lonely for her friend, Zubaida willingly bore the added tension of exchange under conditions of secrecy, time constraint, and heightened risk; in other words, exchange could only proceed if women's routine efforts to avoid and endure male anger were intensified.

Some time after the scandal, Zubaida came to my door. Aliya had been complaining that Zubaida never visited anymore, so Zubaida, anxious to maintain their friendship but nervous about the consequences of such a visit, decided to bring a chaperone. "Come, let's go visit that *moti* (fatty),"[9] she said, and we climbed the stairs together to the fourth floor. In the end, it was a visit like any other. We drank tea and had a few laughs. Aliya and Zubaida talked about their busy schedules and how "tense" they were. Aliya treated us both to her famous hair massage treatment, and we went on our way.

During those weeks in the wake of scandal, it struck me that reading for the insides of others and tentatively allowing oneself to be similarly read were absolute conditions for neighbor exchange. Close kin and extended family members may not need to be "read" in the same manner, for they are "known" by virtue of the fact that they share one's fate in honor. Non-kin neighbors, of course, do not. The sorrow, perplexity, and lack of peace that Zubaida expressed at the interruption of this neighbor exchange—"living without a friend"—convinced me that this reading had itself become exchange's somewhat covert purpose. More than this, it seems that this halting and uncertain intimacy in the form of confessional knowledge is part and parcel of this singular subject, newly outfitted with "nerves" and "feelings" that must be exchanged or "shared" in order to be recognized. Female friendships in this specific civic space were at once the goal, the side effect, and the training ground for this particular peace and the labor through which it was garnered.

In conclusion, I will again remind readers of the conflicted nature of this subject, emergent here at the interstices of potent contradictions: the imperatives of *sharm* and purdah that dictate reticence, silence, secrecy, and inviolability, and the conditions of local exchange that hinge on knowing your neighbors and being known in return. The tension that women labor to hold in suspense emerges not only from the contradictions generated between ethnic and civic discourses (or between an ethos of egalitarianism and the realities of hierarchy) but also from the transformed conditions of self-other knowledge—knowledge unhinged from the shared fates of clan or community and contingent, instead, upon labors both dangerous and sublime.

6

Conclusion
Emotion and the Political Actor

Throughout these pages, I have labored under the assumption that there is a meaningful relationship between emotion and the political actor. We are heir to an intellectual, Enlightenment tradition that has pondered this relationship in scores of treatises, inquiries, essays, and prolegomena. How has this relationship been imagined?

A central tenet of Enlightenment thought held that we could look inside the individual for answers to the how or why of social, moral, or political order. Exemplifying what Émile Durkheim decried as "empirical monism," John Locke reduced moral sentiment to the natural dictates of individual sensation—pleasure directing us to the good, pain protecting us from the bad. Essentially egoistic, self-interested passions were at the root of even our most altruistic or social actions. This found resonance in later Freudian notions of emotion as serving a "signal function," alerting the organism to situations of threat or danger.[1] David Hume struggled to reconcile a similarly atomistic, individualist philosophy with his observations on "social passions" or "virtues." In contrast to Locke, Hume concluded that benevolent actions were positive proof of prior benevolent sentiments; moral passions beget moral order.

Thomas Hobbes, in his infamous *Leviathan*, also sought the origins of political order inside the individual; in his hypothetical state of nature, man, in violent, competitive pursuit of self-interest, lives in perpetual "Feare of Death" and thus willingly sacrifices his liberty for the peace that king and contract secure. For Montesquieu, human passions propel or set in motion distinct political orders—despotism moved by fear, monarchies by honor, republics by virtue—but the relationship is less automatic than ideal typical. Such orders require these underlying emotions for effective governance, and in their absence they will remain "imperfect."

While Enlightenment thinkers largely sought explanations for moral or political order in human nature and natural sentiment, modern social thought turns this proposition on its head. For Durkheim, moral sentiments follow from society. He wrote: "It is not a simple juxtaposition of individuals who bring an intrinsic morality with them, but rather man is a moral being only because he lives in society, since morality consists in being solidary with a group and varying with that solidarity" (1933: 399). Social, benevolent sentiments follow naturally from social formations: "Wherever there are societies, there is altruism, because there is solidarity" (94). The question, here, is not how atomized individuals come to feel bonded, and morally bound, in a group, but how the group creates individuals and individual sentiments (or, in Durkheim's terms, how the group transfers its passions into individual consciousness).

Freud and psychoanalytic thought, for the most part, return us to the individual and human nature. Herein, it is Eros—libidinal, sexual drive—that holds the group together (Freud 1959: 31). An erotic drive toward an object (a leader, an idea) gets diverted on the way to satisfaction and is transformed from sexual desire to "aim-inhibited" Eros, or love. Love for the object generates identification with others in the group who share this same relationship with the object. Altruism is a function of the psychic replacement of the ego-ideal (self-image) by the love object.[2]

With obvious exceptions, the intellectual legacy we have inherited has overwhelmingly cast peace or political community as secured through, or expressed via, sentiments of love, altruism, or benevolence, whether these emerge from egoistic impulses or social passions or forces. (This is an idea we will have to complicate below.) For Freud and Durkheim, the fact of society or groupness explains internal harmony.[3] The problem of political order or of peace, then, can only be whether or not people in a given context constitute a "society." Sentiments of altruism, benevolence, or love operate purely within the boundaries of the group or moral community. Using the church as an example, Freud reminds us that "those people who do not belong to the community of believers, who do not love him [Christ], and whom he does not love, stand outside this tie. Therefore, a religion, even if it calls itself the religion of love, must be hard and unloving to those who do not belong to it" (Freud 1959: 39).

Indeed, to those for whom the fact of society or groupness suffices to create solidarity, morality, or love, the problem then becomes not only how societies come to be constituted but what emotions pertain in relations outside or between groups. Literature on nations and nationalism has noted, with Freud, the tendency for nations to generate sentiments of love, sacrifice, benevolence, and kinship for and between its own members—but hatred, fear, or suspicion for those Others who lie outside its borders. Never mind that intergroup or external relations are as often characterized by mutual trust, respect, and pleasurable congress as they are by antagonism, hostility, and dread. If groupness explains peace, then it also explains war. In this line of thinking, the "conditions of possibility" of violence and those of peace must be seen as identical.

In all these accounts, emotion's relation to the political actor is largely naturally occurring. Emotions either spring naturally from group formations or the natural (and instrumental) emotions of individuals give rise to, or underpin, these social and political orders/groups. There is little sense that emotion may be a product of human action or agency in the world (through relational practices of interpretation, negotiation, and management), even as it is a site of power and constraint (not to mention repression).[4] Similarly lacking is an appreciation for the culturally and historically variable nature of emotions themselves—in terms of "emotion talk" (Harré and Finlay-Jones 1986) and the feeling states such talk purports to represent.

My contribution to this field of thought has been to attempt to link women's labors of emotional regulation with the everyday peace that prevailed in the apartment building. Such an approach is only possible in the wake of extensive work in cultural anthropology that has framed emotion as a domain of cultural construction as much as somatic experience.[5] I have also benefited from those anthropologists who have struggled not to efface the specificity of emotion or reduce it to cognition or construction. William Reddy and Unni Wikan, in particular, have attempted to theorize emotions as reflecting both cultural and natural/biological imperatives. Thus Reddy describes emotion as "neither purely natural nor purely culturally constructed but, rather, as a domain of 'management' and effortful navigation in which the individual, guided by cultural norms and expectations, attempts to achieve or enhance sanctioned states of feeling" (2000: 113). In his account, as in Wikan's (1990), we do not create affect so much as manage it, and this domain of management is where culture, convention, or power comes in.

For Reddy, the management of emotion plays out largely through speech acts which he terms "emotives"—first-person statements (like "I am angry") that describe, imperfectly, internal states; unfold relationally in culturally meaningful "emotion scenarios"; and have a self-exploring or self-altering effect (Reddy 2000: 116). Cultural and political agendas put forward specific "styles" of emotion management that set limits on the type and the intensity of emotions that socially differentiated subjects may express in prescribed contexts. Reddy locates the possibility of political agency in the necessary failure of emotives to represent emotion—a failure that explains both the plasticity of the human subject and the limits of this plasticity. It is not basic emotions that rebel against cultural constraint but a basically emoting subject whose inner feelings never quite line up with external demands.

While I am sympathetic to Reddy's efforts to restore agency to the subject of emotion, I am reluctant to locate this agency in some inner biological residuum that can take on power. Such a formulation is problematic on numerous counts, not the least of which is the alarming way in which it implicitly equates culture with constraint. Wikan similarly seems to find culture disabling. She writes, "The directing and constraining power of customs may interfere with the realization of personal goals and wishes to varying degrees in different societies. In Bali, I have the impression that cultural injunctions are often experienced as a straitjacket that constricts the innermost recesses of 'me' through the actions of 'them'" (1990: 31). Wikan's analysis of women in Bali struggling to manage powerful cultural norms of happy, cheerful self-presentation with powerful sentiments of grief and loss is compelling but ultimately obfuscating. While the imperative to "look happy" is cast as clearly cultural, the sentiments and relationships that generate grief and sorrow are cast as natural and universal.

To reduce the richness of cultural meaning to a kind of sanctioning "they" is a gross impoverishment of what culture means. Such a perspective, less explicit but equally at play in Reddy's account, also returns us to the Enlightenment understandings of natural morality with which we began. Emotion or emotional life is taken to represent or "signal" the individual's authentic interests and highest good, while custom, society, or culture emerges as error (Locke), artifice (Rousseau), repression (Freud), or constraint (Wikan).

To my mind, agency does not lie in some biological residuum, any more than desired ends—the states we wish to be liberated to—lie in some a priori, natural authenticity. Women in the Shipyard may want to be free to re-create a familiar world of female sociality, just as U.S. women may long to fall in love and get married. Both of these are cultural ends, and both are subject to a host of constraints that render their happy actualization fraught with contradiction—not the least of which is the Foucauldian reminder that what we want is itself shaped by power. Freedom does not lie in the triumph of our instinctual or so-envisioned precultural selves winning the day. The good life is culturally defined, hence women's significant efforts to create and preserve female sociality in a new space, with new actors, under new conditions of risk. Of course, nonconformity exists because other discourses of "having a life" are available (e.g., the modern, conjugal, romantic couple; the unmarried, devoted daughter caring for her parents; the religious devotee) and because these cultural discourses are themselves internally contradictory and thus manipulable. Agency emerges in the interstices of these contradictions in the intersubjective moment of navigation, not according to the subject's authentic desires (which are always multiple and conflicting) or unmediated will.

It is by virtue of these contradictions and their navigation that conjugal solidarity and companionship, largely devalued and discouraged in many South Asian contexts, became more of an option for Ruhi. While conjugality may challenge male patrilineal solidarity and generational hierarchies, it also fulfills certain requisites of the sociality that generally prevails in extended or joint family contexts (and which life in the Shipyard rendered less accessible): it keeps women at home and keeps it all "in the family." The converse was true for other women; the normatively muted character of conjugality encouraged women to seek out substitutes for the sociality they would have shared in other nonnuclear contexts, especially the peer group of sisters-in-law and classificatory sisters-in-law (the wives of husband's father's brothers' sons), enabling them to turn "outside" and to redefine that "outside" as comprising a kind of moral community.

Similarly, if I may revisit the central argument developed in the previous chapter, I would suggest that women in the Shipyard are not so much willfully rebelling against an emotion norm that forbids self-disclosure and "sharing" (outside of very specific contexts) as they are navigating between two competing and intersecting cultural plots or two sets of complex circumstances: in one, it is not nice to mix much, to reveal oneself, to confess, to be known; in the other, it is a desired and expected cultural end that one find pleasure and satisfaction—a life—in the company of women (which, in the Shipyard, means one's neighbors). Knowing your neighbors, and being similarly known, as virtuous with good and beautiful hearts is essential to this sociality (in a way that it is not in other contexts, where kin and clan are one's companions, whom you "know" by virtue of a shared fate in honor). Between these two imperatives of secrecy and knowledge, shame and companionship, new possibilities emerge.

The unfortunate notion of culture as constraint that runs through modern and Enlightenment scholarship alike not only impedes our ability to understand the interplay between emotion and political agency; it also fundamentally impairs our ability to theorize peace and moral order. This reductive and disparaged view of culture underpins our reading of the peacemaker, altruist, or rescuer as a lone, individuated, unenculturated figure. All that is good and redemptive, liberating and capable of "saying no" to power is somehow precultural, issuing from some private, inchoate biological residuum—or from an equally natural, transhistorical "will" or "strength of character." That societies may have *created* redemptive, moral, altruistic possibilities—that available narratives for the care of strangers can have normative force—is somehow unimaginable or is taken to diminish our heroes and their acts of sacrifice. But only if we view culture as making automatons can we view it as demeaning to the hero to view him or her as acting according to cherished cultural values (of sacrifice, nurture, etc.).

Such a view has also meant that we have largely failed to subject these acts—of peace, altruism, and rescue—to anthropological analysis: asking when they become available alternatives and exploring the emotion lexicon by virtue of which they "make sense." But an anthropological approach need not—indeed, must not—preclude questions about the individual: Why did this person take up the sword and that one offer sanctuary? Just as we cannot look only inside individuals (or human nature) to explain peace and rescue, neither can we look only at structures, master narratives, or scripture. The complex sets of variegated circumstances that emerge from, and constitute, everyday life mean that this is a matter of on the ground labor, as we witnessed in the Shipyard: the historical particulars that throw women back on their (non-kin) neighbors; the cultural expectation and desired end of female sociality; the perceived dangers of male anger; the contradictions between ethnic and nationalist visions of community; the demands of purdah but the necessity of new forms of self-other knowledge; all these social, historical, and cultural circumstances inform the specific principles, forms, and emotional sensibilities that propel women's labors of peace—not to mention the character of the peace that they labor to produce.

We must also recognize that peace and rescue may not always be secured through, or characterized by, sentiments of love, benevolence, pity, or attachment. As we have seen in the Shipyard, male anger and the fear of this anger were central to women's local peacemaking efforts. In a similar fashion, the "anthropology of peace and nonviolence" (Howell and Willis 1989; Sponsel and Gregor 1994) has demonstrated the way in which witchcraft beliefs, fear, opposition, and antagonism can in fact underpin peaceful coexistence, generating what Gregor (1994) has labeled a "separative" peace (in contrast to a "sociative" peace characterized by amity, exchange, and intergroup engagement). We must also entertain the possibility that peace is not always or exclusively the product of clear intent; it can emerge as the by-product of other ends that subjects pursue or, conceivably, from practice that is essentially uncalculated. For example, peace in the Shipyard may be, in part, a *by-product* of women's efforts to re-create a familiar female sociality under new conditions of risk (which entailed navigating contradictory discourses of community and holding them in suspense, through a new lexicon of emotion management and bodily discipline).

To recap, we have seen how Enlightenment thinkers (and their heirs) sought the origins of morality in human nature. We have also seen modern sociology's rejoinder that the origins of morality lie in society and social forms. What has dropped out of this equation is violence and its putative origins yet again in that familiar bogey "human nature." It is not my intention to participate in the quest for violence's origins (other than to refute its status as natural attribute, biological instinct, or propensity). My specific interest here is the role that "natural" violence and its management are seen to play in the emergence of civilization, meaning, or social life.

For Freud, the irrational predations of the crowd were nothing more than "the manifestations of th[e] unconscious, in which all that is evil in the human mind is contained as a predisposition" (1959: 9). Violent impulses, linked to the libidinal energies of Thanatos, the "death instinct" (or the essentially egoistic drives of Eros, or sexual aggression), need to be redirected, repressed, or sublimated in order for civilization—and peaceful social existence—to emerge. But civilization, thought, and meaning are not imaginable *without* this violent, libidinal energy. Violence is at the root of creative social production.

The essential creativity, or "generativity," of violence is at the heart of René Girard's well-known anthropological work, *Violence and the Sacred*. Sacrificial violence is socially necessary, he contends, in order to vent natural, violent impulses which, uncontrolled, beget "an interminable, infinitely repetitive process" of vengeful reciprocity (1972: 14). The role of ritual violence, or "impartial justice," is "to 'purify' violence, that is, to 'trick' violence into spending itself on victims whose death will provoke no reprisals" (36). Scapegoats, like ethnic minorities, become "surrogate victims" around whom (or by virtue of whose destruction) internal strife and reciprocal violence can give way to social accord. Peace, here, emerges in the wake of spent creativity—on the tail of this "generative act" of violent unanimity.

It is not unusual for peace to appear as the poor relation of social theory, a default, or disparaged "everyday life" offset by the creative, generative, spontaneous forces of violent conflict. This, in fact, is a hallmark of liberalist thought, the opposition between the dull, rule-bound drudgery of quotidian existence and the dynamism of "genius." Thus Max Weber framed charisma and charismatic individuals as revolutionary forces in history, distinct from the pedestrian routines of household, work life, and bureaucracy. Durkheim proposed a notion of collective effervescence to convey the sporadic, spontaneous, public, creative generation of social values and their transfer into individual consciousness—in contrast to the dull tribal wanderings of everyday life. Victor Turner similarly put forward a notion of *communitas*, that creative liminality that momentarily escapes the everyday demands and hierarchies of "structure." In all these accounts, everyday life is denigrated as a kind of passive enactment, lacking in creative, productive, or emancipatory force.[6]

This framework is clearly inadequate for understanding everyday life and its relation to peace in the Shipyard. Peace cannot be said to emerge in the wake of spent creativity. On the contrary, it is the product of relentless labor—in this case, labors of emotional regulation (individual and collective) carried out by women. My position here is perhaps best illustrated with reference to the electrical fire with which I concluded chapter 2. The fire, and the intense sociality, solidarity, and unity that emerged in its wake, has all the drama of Durkheim's collective effervescence or Turner's *communitas*. It was the one occasion of the entire year when I witnessed men engaging in the same sorts of intensive interactions with neighbors as women routinely did: offering, helping, giving. In some accounts, this would be the generative moment from which all other possibilities emerged. In contrast to the tedious drudgery of everyday routine, this would solidify a group feeling that could then carry on in a trace manner into the everyday.

I believe it is precisely the contrary, for it is women's creative, routine management of emotion and their transfer of the goodwill of the household to others in the building that enabled this "spontaneous" expression of unity. The group was imaginable because it had already been imagined. We cannot understand everyday life in the Shipyard as women's rote enactment of the meanings, feelings, and social forms created in the (more masculine oriented) moment of crisis/*communitas*/collective effervescence. This diminishes, yet again, everyday life, not to mention women's work. The repercussions of women's labors of peace must be reckoned with more faith.

To reiterate: Peace is not the automatic endpoint of natural feelings of love or benevolence, nor does the fact of society automatically translate into altruism. Peace is the product of effortful labor, in which both ends and means are culturally constituted. Emotion figures not as peace's underlying principle, nor as its necessary effect, but as a site of relational practice, negotiation, interpretation, and management. With this framework in mind, we can retell the story of peace in the Shipyard in slightly different terms.

In chapter 3, I attempted to draw connections between women's confusion over the norms of reciprocity that were to govern this new dwelling space and transformed understandings of "tension." I have described an emergent "ethic of suspense" that linked practices of generalized reciprocity with the ability to bear in tension, or hold in suspense, contradictory principles of social organization (nation and ethnic group, hierarchy and equality). We can see how kin-based forms of exchange were being brought to bear on these neighbor/stranger relations. The informal, uncalculated character of generalized reciprocity is, after all, usually reserved for close kin and intimates. But this is not to say that it is sentiments of close kinship—attachment, love, nurture—that underlay this exchange and the peace it produced. On the contrary, treating stranger-neighbors as kin depended not on sentiments of love and attachment but on the willingness and ability to bear the tension of contradictory cultural categories of belonging; to put it another way, applying principles of exchange normally reserved for close kin in this new space, with the "wrong" people, generates contradictions that must be held in suspense. This labor of irresolution involves the relational narrativization of "tension" in which, to use Reddy's terms, the emotive "I am tense" serves not just to describe but to alter or construct "tension" as an inner state—one with redemptive, stoic, burden-well-borne connotations. Through these intersubjective emotives and the embodied, pragmatic exchanges within which they unfold, tension is transformed from an external property of the physical and ideational universe into a psychic, bodily, and collective burden. Social, cultural, intergroup tension is thus managed via the bodies and subjectivities of women.

I have proposed, moreover, that this picture of "tension sustained" can radically challenge our notion of peace as emergent in the wake of violent catharsis. While peace is usually seen to follow from a release of tension, either through violent explosion, sublimation, or "conflict resolution," this example links peace to tension's *maintenance*. This finds resonance in object relations theories that distinguish need-based tension—sexual desire or hunger: tensions with teleologies—from the tension of autonomous object interest. Tension, without discharge, is central to the subjective emergence of the object as a subject in its own right, and thus, at least metaphorically, it is a condition of social engagement, self-other knowledge, and peace.

Moreover, as I discussed in chapter 4, local notions of male anger were fundamental to women's efforts at peacemaking in the building. There is a paradoxical sense in which this cultural notion of anger as an inevitable and even celebrated aspect of masculine virility (which is central to group status) makes women's (and men's) lives more dangerous, even as it promotes complex ethics of restraint and containment. On the one hand, the specter of male anger in the Shipyard clearly contributed to a "separative" peace that promoted distance, caution, and avoidance between potential (male) antagonists. On the other hand, this potential anger was a focal point for women's collective lives and labors. Equally paradoxical is the way in which informal exchange or visiting in the Shipyard risked male anger for the individual woman, but simultaneously managed it for the collective, by transferring the goodwill of the family from household to household. Indeed, by virtue of their embodied and affective labors of sustaining sociocultural tension and managing male anger (in large part by containing it in the household), women were able to serve as men's (or the family's) mediators in this local space.

As I have suggested, the specific peace that Shipyard women labored to produce required the negotiation of contradictory discourses of emotion management—so that, for example, one must remain private, secret, closed, to demonstrate shame, but one must know one's neighbors and be known by them if social life (and its peacemaking dimensions) is to be realized safely and with discrimination. Since neighbors are not kin or extended kin who are known by virtue of sharing a common fate in honor, knowing them requires knowing their character, their "insides," their "hearts," anticipating and making judgments about their motives, morals, attitudes, and "true feelings." Careful readings rely largely on inference, but they also aim to elicit confession or revelation. Revelation, however, can allude to the very thing that purdah and *sharm* forbid: loose morals or shamelessness. Similar conflicts are visible in discussions of male anger, where competing cultural discourses of anger—one celebratory, one reproved—render women's practices problematic, no matter what.

Throughout this work, I have alluded to the psychic cost of women's peacemaking labors: taking on and bearing the tension of sociocultural contradiction; managing and enduring male anger; the high stakes of reading for the "insides" of others. In chapter 5, I suggested that it is the possibility of intimacy, in this reconfigured space of female sociality, which makes these labors worthwhile. In some sense, peace in the apartment building may be a side effect of, or necessary condition for, the pursuit of this specific cultural end.

Keeping this "motive" in mind prevents the reduction of our story of the apartment building to one of the sweep of modern Western institutions and their homogenizing cultural effects. For example, the apparent proliferation of new emotion terms in Karachi (tense, like, feel, mind, share) should not be taken to reflect some uniform modernity, where increased differentiation leads to an explosion in the discrimination or variety of emotional expression. I see it, rather, as the recruitment of newly available emotional styles in order to bring forward powerful cultural ends: a life lived in the company of women, in the transformed context of increased (culturally perceived) risk (loss of reputation).

On a final note, I have attempted throughout the text to reconfigure the *zenana* as a site fully permeated by more macropolitical forces and, more crucially, as a site in which women's political subjectivity and agency is both possible and articulable (with reference not simply to gender hierarchy but also to ethnic and national enmities and solidary relations). At the same time, it is clear that the very conditions of emergence of political agency within the *zenana* are the iteration and embodiment of gender difference and subjection. In linking these two concerns, it is possible to go yet further and suggest that in this cultural and historical moment, the symbolic and pragmatic conditions of possibility of peace—as well as those of violence—are irretrievably gendered. By implication, the gendered character of ethnic and national movements and conflicts—in South Asia and beyond—requires urgent attention, as do the gendered systems of everyday peace that contain but also support them.

The everyday sociality that prevailed in the Shipyard constitutes one form of peace, and if anything, our inquiries can show how impacted that word is, how culturally and historically variable, how contingent, how replete with possible means, meanings, and manifestations. I am reminded of a phrase in Amitav Ghosh's *The Shadow Lines*, where the narrator, on pondering the "madness" of riots, refers to "that indivisible sanity that binds people to each other independent of their governments" (1988: 230). I have long appreciated that line and the sentiments behind it. But it is my belief that we cannot afford to view this "sanity" as indivisible or prior, inaccessible or outside of the purview of analytic inquiry. The nature of this sanity or this peace—its forms of authority, narrative properties, sensibilities, and contingencies; the energies we employ to sustain it; our faith in it, and our utter stupefaction at its collapse—deserves the full force of our attention.

Glossary

aql (ʿaql). Wisdom, reason
baji (bājī). Elder sister
batin (bāṭin). Inner, hidden, secret
bhabi (bhābī). Brother's wife
bhai (bhāʾī). Brother
biradari (birādarī). Lineage, kin group, extended family
bura manna (burā mānnā). To take offense
burqa (burqaʿ). A garment that covers a woman's face and body; a veil
chapati (ćapātī). Unleavened flatbread
chowkidar (ćaukīdār). Watchman, guard, or gatekeeper
daku (ḍākū). Bandit
dastarkhan (dastar-khwān). A cloth spread on the floor, on which food and dishes
    are placed
devar (devar). Husband's younger brother
devrani (devrānī). Husband's younger brother's wife
dupatta (ḍupaṭṭa). A long cloth or scarf that women wear across their shoulders
    or over their hair
faqir (faqīr). Religious devotee, ascetic, holy man
gaon (gāṅʾoṅ). Village
ghair (gair). Outsider, stranger
ghussa (guṣṣa). Anger; rage
hadith (ḥadīṣ). Acts and sayings of the prophet Mohammad
ham sayah (ham sāyah). Neighbor; under the same shade
hijab (ḥijāb). Veil
Holi (Holī). Hindu festival in which participants sprinkle each other with colored
    powder
ishq (ʿishq). Excessive love; passion
jahalat (jahālat). Ignorance; barbarism
jethani (jeṭhānī). Husband's elder brother's wife
jora (joṛa). Suit of clothes
kash (kash). Anxious, harassed, perplexed
khandan (khandān). Family, household, lineage
khichao (khićāʾo). State of being stretched, drawn out, extended
khushi (khushī). Happiness

kurta (*kurta*). Long shirt or tunic

mandir (*mandir*). Temple; dwelling place of Hindu ascetics

mardana (*mardāna*). Pertaining to men; men's space

masi (*māsī*). Mother's sister

mastani (*mastānī*). Female religious ecstatic

mazar (*mazār*). Shrine of a saint

mithai (*miṭhā'ī*). Candy; sweets

mohalla (*maḥalla*). City or town quarter

nafs (*nafs*). Bodily desire; the lower soul

purdah (*parda*). Screen, veil, curtain; the veiling and seclusion of women

rakhwala (*rakhwālā*). Caretaker

rishta (*rishta*). Relationship, connection, kinship

riwaj (*riwāj*). Custom, practice, fashion

roti (*roṭī*). Bread

shalwar kameez (*shalwār qamīṣ*). A suit comprised of loose trousers and a long tunic

shariat (*sharī'at*). Muslim religious law

sharif (*sharīf*). Noble, refined

sharm (*sharm*). Shame, modesty

tannao (*tannā'o*). Tension; state of being pulled, stretched

tez (*tez*). Sharp, cunning, swift

uljhan (*uljhan*). Anxiety, perplexity, uneasiness

zahir (*ẓāhir*). Manifest, external, evident

zat (*ẕāt*). Caste, lineage group

zenana (*zanāna*). Women's quarters

zina (*zinā*). Fornication; adultery

Notes

1. Introduction

1. See, e.g., Appadurai 1996, 1998; Aretxaga 1997; Daniel 1996; Das et al. 2000; Devisch 1995; Feldman 1991; Jeganathan 1997; Malkki 1995; Tambiah 1996.

2. At the time of the 1998 census, 48.52 percent of Karachi's population was Muhajir/Urdu-speaking, 13.94 percent Punjabi, 11.42 percent Pathan, and 7.22 percent Sindhi.

3. In *sharif* national discourse, ethnic identifications are also represented as remnants of a feudal, medieval past, Muhajir identity thus becoming equated in popular discourse with modernity.

4. This policy—known as One Unit—was in effect from 1955 to 1970.

5. The equation between "Muhajir identity" and "*sharif* discourse" is a simplification that I will complicate in the chapters that follow.

6. I wish to note here, for the record, that all my informants' names have been changed in order to protect their confidentiality. Furthermore, I have changed certain building and street names (and other minor geographical details) in order to preserve the anonymity of the field site.

7. Of course, some of these social forms—notably "ethnicity"—are modern products. Furthermore, it has been argued (Chandra 1977) that in some ways urban enclaves are vastly *more* homogeneous than their village counterparts.

8. Laws in Pakistan favor tenants over landlords, and it is close to impossible to evict someone. This is one reason why landlords prefer foreign tenants and "multinationals," because they are seen as less permanent dwellers.

9. Urdu is the national language of Pakistan and is actively promoted by the state (over the vernacular languages favored by many Pakistanis, especially in rural areas) to replace English as the lingua franca and language of government and administration. Many Pakistanis view Urdu as a foreign language, arguing that it is not "native" to the area that is now Pakistan and that its only native speakers are Muhajirs. Nevertheless, Urdu is a central feature of dominant Pakistani nationalism. "Urdu-medium" (i.e., educated in Urdu, rather than vernacular or English-medium school systems) marks a boundary that separates Karachi's middle class from the uneducated or rural population and from the Western educated, English-speaking elite.

10. The government holds a lottery each year whose winners are sent for Hajj—the ritual pilgrimage to Mecca—at state expense.

11. Readers familiar with South Asian Muslim names may protest that Iqbal is a "man's" name. However, many communities in Pakistan—particularly Punjabi Christians and Pashto speakers, but also Sindhis—give women "men's" names, sometimes adding Bibi (Lady) or another qualifier to the end of it, but just as often not. I have tried to preserve this aspect of my informant's name in my choice of pseudonym.

12. This is a reference to a genre of eighteenth-century Urdu poetry known as *shahr ashob*, or the ruined city, which lamented the decline of Delhi and its urban, educated, "noble" Muslim class.

13. Aga Khani, or Ismaili, refers to a liberal Shia sect of Islam.

14. Suit, or *jora*, refers to the ubiquitous *shalwar kameez*, which I describe in more detail in chapter 2.

15. Literally, everyone is our own, meaning they are all "our people."

16. "Sahib" is a respectful mode of address for men used throughout Pakistan. It is roughly equivalent to "Sir" or "Mr."

17. In cases where other neighbors and I referred to a woman teknonymically—through reference to husband or child, e.g., "Hina's mother"—I have sought to represent that in my choice of pseudonyms.

18. Strikes in Karachi aim to stop all activity in the city. Thus stores that remain open in defiance of the strike risk being looted or burned; drivers who venture onto the street risk similar retaliatory action.

19. By leaving behind tape recorder and notebook, I intended no deception. My informants were well aware of my scholarly objectives, but in the absence of such formal, distancing props, these objectives became part of routine visits and neighborly interactions.

2. A Day in the Life

1. The reasons women gave for bathing children in the morning as opposed to the evening had to do with the night chill and the dangers of going to bed with a wet head. But a Pakistani friend alluded to beliefs in supernatural child-snatching beings like tree spirits that came out at night and were attracted to clean-smelling children and repelled by dirty ones.

2. Most of the women driving cars in Karachi are quite elite, and among less elite families that own cars, one usually sees men driving. Zubaida, however, insisted that she would be free to go shopping and to visit relatives in the city if only they owned a car, for her husband would give her permission to drive to such places, but not to take public transportation.

3. On special occasions like weddings, women would often wear *sari*s or other

wedding attire like *shararas* or *ghararas*. Very few women other than Hindus or Parsis would wear *saris* on a daily basis. Those who did were almost invariably Muhajir or even more recent immigrants from India. Women's dress marked so many things: adulthood vs. childhood, respectable vs. shameless, and modern vs. retrograde (not to mention Hindu vs. Muslim or Pakistani vs. Indian). That little girls could wear dresses and pants served to further demarcate the significance of their abandonment at puberty. Women were risking their reputations if they donned pants, skirts, or even sleeveless *shalwar kameezes* or *dupatta*-less ensembles. At the same time, women who wore *hijab* (headscarf) or *burqa* (full body covering) risked being viewed as relics in the city, even while their attire could be deemed proper from a small town or village perspective.

4. Pakistani society is usually presented to the outside world as highly status conscious, characterized by a kind of castelike hierarchy (Lindholm 1995; Werbner 1990, 1995) and an obsession with "besting" one's neighbors (Grima 1992). The actions and words of my neighbors, nevertheless, bespeak a definite discomfort with obvious practices of ranking. Some of this awkwardness is rooted in the fact that people bring a widely divergent set of expectations about social relationships with them to this new context: patron-client relations (Barth 1959); the castelike complementarity and rank of village labor-exchange systems (Eglar 1960; Werbner 1990); the deferential, hierarchical elevation of others common to *sharif* values (Metcalf 1990); and transformations in the meaning of *sharif* itself, from noble lineage to middle-class respectability. Suffice it to say that in the Shipyard, there is an express ethos of egalitarianism that is repeatedly offset by the expectation and assumption of rank.

5. Sheheryar's mother is Aga Khani; his father's family, and Sheheryar himself, are straight Shia (also referred to as twelver Shia).

6. The literature on nationalism is both mammoth and well known. In my thinking about these specific issues, I am most indebted to the work of Anderson 1983, Gellner 1983, and Hobsbawm 1990.

3. Tension

1. Sahlins (1972) has argued that reciprocity, the moral norm that governs exchange, "is a whole class of exchanges, a continuum of forms" (29) ranging from "generalized reciprocity," the informal exchange between intimates, in which the expectation of a return is "weak" and "indefinite," to "balanced reciprocity," a more exacting exchange between allied but not "close" parties, to "negative reciprocity" or "self-interested seizure" (29). The nature of the exchange and its return thus makes statements about—and constructs—the nature of the relationship between the trading parties. As Marilyn Strathern states, "Things move between people as encoded relationships" (1984: 44).

2. *Hadith* refers to the collected sayings and acts of the prophet Mohammad.

3. *Nari* is actually the Sindhi term for "tap"; the Urdu term is *nal* or *nalka*.

4. On another front, in the wake of sectarian violence in Karachi and other areas, leaders of the current military regime called on citizens to live together as neighbors by sacrificing their ethnic, sectarian, and other "parochial" commitments. Wrote a *Dawn* reporter, "President Rafique Tarar and Chief Executive General Pervez Musharraf have called on the nation to forge unity in their ranks and reaffirm their pledge to sacrifice everything for the cause of Islam and the country." (Of course, the equation of serving the nation with serving Islam should not be overlooked.) Drawing on the images of Karbala and the martyrdom of Imam Hussain, Musharraf urged citizens to "do away with all linguistic, sectarian, regional, and community differences and serve the country" (*Dawn Internet Edition*, 15 April 2000). Becoming neighbors, then, is in many ways about becoming national.

5. There are two Eid celebrations in the Islamic calendar year: one to celebrate the end of the month of fasting (Ramzan) and one to celebrate Abraham's willingness to sacrifice his son Ishmael at God's request.

6. The tenth of Moharrum (Ashurah) commemorates the martyrdom of the Prophet's grandson, Husain, at the Battle of Karbala.

7. Marriage practices in Pakistan are dramatically heterogeneous, varying not only from region to region but also from family to family. From an anthropological perspective, a main imperative of marriage exchange is to manage the problem of "bride-giving"—bride-givers always being subordinate to bride-takers. Numerous marriage practices common in Pakistan—particularly *biradari* endogamy and dowry—have been described as separate strategies designed to manage the same problem (Eglar 1960; Werbner 1990). Endogamy and a corresponding rejection of dowry could constitute a denial of exchange: "We don't give dowry because we're one family." Dowry, on the other hand, may mark the bride-giver's attempt to recuperate social status by showering the groom's family with lavish, unreciprocated gifts. The picture is complicated, however, by the not infrequent confluence of both strategies in the same exchange. Thus even those marriages that are endogamous—where there is no "bride-giver," so to speak—are often embedded in exchange practices (like dowry) that proceed as if they are sided and hierarchical.

8. These terms are taken directly from Webster's definitions of "tense" and "tension."

9. Freud contended that the origins of neuroses lay in the anxiety created by "unconsummated excitation," where "libidinal excitation is aroused but not satisfied, not employed." The subject is "unable to control this libidinal excitation[;] *he cannot hold it in suspense* but changes it into anxiety" (1965: 73; italics added).

10. Personal communication. The term *tannao*, however, is not in common usage in Karachi and would undoubtedly be deemed too elite or obscure for the

majority of my non-Urdu-speaking informants. My thanks to Kamran Ali for this point.

11. Indian Muslim social reform movements of the nineteenth century marked a response to British colonialism and Muslim disenfranchisement. "Reform" upheld the philosophy of social change through internal, individual, and community development or self-improvement. Important nineteenth-century reformers who concerned themselves with women's conduct and education included Maulana Ashraf Ali Thanawi, Sayid Mumtaz Ali, Nazir Ahmad Dehlavi, and Altaf Husain Hali. It should be noted that these reform efforts developed largely in North India and other Urdu-speaking centers, thus arguably speaking more to Muhajir heritage and dominant Pakistani national imaginaries than to Pakistani provincial or rural histories.

12. "*Sindhi log to masjid nahin jate, mazar jate hain, aur wahan bura kam karte hain: charas,* male prostitution, dancing girls; *mazhabi log to nahin.*"

13. Oscar Verkaaik (1999) argues that a kind of ludic play with ambiguity is characteristic of much of his Muhajir informants' political activity but that extreme violence seems to forbid such play.

4. Anger

1. The literal translation is "she did a wrong thing."

2. The vocabulary of *nafs* and *aql,* with its moral indictment of anger and emotional display or excess in general, has broad salience in a range of Islamic contexts. Of Iraqi society, Eickelman writes, "In almost all social situations a respectable man is expected to show reason and self-control" (1981: 194). For Morocco, see Rosen 1980; for Iran, see Beeman 1976.

3. This is a very condensed and simplified account of what is, of course, a complex and contested field of kinship hierarchies. Because of the preference for clan endogamy, affinal kin are often also consanguinal. Moreover, while men are expected to be deferent toward superordinate affines, there is also an expected degree of distance, if not outright hostility, between men and their wives' brothers. Furthermore, there is a greater expectation of deference on the part of women toward their superordinate affines. This brief discussion of kinship hierarchies takes up general principles of kinship organization that Pakistan's major ethnic groups share for the most part, but these systems are not identical. In fact, the sense that "those people" (*woh log*) do not know the proper order of things, do not know how or to whom to show respect (*izzat* or *lehaz*), is a key mode of drawing boundaries around the moral community.

Finally, relations of deference are sufficiently ambiguous to require repeated negotiation. While visiting my *jethani* Humaira, my husband's classificatory elder brother's wife (the wife of Sheheryar's father's elder brother's son), I heard her complaining to her sister-in-law that she could not be expected to call her husband's elder brother's new wife *bhabi* (an honorific for brother's wife) because, while she was indeed higher in structural "rank," she was many years younger than Humaira. Clearly, then, these relations are not prior to negotiated practice.

4. I am not using "totemic" in its traditional sense, to signify the symbolic classification of egalitarian groups, but to suggest a symbolic mode of marking ethnic difference, difference that is ranked (see Comaroff and Comaroff 1992).

5. As suggested by Pastner's 1982 allusion to the absent anger of the Baluch, anger does not simply separate national "Urdu" culture from the vernacular; it also divides and ranks the many asymmetrically placed groups that make up this "vernacular."

6. Pastner (1990) has argued that "honor" and the practices of purdah grew in importance for the Baluch as they were integrated asymmetrically into the Pakistani state—incorporated but politically and culturally disenfranchised and denigrated. Very crudely, one could attempt a history of male anger by compiling and correlating "honor killing" statistics with periods of relative ethnic peace and parity and periods of grievance and enmity.

5. Intimacy

1. The saying is taken from a couplet by the Urdu poet Ahmad Faraz. I am grateful to Kamran Ali for this reference.

2. The expression *log bat karenge*—people will talk—is frequently used by women to explain why they veil or act shy in particular circumstances.

3. One group of women that did veil almost all the time were domestic servants, whose reputations were always at risk and from whom deference was always expected.

4. The *mehndi* ceremony is a festive prewedding ritual in which henna is applied to the bride's hands and feet while her female relatives dance and sing.

5. I am using the term "true love" for *ishq*, although it is not an accurate translation. I am trying to convey to an English-speaking audience the distinction between this kind of all-encompassing, romantic love and more tepid versions; perhaps a better phrase would be "mad love," which more accurately portrays the cultural evaluation of *ishq* as excessive and threatening.

6. *Nazar lagna* is referred to in anthropological literature as "the evil eye," but my informants understood *nazar lagna* less as a malign force born of envy or ill will than as the inadvertent physical or material effects of inadequately controlled senses. Thus Urdu speakers use the term *nazar ka pardah* (purdah of the eye) and also *zabaan ka pardah* (purdah of the tongue) to signify the willful control or veiling of sensory perception as well as expression (which suggests that percep-

tion—e.g., vision and hearing—is as materially present in and transformative of the physical world as is touch or speech). There is a whole body of literature on vision in Islam and the nature of the senses in South Asia that I am not going to address here; see especially Babb 1981; Eck 1981; Maloney 1976.

7. Positive or friendly relationships between a bride and her husband's brothers' wives are generally approved of by senior affines and husbands, although these relationships are embedded within generational hierarchies, where the wives of elder brothers exercise control over the wives of younger brothers. These relationships are thus often a site of conflict—conflict which is blamed for the breakup of joint family households. Nevertheless, many of my informants had warm friendships with their sisters-in-law, as Zubaida did with her *devrani* Tahira and as Hina's mother did with her *devrani* Seema, as I discuss below.

8. These terms refer to Shia ceremonies held at private homes during certain times of the year.

9. This is meant affectionately.

6. Conclusion

1. See Hochschild 1983: 208–10.

2. On the other hand, the marauding crowd of Le Bon's psychology is reframed by Freud as the setting free of the id, a disruption of the repression of individual impulse and aggression so necessary for "civilization." The place of emotion or passion in political order thus hinges on the nature, duration, and form of this order, society, or group: "The essence of a group lies in the libidinal ties existing in it" (Freud 1959: 35).

3. I am simplifying here. Freud envisions the operation of psychic processes as necessary to the emergence of a "psychological group," and Durkheim contrasts mechanical with organic solidarity, the latter requiring specialization and the division of labor. Both, however, grant little need for actors to produce solidarity by virtue of initiative and mindful effort.

4. One early exception can be found in Aristotelian rhetoric, where the appeal to emotion is pivotal to the orator's ability to persuade. Similar formulations appear in the literature on crowd psychology, social movements, and collective violence or rebellion, where leaders or conspirators make use of base, irrational sentiment in order to manipulate the group (whose members, however, remain mere automatons, hypnotized or psychically fused with the will of the leader). Moreover, the literature on nationalism, particularly that following in the footsteps of Benedict Anderson, has questioned precisely how the nation comes to be "imagined." But while the processes of producing solidarity, national identity, or collective consciousness has attracted our attention, the sentiments or emotions emerging therein are rarely subject to the same practice-oriented or constructivist analysis.

5. See especially Abu-Lughod and Lutz 1990; Briggs 1970; Geertz 1973; Grima 1992; Rosaldo 1980, 1984; Shweder and LeVine 1984.

6. Thanks to the work of thinkers like Bourdieu (1977), de Certeau (1984), and Lefebvre (1991), the productive character of everyday life and practice is becoming increasingly clear, although the tendency to grant nearly hegemonic power to "structure" and subversive, "tactical" power to everyday consumption is a danger we must avoid. There has also been important work in feminist theory and anthropology on everyday life and violence. See Das and Kleinman (2000) and Iris Jean-Klein (2001).

Bibliography

Abu-Lughod, Lila. 1986. *Veiled Sentiments: Honor and Poetry in a Bedouin Society.* Berkeley: University of California Press.

———. 1993. *Writing Women's Worlds: Bedouin Stories.* Berkeley: University of California Press.

Ahmed, Feroz. 1988. "Ethnicity and Politics: The Rise of Muhajir Separatism." *South Asia Bulletin* 8:33–45.

Alavi, Hamza. 1987. "Politics of Ethnicity in Pakistan." *Pakistan Progressive* 9 (1): 4–25.

Allen, Danielle S. 2000. *The World of Prometheus: The Politics of Punishing in Democratic Athens.* Princeton, N.J.: Princeton University Press.

Anderson, Benedict. 1983. *Imagined Communities: Reflections on the Origin and Spread of Nationalism.* London: Verso.

Ansari, Sarah. 1992. *Sufi Saints and State Power: The Pirs of Sind, 1843–1947.* New York: Cambridge University Press.

Appadurai, Arjun. 1996. *Modernity at Large: Cultural Dimensions of Modernization.* Minneapolis: University of Minnesota Press.

———. 1998. "Dead Certainty: Ethnic Violence in the Era of Globalization." *Public Culture* 10 (2):225–47.

Aretxaga, Begoña. 1997. *Shattering Silence: Women, Nationalism, and Political Subjectivity in Northern Ireland.* Princeton, N.J.: Princeton University Press.

Babb, Lawrence. 1981. "Glancing: Visual Interaction in Hinduism." *Journal of Anthropological Research* 37 (4):387–401.

Barth, Fredrik. 1959. *Political Leadership among Swat Pathans.* London: Athlone.

Beeman, William O. 1976. "Status, Style, and Strategy in Iranian Interaction." *Anthropological Linguistics* 18:305–22.

Benhabib, Seyla. 1992. *Situating the Self: Gender, Community, and Postmodernism in Contemporary Ethics.* New York: Routledge.

Berlant, Lauren. 1998. "Intimacy: A Special Issue." *Critical Inquiry* 24 (Winter): 281–88.

Berlin, Isaiah, Sir. 2000. *Three Critics of the Enlightenment: Vico, Hamann, Herder.* Ed. Henry Hardy. Princeton, N.J.: Princeton University Press.

Bouhdiba, Abdelwahab. 1998. *Sexuality in Islam.* London: Saqi Books.

Bourdieu, Pierre. 1977. *Outline of a Theory of Practice.* Trans. Richard Nice. Cambridge: Cambridge University Press.

———. 1990. *The Logic of Practice.* Trans. Richard Nice. Stanford: Stanford University Press.

Brenneis, Donald. 1990. "Shared and Solitary Sentiments: The Discourse of Friendship, Play, and Anger in Bhatgaon." In *Language and the Politics of Emotion*, ed. Catherine Lutz and Lila Abu-Lughod. Cambridge: Cambridge University Press.

Briggs, Jean L. 1970. *Never in Anger: Portrait of an Eskimo Family.* Cambridge, Mass.: Harvard University Press.

———. 1994. "Why Don't You Kill Your Baby Brother?" In *The Anthropology of Peace and Nonviolence*, ed. Leslie E. Sponsel and Thomas Gregor, 155–82. Boulder, Colo.: Lynne Rienner.

Buckley, Anthony D. 1989. "'You Only *Live* in Your Body': Peace, Exchange, and the Siege Mentality in Ulster." In *Societies at Peace: Anthropological Perspectives*, ed. Signe Howell and Roy Willis, 146–64. London: Routledge.

Burton, John. 1994. *An Introduction to the Hadith.* Edinburgh: Edinburgh University Press.

Certeau, Michel de. 1984. *The Practice of Everyday Life.* Berkeley: University of California Press.

Chandra, Subhash. 1977. *Social Participation in Urban Neighborhoods.* New Delhi: National Publishing House.

Chatterjee, Partha. 1993. *The Nation and Its Fragments: Colonial and Postcolonial Histories.* Princeton, N.J.: Princeton University Press.

Comaroff, John, and Jean Comaroff. 1992. "Of Totemism and Ethnicity." In *Ethnography and the Historical Imagination.* Boulder, Colo.: Westview.

Daniel, E. Valentine. 1996. *Charred Lullabies: Chapters in an Anthropography of Violence.* Princeton, N.J.: Princeton University Press.

Das, Veena, Arthur Kleinman, Mamphela Ramphele, and Pamela Reynolds, eds. 2000. *Violence and Subjectivity.* Berkeley: University of California Press.

Dawn. 1997. "11 Students Wounded in Group Clash." 8 July.

———. 1997. "Murder at DMC: LMC Students Boycott Classes, Hold Rally." 11 July.

Dentan, Robert Knox. 1994. "Surrendered Man: Peaceable Enclaves in the Post-Enlightenment West." In *The Anthropology of Peace and Nonviolence*, ed. Leslie E. Sponsel and Thomas Gregor, 69–108. Boulder, Colo.: Lynne Rienner.

Devisch, René. 1995. "Frenzy, Violence, and Ethical Renewal in Kinshasa." *Public Culture* 7 (3):593–629.

Devji, Faisal F. 1991. "Gender and the Politics of Space: The Movement for Women's Reform in Muslim India, 1857–1900." *South Asia* 14 (1):141–53.

———. 1993. "Muslim Nationalism: Founding Identity in Colonial India." Ph.D. diss., University of Chicago.

Durkheim, Émile. 1915. *The Elementary Forms of the Religious Life.* New York: Macmillan.

———. 1933. *The Division of Labor in Society.* Trans. George Simpson. New York: Macmillan (orig. pub. 1893).

———. 1973. "The Dualism of Human Nature and Its Social Conditions." In *Emile Durkheim: On Morality and Society,* ed. Robert N. Bellah, 149–63. Chicago: University of Chicago Press (orig. pub. 1914).

Eck, Diana L. 1981. *Darśán: Seeing the Divine Image in India.* Chambersburg, Pa.: Anima Books.

Eglar, Zekiye. 1960. *A Punjabi Village in Pakistan.* New York: Columbia University Press.

Eickelman, Dale F. 1981. *The Middle East: An Anthropological Approach.* Englewood Cliffs, N.J.: Prentice-Hall.

Evans-Pritchard, E. E. 1965. *Theories of Primitive Religion.* Oxford: Clarendon.

Feldman, Allen. 1991. *Formations of Violence: The Narrative of the Body and Political Terror in Northern Ireland.* Chicago: University of Chicago Press.

Fernea, Elizabeth W. 1965. *Guests of the Sheik.* Garden City, N.Y.: Doubleday.

Freud, Sigmund. 1959. *Group Psychology and the Analysis of the Ego.* Trans. James Strachey. New York: W. W. Norton (orig. pub. 1922).

———. 1961. *Civilization and Its Discontents.* Trans. James Strachey. New York: W. W. Norton (orig. pub. 1930).

———. 1965. *New Introductory Lectures on Psychoanalysis.* Trans. James Strachey. New York: W. W. Norton.

Geertz, Clifford. 1973. *The Interpretation of Cultures.* New York: Basic Books.

Gellner, Ernest. 1983. *Nations and Nationalism.* Ithaca, N.Y.: Cornell University Press.

Ghosh, Amitav. 1988. *The Shadow Lines.* New Delhi: Oxford University Press.

Gilligan, Carol. 1982. *In a Different Voice: Psychological Theory and Women's Development.* Cambridge, Mass.: Harvard University Press.

Girard, René. 1972. *Violence and the Sacred.* Trans. Patrick Gregory. Baltimore, Md.: Johns Hopkins University Press.

Goffman, Erving. 1959. *The Presentation of Self in Everyday Life.* New York: Doubleday.

———. 1967. *Interaction Ritual: Essays on Face-to-Face Behavior.* New York: Pantheon Books.

———. 1974. *Frame Analysis: An Essay on the Organization of Experience.* Boston: Northeastern University Press.

Gregor, Thomas. 1994. "Symbols and Rituals of Peace in Brazil's Upper Xingu." In *The Anthropology of Peace and Nonviolence,* ed. Leslie E. Sponsel and Thomas Gregor, 241–58. Boulder, Colo.: Lynne Rienner.

Grima, Benedicte. 1992. *The Performance of Emotion among Paxtun Women: "The Misfortunes Which Have Befallen Me."* Austin: University of Texas Press.

Harré, Rom, and Robert Finlay-Jones. 1986. "Emotion Talk across Times." In

The Social Construction of Emotions, ed. Rom Harré, 220–33. Oxford: Basil Blackwell.

Hasan, Mohammad. 1976. *The Social Organization of Residence in Urban India.* Discussion Paper Series no. 17. Syracuse University, Department of Geography.

Heelas, Paul. 1986. "Emotion Talk across Cultures." In *The Social Construction of Emotions*, ed. Rom Harré, 234–66. Oxford: Basil Blackwell.

Hobbes, Thomas. 1968. *Leviathan.* London: Penguin (orig. pub. 1651).

Hobsbawm, Eric. 1990. *Nations and Nationalism since 1780.* Cambridge: Cambridge University Press.

Hochschild, Arlie Russell. 1983. *The Managed Heart: Commercialization of Human Feeling.* Berkeley: University of California Press.

Howell, Signe, and Roy Willis. 1989. "Introduction." In *Societies at Peace: Anthropological Perspectives*, ed. Signe Howell and Roy Willis. London: Routledge.

Hull, Matthew. 1995. "Urban Villagers into Urban Citizens: American Techniques of Democracy and Change in Post-Independence Delhi." Master's thesis, University of Chicago.

Hume, David. 1968. *A Treatise of Human Nature.* Oxford: Clarendon (orig. pub. 1739, 1740).

Jayawardena, Kumari. 1986. *Feminism and Nationalism in the Third World.* London: Zed Books.

Jean-Klein, Iris. 2001. "Nationalism and Resistance: The Two Faces of Everyday Activism in Palestine during the Intifada." *Cultural Anthropology* 16 (1):83–126.

Jeganathan, Pradeep. 1997. "After a Riot: Anthropological Locations of Violence in an Urban Sri Lankan Community." Ph.D. diss., University of Chicago.

Kakar, Sudhir. 1981. *The Inner World.* Delhi: Oxford University Press.

———. 1990. *Intimate Relations.* Chicago: University of Chicago Press.

———. 1996. *The Colors of Violence: Cultural Identities, Religion, and Conflict.* Chicago: University of Chicago Press.

Kapferer, Bruce. 1976. *Transaction and Meaning: Directions in the Anthropology of Exchange and Symbolic Behavior.* Philadelphia: Institute for the Study of Human Issues.

Khuhro, Hamida. 1978. *The Making of Modern Sind: British Policy and Social Change in the Nineteenth Century.* Karachi: Indus.

Kleinman, Arthur. 2000. "The Violences of Everyday Life: The Multiple Forms and Dynamics of Social Violence." In *Violence and Subjectivity*, ed. Veena Das, Arthur Kleinman, Mamphela Ramphele, and Pamela Reynolds. Berkeley: University of California Press.

Komter, Aafke E. 1996. *The Gift: An Interdisciplinary Perspective.* Amsterdam: Amsterdam University Press.

Kurin, Richard. 1981. "Person, Family, and Kin in Two Pakistani Communities." Ph.D. diss., University of Chicago.

Lari, Mihail. 1998. "Appropriate Housing Solutions for the Fast-Growing Middle Class in Karachi (Pakistan)." Master's thesis, Rice University.

Le Bon, Gustave. 1960. *The Crowd: A Study of the Popular Mind.* New York: Viking (orig. pub. 1897).

Lefebvre, Henri. 1991. *Critique of Everyday Life,* vol. 1. Trans. John Moore. London: Verso (orig. pub. 1947).

Lévi-Strauss, Claude. 1969. *The Elementary Structures of Kinship.* Rev. ed. Trans. James Harle Bell, John Richard von Sturmer, and Rodney Needham. Boston: Beacon (orig. pub. 1949).

LeVine, Robert A. 1984. "Properties of Culture: An Ethnographic View." In *Culture Theory: Essays on Mind, Self, and Emotion,* ed. Richard Shweder and Robert A. LeVine. Cambridge: Cambridge University Press.

Levy, Robert I. 1984. "Emotion, Knowing, and Culture." In *Culture Theory: Essays on Mind, Self, and Emotion,* ed. Richard Shweder and Robert A. LeVine. Cambridge: Cambridge University Press.

Lindholm, Charles. 1995. "Caste in Islam and the Problem of Deviant Systems: A Critique of Recent Theory." In *Muslim Communities of South Asia,* ed. T. N. Madan. New Delhi: Manohar.

———. 1996. "The Social Structure of Emotional Constraint: The Court of Louis XIV and the Pukhtun of Northern Pakistan." In *Frontier Perspectives: Essays in Comparative Anthropology,* 187–205. Karachi: Oxford University Press.

Locke, John. 1975. *An Essay Concerning Human Understanding.* Oxford: Clarendon (orig. pub. 1690).

Luhrmann, Tanya. 1996. *The Good Parsi: The Fate of a Colonial Elite in a Postcolonial Society.* Cambridge, Mass.: Harvard University Press.

Lukose, Ritty. 2001. "Learning Modernity: Youth Culture in Kerala, India." Ph.D. diss., University of Chicago.

Lutz, Catherine. 1990. "Engendered Emotion: Gender, Power, and the Rhetoric of Emotional Control in American Discourse." In *Language and the Politics of Emotion,* ed. Catherine Lutz and Lila Abu-Lughod. Cambridge: Cambridge University Press.

Lutz, Catherine, and Lila Abu-Lughod, eds. 1990. *Language and the Politics of Emotion.* Cambridge: Cambridge University Press.

Lutz, Catherine, and Geoffrey White. 1986. "The Anthropology of Emotions." *Annual Review of Anthropology* 15:405–36.

Malinowski, Bronislaw. 1961. *Argonauts of the Western Pacific.* New York: E. P. Dutton.

Malkki, Liisa. 1995. *Purity and Exile: Violence, Memory, and National Cosmology among Hutu Refugees in Tanzania.* Chicago: University of Chicago Press.

Maloney, Clarence. 1976. "Don't Say 'Pretty Baby' Lest You Zap It with the Evil Eye: The Evil Eye in South Asia." In *The Evil Eye*, ed. Clarence Maloney, 102–48. New York: Columbia University Press.

Maniruzzaman, Talukder. 1971. *The Politics of Development: The Case of Pakistan (1947–1958)*. Dacca: Green Book House.

Marriott, McKim. 1976. "Hindu Transactions: Diversity without Dualism." In *Transaction and Meaning: Directions in the Anthropology of Exchange and Symbolic Behavior*. Philadelphia: Institute for the Study of Human Issues.

Maschio, Thomas. 1998. "The Narrative and Counter-narrative of the Gift: Emotional Dimensions of Ceremonial Exchange in Southwestern New Britain." *Journal of the Royal Anthropological Institute* (n.s.) 4:83–100.

Mauss, Marcel. 1990. *The Gift: The Form and Reason for Exchange in Archaic Societies*. New York: W. W. Norton.

Metcalf, Barbara D. 1990. *Perfecting Women: Maulana Ashraf 'Ali Thanawi's Bihishti Zewar*. Berkeley: University of California Press.

Minault, Gail. 1998. *Secluded Scholars: Women's Education and Muslim Social Reform in Colonial India*. Oxford: Oxford University Press.

Miner, Horace. 1952. "The Folk-Urban Continuum." *American Sociological Review* 17: 529–37.

Montesquieu. 1977. *The Spirit of Laws*. Berkeley: University of California Press (orig. pub. 1748).

Munn, Nancy. 1986. *The Fame of Gawa: A Symbolic Study of Value Transformation in a Massim (Papua New Guinea) Society*. Durham, N.C.: Duke University Press.

Naim, C. M. 1987. "How Bibi Ashraf Learned to Read and Write." *Annual of Urdu Studies* 6:99–115.

Papanek, Hanna. 1979. "Family Status Production: The 'Work' and 'Non-Work' of Women." *Signs* 4 (4):775–81.

———. 1982. "Purdah: Separate Worlds and Symbolic Shelter." In *Separate Worlds: Studies of Purdah in South Asia*, ed. Hanna Papanek and Gail Minault, 3–53. Delhi: Chanakya.

Papanek, Hanna, and Gail Minault, eds. 1982. *Separate World: Studies of Purdah in South Asia*. Delhi: Chanakya.

Park, George. 1994. "Peace and Power in an African Proto-State." In *The Anthropology of Peace and Nonviolence*, ed. Leslie E. Sponsel and Thomas Gregor, 197–212. Boulder, Colo.: Lynne Rienner.

Pastner, Carroll McC. 1982. "Gradations of Purdah and the Creation of Social Boundaries on a Baluchistan Oasis." In *Separate Worlds: Studies of Purdah in South Asia*, ed. Hanna Papanek and Gail Minault, 164–89. Delhi: Chanakya.

———. 1990. "A Social Structural and Historical Analysis of Honour, Shame, and Purdah in Baluchistan." In *Pakistan: The Social Sciences' Perspective*, ed. Akbar S. Ahmed, 247–59. Karachi: Oxford University Press.

Radcliffe-Brown, A. R. 1952. *Structure and Function in Primitive Society*. London: Routledge and Kegan Paul.

Raheja, Gloria Goodwin. 1988. *The Poison in the Gift: Ritual, Prestation, and the Dominant Caste in a North Indian Village*. Chicago: University of Chicago Press.

Raheja, Gloria Goodwin, and Ann Grodzins Gold. 1994. *Listen to the Heron's Words: Reimagining Gender and Kinship in North India*. Berkeley: University of California Press.

Raju, Saraswati. 1982. *A Place for Everyone: Social Order and Residential Pattern in Urban India*. Discussion Paper Series no. 73. Syracuse University, Department of Geography.

Reddy, William M. 1997. "Against Constructionism: The Historical Ethnography of Emotions." *Current Anthropology* 38 (3):327–51.

———. 1999. "Emotional Liberty: Politics and History in the Anthropology of Emotions." *Cultural Anthropology* 14 (2):256–88.

———. 2000. "Sentimentalism and Its Erasure: The Role of Emotions in the Era of the French Revolution." *Journal of Modern History* 72 (March 2000): 109–52.

Redfield, Robert. 1947. "The Folk Society." *American Journal of Sociology* 41:293–308.

Robarchek, Clayton A. 1989. "Hobbesian and Rousseauan Images of Man: Autonomy and Individualism in a Peaceful Society." In *Societies at Peace: Anthropological Perspectives*, ed. Signe Howell and Roy Willis, 31–44. London: Routledge.

Rosaldo, Michelle. 1980. *Knowledge and Passion: Ilongot Notions of Self and Social Life*. Cambridge: Cambridge University Press.

———. 1984. "Toward an Anthropology of Self and Feeling." In *Culture Theory: Essays on Mind, Self, and Emotion*, ed. Richard Shweder and Robert A. LeVine, 137–57. Cambridge: Cambridge University Press.

Rosen, Lawrence. 1980. "The Negotiation of Reality: Male-Female Relations in Sefrou, Morocco." In *Women in the Muslim World*, ed. Lois Beck and Nikki Keddie. Cambridge: Cambridge University Press.

Rousseau, Jean-Jacques. 1964. *The First and Second Discourses*. New York: St. Martin's (orig. pub. 1750, 1755).

Sahlins, Marshall D. 1972. *Stone Age Economics*. Chicago: Aldine-Atherton.

Schachtel, Ernest G. 1984. *Metamorphosis: On the Development of Affect, Perception, Attention, and Memory*. New York: Basic Books.

Scheper-Hughes, Nancy. 1992. *Death without Weeping: The Violence of Everyday Life in Brazil*. Berkeley: University of California Press.

Scheper-Hughes, Nancy, and Margaret Lock. 1987. "The Mindful Body: A Prolegomenon to Future Work in Medical Anthropology." *Medical Anthropology Quarterly* (n.s.) 1:6–41.

Shweder, Richard, and Robert LeVine, eds. 1984. *Culture Theory: Essays on Mind, Self, and Emotion.* Cambridge: Cambridge University Press.

Singh, Uma. 1986. "Ethnic Conflicts in Pakistan: Sind as a Factor in Pakistani Politics." In *Domestic Conflicts in South Asia,* vol. 2: *Economic and Ethnic Dimensions,* ed. Urmila Phadnis, S. D. Muni, and Kalim Bahadur. New Delhi: South Asian.

Solomon, Robert C. 1984. "Getting Angry: The Jamesian Theory of Emotion in Anthropology." In *Culture Theory: Essays on Mind, Self, and Emotion,* ed. Richard Shweder and Robert A. LeVine, 238–56. Cambridge: Cambridge University Press.

Sponsel, Leslie E. 1994. "The Mutual Relevance of Anthropology and Peace Studies." In *The Anthropology of Peace and Nonviolence,* ed. Leslie E. Sponsel and Thomas Gregor. Boulder, Colo.: Lynne Rienner.

Sponsel, Leslie E., and Thomas Gregor, eds. 1994. "Preface in *The Anthropology of Peace and Nonviolence,* xv–xiv. Boulder, Colo.: Lynne Rienner.

Strathern, Marilyn. 1984. "Marriage Exchanges: A Melanesian Comment." *Annual Review of Anthropology* 13:41–73.

———. 1988. *The Gender of the Gift: Problems with Women and Problems with Society in Melanesia.* Berkeley: University of California Press.

Stree Shakti Sanghatana. 1989. *We Were Making History: Life Stories of Women in the Telangana People's Struggle.* London: Zed Books.

Tambiah, Stanley J. 1996. *Leveling Crowds: Ethnonationalist Conflicts and Collective Violence in South Asia.* Berkeley: University of California Press.

Turner, Victor. 1969. *The Ritual Process: Structure and Anti-Structure.* Ithaca, N.Y.: Cornell University Press.

Verkaaik, Oscar. 1999. "Inside the Citadel: Fun, Violence, and Religious Nationalism in Hyderabad, Pakistan." Ph.D. diss., University of Amsterdam.

Weber, Max. 1946. "The Sociology of Charismatic Authority." In *From Max Weber: Essays in Sociology,* ed. H. H. Gerth and C. Wright Mills. New York: Oxford University Press (orig. pub. 1922).

Werbner, Pnina. 1990. "Economic Rationality and Hierarchical Gift Economies: Value and Ranking among British Pakistanis." *Man* (n.s.) 25 (2): 266–85.

———. 1995. "The Ranking of Brotherhoods: The Dialectics of Muslim Caste among Overseas Pakistanis." In *Muslim Communities of South Asia,* ed. T. N. Madan. New Delhi: Manohar.

Wikan, Unni. 1984. "Shame and Honour: A Contestable Pair." *Man* (n.s.) 19 (4):635–52.

———. 1990. *Managing Turbulent Hearts: A Balinese Formula for Living.* Chicago: University of Chicago Press.

Williams, Raymond. 1973. *The Country and the City.* New York: Oxford University Press.

Winnicott, D. W. 1971. *Playing and Reality.* London: Routledge.

Yngvesson, Barbara. 1993. *Virtuous Citizens, Disruptive Subjects: Order and Complaint in a New England Court.* New York: Routledge.

Index

Laura A. Ring lives in Chicago with her husband, photographer Sheheryar Hasnain, and their two sons. She received a Ph.D. in anthropology from the University of Chicago, and continues to research and write about everyday life in Karachi.

CPSIA information can be obtained at www.ICGtesting.com
Printed in the USA
LVOW070242240812

295599LV00003B/2/P